TEACHERS' WORKPLACE

Research on Teaching Monograph Series

PUBLISHED TITLES

JERE E. BROPHY AND CAROLYN M. EVERTSON, *Student Characteristics and Teaching*

SUSAN URMSTON PHILIPS, *The Invisible Culture: Communication in Classroom and Community on the Warm Springs Indian Reservation*

HARRIS M. COOPER AND THOMAS L. GOOD, *Pygmalion Grows Up: Studies in the Expectation Communication Process*

THOMAS L. GOOD, DOUGLAS GROUWS, AND HOWARD EBMEIER, *Active Mathematics Teaching*

ROBERT E. SLAVIN, *Cooperative Learning*

LEONARD S. CAHEN, NIKOLA FILBY, GAIL McCUTHEON, AND DIANE W. KYLE, *Class Size and Instruction*

PHILIP A. CUSICK, *The Egalitarian Ideal and the American High School*

LARRY CUBAN, *How Teachers Taught: Constancy and Change in American Classrooms: 1890–1980*

GARY NATRIELLO AND SANFORD M. DORNBUSCH, *Teacher Evaluative Standards and Student Efforts*

CHARLES W. FISHER AND DAVID C. BERLINER, *Perspectives on Instructional Time*

BARBARA LARRIVEE, *Effective Teaching for Successful Mainstreaming*

GRETA MORINE-DERSHIMER, *Speaking, Listening, and Learning in Elementary Classrooms*

DEE ANN SPENCER, *Contemporary Women Teachers: Balancing School and Home*

PATRICIA T. ASHTON AND RODMAN B. WEBB, *Making a Difference: Teachers' Sense of Efficacy and Student Achievement*

HARRIS M. COOPER, *Homework*

TEACHERS' WORKPLACE

THE SOCIAL ORGANIZATION OF SCHOOLS

Susan J. Rosenholtz

University of Illinois at Champaign–Urbana

Longman
New York & London

Teachers' Workplace: The Social Organization of Schools

Longman Inc., 95 Church Street, White Plains, N.Y. 10601

Associated companies:
Longman Group Ltd., London
Longman Cheshire Pty., Melbourne
Longman Paul Pty., Auckland
Copp Clark Pitman, Toronto
Pitman Publishing Inc., New York

Executive editor: Naomi Silverman
Production editor: Ann P. Kearns
Text art: Edward Jasmin
Production supervisor: Kathleen Ryan

Library of Congress Cataloging-in-Publication Data

Rosenholtz, Susan J.
    Teachers' workplace.

    (Research on teaching monograph series)
    Bibliography: p.
    Includes index.
    1. Schools—Social aspects—Case studies.   2. School
management and organization—Social aspects—Case
studies.   3. Social structure—Case studies.
4. Teachers—Attitudes—Case studies.   5. Academic
achievement—Case studies.   I. Title.   II. Series.
LB2806.R65   1989   371   88-23113

ISBN 0-8013-0115-7
ISBN 0-8013-0114-9 (pbk.)

89 90 91 92 93 94 9 8 7 6 5 4 3 2

DEDICATION

To the memory of my father,
who taught me always
to strive for excellence,
and to my husband and mother,
who love and encourage me in the attempt.

Contents

Foreword

This is an important book. In time, I am confident that history will demonstrate that Susan Rosenholtz's work will have had an enduring effect on educational research, practice, and policy. Considering this enthusiastic judgment, it will come as no surprise that I believe the book should be required reading for both policymakers and practitioners. It presents an intriguing account of a study of the social organization of schools and the effects of school organization on school ambiance and performance. Due to its empirical data, theoretical logic and structure, and eloquent writing, the book successfully demonstrates marked variation in the social organization of schools. The picturesque images that Rosenholtz creates demonstrate how a facilitating or inhibiting normative climate can permeate a particular district, school, or classroom. The book provides prima facie evidence that variation in school organization affects the lives of all participants (administrators, teachers, and students) in cumulative and reciprocal ways so that both the setting and attainment of academic goals are highly influenced by the social organization in which teaching and learning occur. We can take comfort in the fact that Rosenholtz identifies schools in which participants are encouraged to think and grow, but her finding that in some schools neither teachers nor students received more than minimal intellectual stimulation is depressing.

In 1970, it was still popular for many social scientists and educators to question whether teachers could affect student achievement, given the unequal backgrounds and aptitudes that students brought to the classroom. Although student and home variables place certain restrictions on what can be accomplished in the classroom, data collected in the 1970s and 1980s provide compelling evidence that teachers can have important, verifiable effects on student achievement.[1] Although this research on instructional behavior and classroom learning has not led to "rules of practice," it has produced concepts, findings, and models that are of immense value to teachers who act as decision makers and engage in reflective teaching. Because of this research and the discussion it has created (including criticisms of the research as well as discussion of the influence of research on educational practice and policy), the study of teaching is a much more complex and sophisticated enterprise than it was 20 years ago. New concepts, increased awareness of variation in instructional behavior from classroom to classroom, and more attention to teacher and student thinking and decision making have led to the development of more comprehensive models to describe teaching.

I include this brief historical reference to research on teaching in order to provide a framework for examining the contribution of Rosenholtz's book. Although several useful books on school effects have been published recently, this is the first book to provide a coherent description of how school organization at the district, school, and classroom levels influences instructional practice. Rosenholtz demonstrates in rich detail how certain school practices (e.g., teacher involvement in the recruitment of other teachers) influence decisions and practices that occur at other levels of schooling (to what extent teachers exchange information with one another and how helpful this process is in producing viable instructional alternatives). Cogent arguments illustrate the dynamic relations in schools (e.g., between goal consensus, learning opportunities, and evaluative activities), offering a sophisticated view of differences in functioning between schools that are changing and improving ("moving" schools) and those that are not ("stuck"). Too often, descriptions of schooling discuss single variables (e.g., communication of expectations, goal setting, leadership) without examining the relationships between variables. Because of Rosenholtz's rich and integrative descriptions of school processes, it is my judgment that her book will set the terms of the debate for some of the school research that will occur in the 1990s.

Rosenholtz's analysis points to a number of ways in which schools dif-

---

[1]Jere Brophy and I have written extensively about the strengths and weaknesses of classroom research. The practical implications of this research are discussed in *Looking in Classrooms* (Good, T. & Brophy, J. New York: Harper & Row, 4th ed., 1987). The technical issues associated with this research are presented elsewhere (Brophy, J. & Good, T. "Teacher Behavior and Student Achievement," pp. 328–375. In M. Wittrock (ed.), *Handbook of Research on Teaching,* 3rd ed., New York: Macmillan, 1986). Rosenholtz's book provides arguments and data that connect school processes with classroom findings. Hence, her research builds on, extends, and integrates previous research.

fer in internal organization and in the values they hold with regard to student learning and necessary and appropriate instructional conditions. For example, using both quantitative and qualitative research strategies in an innovative way, she identifies some schools in which teachers have a common purpose and work openly and cooperatively. Rosenholtz notes that several factors helped to explain the attractiveness of cohesive, high-consensus schools. In these schools, "students' mastery of basic skills was the common factor that united them, the force that welded all the separate autonomous teachers into one common voice." Other factors supported and sustained this focus. For example, teachers in high-consensus schools believed that teachers affect student learning and thus that teaching is important. These teachers were open to comments about their teaching and to suggestions about alternative instructional practices that might improve their efforts. Peers were seen as a resource, and teachers had a sense of community that allowed them to persist when they encountered instructional difficulties. High-consensus and forward-moving schools were enriched by a marked spirit of continuous improvement in which no teacher ever stopped learning how to teach.

In contrast, teachers in low-consensus schools did not enjoy a sense of community and suffered the consequences. In particular, principals in these schools were unsure of their knowledge of instruction and did not assist teachers in identifying and solving classroom problems.

How do these differences between schools emerge? What factors create high- and low-consensus schools? Why do some schools encourage commitment and effort from faculty and students and other schools seem to breed only expectations for minimal performance? Why do teachers want to transfer from some schools while teachers in other schools that serve comparable students not only are content but also want to participate in school life—to talk and to learn with peers? Why do teachers in some schools acknowledge their instructional problems and obtain appropriate feedback, whereas teachers in other schools feel threatened if they ask for help?

Rosenholtz's book provides important, plausible answers to such questions, at least regarding the schools that she studied. However, readers should examine the book not to obtain "rules" for establishing effective schools but rather to gain a framework for thinking about human resources in schools. The book does not—and cannot—answer specific questions about what should occur in a particular classroom in a given school. There is no single answer to a question like, What is the best way to encourage teachers to exchange instructional information with other teachers? In time, if researchers are careful and conduct broad studies, they will find that some schools have successfully answered this and related questions in diverse ways and, at times, in ways that may even appear to be contradictory.

What the Rosenholtz book does demonstrate is that answers are possible. Some schools have found ways to stimulate teacher and student performance, and the existence of these schools demonstrates that low efficacy and low performance need not be the norm.[2] Schools may need to explore different means of promoting individual teacher excellence in ways that not only improve instruction but also inspire community (e.g., a willingness to help other teachers), because school context can vary considerably.

This book will lead to much productive debate and policy discussion as schools search for ways to improve the workplace conditions of teaching in order to create more commitment and less early defection by the most capable teachers. The Rosenholtz work provides a vivid and vital model of the school as a workplace that demands more teacher participation in its governance, especially concerning professional practice (e.g., classroom evaluation, peer exchange, inservice education). How such models work in practice will no doubt vary with school context.

The fundamental value of Susan Rosenholtz's work lies in the evidence it provides that researchers need to study seriously and attempt to improve the social organization of schools. In no sense do I want to devalue the empirical contribution of her research. Much of the evidence will apply to a range of school contexts. However, in a sensitive and eloquently written final chapter, Rosenholtz cautions readers not to overgeneralize her findings and to avoid the temptation of turning tentative, provocative images into narrow, technical rules. Readers should heed her advice. The book is an important beginning for informed debate that will inspire improved conceptualization and more research, which will in turn lead to greater understanding of effective social organizations in schools.

THOMAS L. GOOD

[2]Two other important books in the Longman Research on Teaching Monograph Series provide clear evidence that many teachers face lonely and professionally empty lives. For a valuable analysis of why many teachers feel powerless, I recommend the following two books from the Longman series: *Contemporary Women Teachers: Balancing School and Home,* by Dee Ann Spencer, and *Making a Difference: Teachers' Sense of Efficacy and Student Achievement,* by Patricia T. Ashton and Rodman B. Webb. Rosenholtz's book provides evidence that teachers' levels of efficacy and feelings of professional fulfillment can be increased in certain school environments.

Preface

In the beginning, I held only passing interest in the research on effective schools. As an assistant professor of Education and Sociology at Vanderbilt University, I was perfectly content in my ongoing study of the social construction of ability in elementary school classrooms (in collaboration with my colleague Carl Simpson). At that same time, 1981, the Dean of Peabody College at Vanderbilt, as part of a contract we had won with the Federal Department of Education, asked among other things that I abridge the summaries of the "effective schools" research. I lacked initial enthusiasm for the task. In the main, I found the summaries proper in their methodological critique, but wanting conceptually.

A sociologist without a conceptual framework is like an orphaned child without toys. Thus, laboriously I read the original studies themselves. Few had a theoretical framework of any sort, but by weaving all the different studies together, and adding knowledge from organizational theory and the sociology of teaching, I found one begging to be told. The end result was a paper entitled "Effective Schools: Interpreting the Evidence" (see References).

The abrupt interruption in my original scholarship was not to end there. Shortly after acceptance of the paper by the *American Journal of Education,* the National Institute of Education (NIE) issued a call for proposals that included policy studies of effective schooling. Having by now become quite taken with the subject, I could not resist the adventurous impulse. A study based on the theoretical framework was thereafter funded. Adding new conceptual grist to my first formulation led to the study of teaching as a social construction, the results of which comprise this book. Thus I owe no small debt of gratitude to Bill Hawley, Dean of Peabody College, Vanderbilt University, for dragging me, silently kicking and screaming, into our initial contract and a new intellectual pursuit.

ACKNOWLEDGMENTS

This study, as do most, involved an orchestration of many different voices. With a conductor's grace, Tom Good, in reviewing the manuscript for the editorial board of this monograph series, held me to high expectations, challenged me to reach, and never wavered in his interest and syncopated rhythm.

Many graduate students deserve heartfelt thanks for the ensemble of massive data sets: Susan Kyle, Amy McAninch, Jan Doherty, Robert Kleinsasser, Ian Wilkinson, Dan Foertsch, Eunice Greer, Mary Prignano, and Gina Carrona.

I am also grateful to Kathy Hoover-Dempsey and Otto Bassler for their initial assistance in subduing and muting my overenthusiastic need to ask every question.

For his sounding board of support and exacting measure of each chapter, I am indebted to my brother, Stephen Rosenholtz.

Finally, a special note of gratitude to Dane Shepard, Gary Griffin, Ted Manolakes, and Paul Nelson for their encouragement that cheered me on; for their help through difficult passages that made completion of this research possible.

1

The Conceptual Framework and Design of the Study

This is a study of the school as a workplace. In a whirlwind panorama, we expose to view teachers' varied understandings, expectations, and cognitions of school life, and their behaviors that then follow suit. We will come to see just how good schools can be at their best, and how bad they can be at their worst: Schools where teachers share common goals, and schools more like organized anarchies; schools where colleagues help one another, and schools of professional isolation; schools where teachers and students learn and grow, and schools where most of them stagnate; schools where teachers believe in themselves, and schools of contagious uncertainty; schools where teachers spark enthusiasm and hope, and schools where they only despair. To account for these differences between elementary schools and to explain their various effects is at the core of our purpose here.

BACKGROUND OF THE STUDY

Broadly conceived, ours might be viewed as a study of "effective" schools. This is a topic with voluminous literature (and much commentary), but precious little theory to guide it. Studies have been episodic, not consciously building on each other. There has been much independent ploughing and reploughing of the same ground. Moreover, an air of methodological criticism hovers about it, as though the central problem were that of merely refining output measures, of controlling for previously overlooked variables, of quantifying what are largely case-study findings, or of sampling still wider populations to assure generalizability.

But the most interesting questions in this area are not at all methodological, they are conceptual. Not *how* to measure school effectiveness but *what* to measure; the manner in which school structure interrelates with its functioning and its productivity. Problems plaguing this literature are not mere inconveniences to be brushed aside until more rigorously designed studies come along. Instead, they are fundamental to school life itself.

Among the most important conceptual issues is that student learning gains have been associated with a handful of school characteristics without convincing rationales and empirical support for how those specific characteristics actually come to affect the internal dynamics of schools. That is, although we have had much attention directed toward what constitutes an "effective" school, information about within-school variation has been strikingly sparse. Is it possible, for example, that differences between schools might be due to only a handful of teachers rather than to shared, schoolwide goals? If not, how are shared cultures forged? And why are they central to school success?

A related concern is the very definition of school effectiveness. To be sure, productivity as measured by student learning is one dimension in the character of a successful school. Yet it is apparent to most organizational theorists that effectiveness is more a multidimensional than a unidimensional construct (see Kanter & Brinkerhoff 1981). Indeed, multiple measures are both useful and necessary; if we look only at the outputs of schools and not at the structures and processes influencing them, we will never learn *why* organizations such as schools work, and how positive outcomes are brought about. We suggest, then, that a more expansive definition of school success, one that addresses its social organization, will help us better understand how it works.

Accordingly, the present study flushes out one critical story of school success by relying on four measures of organizational effectiveness: (1) schools' problem-solving and renewal capabilities, defined here as teachers' opportunities to learn; (2) the satisfaction of individual needs and organizational tasks, viewed here as teachers' certainty about their instructional practice; (3) maintaining the motivation and values of the school, as indicated by teachers' workplace commitment; and (4) school productivity, measured by student learning outcomes. Even with multiple measures, however, all organizational outcomes and their symbiotic relationships depend at heart on the guiding theoretical framework. Next we offer such a conceptual scaffolding for our look at elementary schools and the work of teachers within them.

THEORETICAL OVERVIEW

Teachers, like members of most organizations, shape their beliefs and actions largely in conformance with the structures, policies, and traditions of the workaday world around them. A social organizational perspective, which we take here, asks whether commonly observed associations, such as that between teaching and learning, are conditionalized by variations in those structures, policies, and traditions (Bidwell & Kasarda 1980). The ultimate social organizational variable is the meaning that the organization has for those who work within it. To understand schools, we must understand them as teachers do, that is, we must attempt to construe how schools appear to teachers who inhabit them.

People come to define their workday realities through a set of shared assumptions about appropriate attitudes and behaviors constructed within them. Meanings of work are exchanged, negotiated, and modified through the communications people have with, or the observations they make of, others. Thus teachers learn through everyday interactions how to name and classify things, and in that process learn how they are expected to behave with reference to those things. In this way teachers define the nature of their work, their sentiments toward their work, the substance of their work. Teaching beliefs and behaviors become necessary, natural, and proper to the social organization of the school (Berger & Luckmann 1966).

Meanings not only are forged in the crucible of everyday interaction, they also form that interaction. That is, the reality of the taken-for-granted workplace is continually made apparent in the actions of its members. Teachers in a particular school have always acted in certain ways, and they will go on acting in those ways because it is "natural" that they should do so. Stability in social meanings and actions gives teachers a sure-footed sense of their organizational lives that protects, maintains, or further extends beliefs about themselves and their reality (Blankenship 1973).

If new and stable forms of organizational behavior emerge, transformations of meanings invariably accompany them. Teachers develop new conceptions of their work through communications in which their principal or colleagues point out new aspects of experience to them with fresh interpretations. It is only when teachers adopt these fresh perspectives that their behavior becomes subject to change (Becker 1953).

Social organizations vary enormously from school to school. This means that teachers from different settings may hold altogether different definitions of school reality. Teachers' situated activities and the interpretation that is made of them, then, allow for different but equally valid conceptions of teaching from their varied points of view. These multiple definitions of teaching, contoured by the social organization of schools, is what this study is about. We are interested not only in ways that the structure of their daily experiences affects teachers' beliefs, cognitions, and behaviors, but also in the reciprocal effect of those beliefs, cognitions, and behaviors on their school's social organization.

The perspective that reality is socially constructed and maintained through everyday organizational life deemphasizes individual members per se. We are quick to acknowledge that teachers differ substantially in their individual biographies, and even that those biographies may produce variations in teachers' perceptions of reality. Nonetheless our perspective holds that there are shared aspects of work that cut across individual biographies with sufficient force to explain the pattern of beliefs and behaviors in schools. Indeed, we may well argue that teachers' attitudes, cognitions, and behavior have less to do with the individual biographies teachers bring with them to the workplace than with the social organization of the workplace itself—social organizations that are not characteristics of individual teachers but that teachers have helped to shape; social organizations that then have consequences for teachers' perceptions and behaviors.

Recurring Conceptual Themes

Teaching Uncertainty. This look at different school realities juxtaposes several distinct bodies of sociological and social psychological theory. One has to do with the uncertainty many teachers face as they go about their work—uncertainty about how teaching should best be done in ways that enable their student charges to learn and grow.

Uncertainty arises from the absence of a technical culture, the processes designed to accomplish an organization's goals (Perrow 1970; Thompson 1967). For teachers, technical knowledge encompasses the skills, procedures, and methods that help pupils progress academically. A technical culture is labeled *uncertain* if the outcomes of work are highly unpredictable; where, because of variability in their students, for example, teachers do not reach automatically for solutions to the myriad learning problems they confront. Uncertainty means there are few well-established techniques—codified technical knowledge—to help teachers meet students' widely varying needs. In such cases, work is said to be *nonroutine*. With *routine* work, well-established techniques and procedures can be applied over and over to essentially the same "raw" materials to produce the same result (Perrow 1970).

Lest readers conclude too hastily that the uncertainties of teaching make it nonroutine work (thereby missing much of the story we have to tell) they need only consult the organizational literature. Especially in service organizations, whether a technical culture is defined as routine or nonroutine depends heavily on people's conceptions of their work. We see this point illustrated in Perrow's (1970) comparison of two juvenile correction institutions where dramatic differences existed in the definition of the delinquent. In one facility, the staff viewed all delinquents as lacking respect for authority, ill-socialized to conform to rules, and highly untrustworthy. To rehabilitate them, they treated all youngsters in identical fashion, using strict and punitive measures. Moreover, because anyone could follow the institutional rules and procedures designed to instill obedience to authority, the staff required no specialized training—a routine technical culture. In the other facility, the staff perceived each youngster as unique psychologically and held that reasons for their delinquency varied from case to case. After extensive information-gathering on each client, requiring specialized diagnostic skills, the staff prescribed individual programs and activities—a nonroutine technical culture.

A second conceptual thread that weaves throughout this study follows organizational uncertainty to its social psychological consequences. It is that uncertainty about a technical culture and one's capacity to help students learn leads teachers and principals to self-defensive posturing—in social psychological terms—threatened self-esteem.

Threatened Self-Esteem. Most formulations of the "threatened self-esteem" model begin with the assumption that most of us like to think well of ourselves. Indeed, we maximize our opportunities to do so. We therefore avoid situations where our performance adequacy, and thus our sense of self-esteem, may conceivably be called into question (Fisher, DePaulo & Nadler 1981). The task at hand is not merely to prevent damage to our sense of self-worth; it also involves our need to maintain control. For not only are we motivated to cast ourselves in the best possible light; we are also motivated to experience ourselves as causal agents in our performance—to feel that we can make things happen with our own deliberate striving (Gecas & Schwalbe 1983).

We are unable to control situations, to make things happen, where our abilities are found wanting. We thus devise self-protective strategies to avoid such occasions. We may refuse to participate, for example, or simply not try. And since any lack of effort or engagement is under *our* control, we are not obliged to accept any self-limiting implications about our abilities (Snyder & Wicklund 1981).

In a like manner, where the uncertainties of teaching threaten to disclose teachers' or principals' professional inadequacies, they too engage self-defensive tactics to protect their sense of control and their social and personal worth. The particular manifestations of these maneuvers, the school conditions under which they occur, and their consequences for teachers and students are also at the heart of this study.

OVERVIEW OF THE STUDY

Our look at different school realities—as teachers subjectively experience them—begins in Chapter 2 with a strategic problem plaguing most elementary schools: how to unify and mobilize teachers in pursuit of the same instructional goals. More broadly, how are teaching goals defined? How do they come to be commonly shared? School goals (or their absence) serve as general referents for organizational beliefs and actions, that is, how teachers should define their work, what they should emphasize instructionally, and how they should gauge their performance success. When they are shared, school goals have tremendous power as moral suasions or norms—to do X is good, to do Y is bad—and as sanctions that can be visited on transgressors of them.

Although there may be professed goals about school purpose, they are often not apparent in the everyday activity of organizational members. That is, teachers' and principals' behavior is not necessarily guided by the goals of student learning. Thus much can be understood about the nature and purpose of schools from the workaday routines within them. Our argument here is straightforward: to the degree that teachers' everyday activity converges into a single harmony of organizational interests—underscoring what they should emphasize in teaching and how their success should be gauged—and to the extent that principals facilitate these everyday activities, teachers will come to identify those interests as their own instructional priorities. In particular, where teachers help principals define school goals and interact about how best to pursue them, where they help determine school policies that facilitate goal attainment, such as how students ought to behave, or help to socialize new recruits, teachers engage actively in constructing their school reality. Through these means school goals should come to be mutually shared.

Goal consensus figures prominently in the extent of teacher collaboration, the topic of Chapter 3. Here we argue that ambiguous goals, unclear, infrequent evaluation, and a lack of common purpose lead to greater instructional uncertainty and, at the same time, grant teachers wide latitude to define and independently pursue their own goals. In other words, goal multiformity encourages norms of self-reliance and, as a consequence, professional isolation from colleagues. The absence of professional interaction, of substantive dialogue about their work, carries profound implications: individuals may come to perceive that comparatively few colleagues suffer similar uncertainties about teaching, that they endure fewer instructional problems; and that if others experience few problems, there is embarrassment in admitting one's own. Thus, to protect their self-esteem in isolated settings, colleagues neither ask for nor expect any help, and cannot be imposed upon by others. In collaborative settings, on the contrary, teaching is defined as an inherently difficult undertaking; one that challenges the best of teachers. And if even the most capable teachers need help in similar situations, there is little reason to question one's own sense of professional worth. Stated differently, the less ego-endangering teachers' workplace circumstances, the more they will request and offer advice and assistance to accomplish agreed-upon goals.

Chapter 4 carries still further the implications of shared teaching goals, useful evaluation criteria, and norms of collaboration in examining teachers' learning opportunities. Here we assert that goal-setting activities accentuate those instructional objectives toward which teachers should aim their improvement efforts; that principals, through their frequent monitoring of teachers' progress, specify improvement needs and mobilize school resources, particularly teacher leaders, to render needed help; that shared goals confer legitimacy, support, and pressure not to deviate from norms of school renewal; and finally, that norms of collaboration enable if not compel teachers to request and offer advice and assistance in helping their colleagues improve. We also find that the greater teachers' opportunities for learning, the more their students tend to learn.

Components of teachers' learning opportunities are heavily implicated in their belief in a technical culture and their certainty about instructional practice, the subject of Chapter 5. The uncertainty endemic to teaching, we assert, can be diminished by two conditions. First, the school setting should provide positive feedback to teachers about their performance. Second, schools should mobilize those resources that help teachers acquire greater technical knowledge, that involve parents in their children's learning, and that optimize pupils' on-task behavior through schoolwide standards for student conduct. Without such resources, teachers suffer a range of classroom difficulties, and they are dwarfed by the technically unknown. To protect their self-esteem and their sense of professional competence, they attribute most classroom problems to ill-begotten circumstances and people other than themselves—specifically, to principals, parents, and students. Through consoling conversation about their trying workplace circumstances, colleagues tend to convince each other that no teacher can reasonably expect to succeed. And the strength of their conviction is manifested in students' learning problems.

Teachers' workplace commitment is at issue in Chapter 6. Here we argue that teachers' commitment, a direct function of their professional fulfillment, is determined by three workplace conditions. First, teachers' empowerment—their task autonomy and discretion—gives them the sense that student growth and development results directly from their own instructional efforts. Second, teachers' learning opportunities offer them a sense of ongoing challenge and continuous growth that makes greater mastery and control of their environment possible. Third, teachers' psychic rewards ensure their continuous contributions to the school. The absence of these workplace conditions carries negative and far-reaching consequences for teachers. They become dissaffected and alienated from their work, they absent themselves frequently, or they desire to leave the workplace altogether. Teachers' lack of motivation and commitment, as manifest in a lack of future planning and in complacency with the present, is visited upon students through their diminished opportunity to learn basic skills.

Finally, in Chapter 7 we depart from the school as the level of analysis to examine district-level differences in teacher commitment. Here we see how superintendents' beliefs and policies may directly and indirectly affect teachers' cognitions and behavior. We examine district procedures and practices for setting and monitoring individual school goals, for selecting principals and teachers and for evaluating them in order that they may learn. The analysis makes clear that teacher commitment is not only embedded in workplace circumstances; it is also governed, at least in part, by a larger environment, and an equally compelling reality.

DESIGN AND PROCEDURES

The Sample

We recruited eight Tennessee districts whose superintendent supported the participation of all elementary schools. In exchange for their cooperation, we offered an inservice on our major quantitative findings for principals within each district, as well as individual school improvement goals.

Tennessee, like many agricultural states, is two-thirds rural. It is also fiscally poor, among the poorest in the nation. In 1984, Tennessee's per-pupil expenditure ranked *third lowest* nationwide (U.S. Department of Education 1985). Most rural districts rely on the state as their sole source of funding and the state does not serve their interests well. Often there are insufficient funds for textbooks and other ordinary classroom supplies. It is not uncommon to find a workbook shared by two or three students; scissors, paste, crayons, pencils, and ordinary writing paper are either furnished by parents or sometimes parcelled out sparingly from teachers' meager salaries. Teachers in such districts spend all day with their students, including recess, lunch, bus detail, and more. Nor do many teachers enjoy planning periods to relieve the tedium of these everyday responsibilities; only five days of inservice is required by the state.

Districts represented a random sample of the state, with its distinct geographic and cultural regions, its impoverished county and wealthier city school systems, and its elected and appointed superintendents. Although the largest city school systems in the state did not participate in this study, 5 rural and 3 urban/suburban districts did; in all, 78 elementary schools.

At the individual level, teachers in the main were locals; over 70% taught in schools close to their degree-granting undergraduate institutions, and most taught in the same school for their entire professional careers. (The correlation between teachers' years of experience and their tenure in schools was .79.) Over 80% reported that their class composition was mixed academically.

At the school level, there was negligible teacher turnover for the three previous years samplewide, but schools varied substantially in range on school demographic and teachers' background variables. The status of teachers' undergraduate institutions, as revealed by the highest degree granted, ranged from schools where all teachers held either no degree or a B.A., to schools where all teachers held either an M.A. or an Ed.D. Teachers' mean experience ran from 6 to 25 years. School size varied from 5 to 42 teachers, and mean teacher–pupil ratio from 19:1 to 33:1. All schools served some low socioeconomic status (SES) youngsters—from 4% to 94%.

The lowest SES schools were rural; the highest were surburban. Only urban schools, desegregated by court order, served substantial proportions of ethnically diverse students.

Data Sources and Methodologies

Teacher Questionnaire Data. To investigate specific social organizational features of schools that inspire and give meaning to life within them, we combined two distinct research methodologies. In the first year of the study, mindful of research conducted by others, we constructed and administered a teacher questionnaire. It consisted of 164 items designed primarily with five-point Likert responses ranging from strongly disagree to strongly agree or from almost never to almost always. We alternated negatively and positively worded items throughout to avoid generalized response patterns.

Two types of information were collected on the questionnaire: teachers' perceptions of their workplace conditions (e.g., "I don't seem to have as much enthusiasm now as I did when I began teaching." "At this school I have many opportunities to learn new things." "Other teachers at this school come to me for help or advice when they need it.") and information on a number of teacher background characteristics, such as their total years of teaching experience, the number of years in their present school, the institution from which they obtained their undergraduate degree, their level of educational attainment, their present class size and its academic composition.

With support from superintendents, we contacted all elementary school principals within each district of our sample. After explaining study purposes and procedures, we requested that they administer the questionnaire at a routine faculty meeting. At that time, teachers read a letter explaining study purposes and methods to protect their anonymity. The questionnaire took approximately 30 minutes to complete. Response rates averaged 70% per school; in all, 1,213 teachers.

From questionnaire items we constructed scales measuring specific social organizational variables of schools (e.g., goal-setting, collaboration, schoolwide standards for student conduct, etc.). Our analysis of quantitative data was conducted at the school level. We aggregated each social organizational and teacher background variable to derive mean school scores. To determine the internal consistency of teacher responses within each school, the skewness of our five outcome measures—goal consensus, teacher collaboration, teachers' learning opportunities, teachers' instructional certainty, and teacher commitment—were each divided by their standard error of skewness. We considered schools extreme outliers (as indicated by a nonhomogeneous response pattern among teachers) if the quotient exceeded 2.54 (a 95% level of confidence). Only 6 of the 78 schools in our sample showed this consistent tendency. That is, teacher perceptions of their workplace conditions wavered only marginally within each school.

Furthermore, variables in the study showed strong communality (averaging .62) as revealed through factor analysis. The Eigenvalue was 8.58, explaining 89% of the variance. In other words, where teachers tended to perceive a high degree of goal consensus in their school, they also perceived a high level of collaboration, commitment, and so forth.

School Demographic Data. Concomitantly, we also gathered demographic data on each school using district archival records. Data included one student cohort's reading and math achievement test scores for the past three years (grades 2 through 4), the total number of teachers' one day absences for the current year, school size as measured by the number of full-time teachers, and school SES (as indicated by the proportion of students receiving Aid to Families with Dependent Children).

Teacher Interview Data. We computed z-scores on all social organizational variables for schools districtwide, and because they tended to be moderately and positively correlated, we identified the most disparate outliers. From each of these schools, and again with superintendent support (in the form of school personnel lists and memos sent to teachers), we interviewed an average of three teachers selected via a random numbers table. This occurred during the second year of the study. Fewer than 20% of the teachers contacted declined our invitation to be interviewed. We selected schools on a district- rather than samplewide basis to control for district-level differences.

To tap the way in which teachers organize and define their workaday worlds, we designed the interview protocol with two types of open-ended questions: those that expanded or clarified quantitative findings (e.g., "Do you share things with other teachers?" "Do you ever have to do things that are against the rules in order to do what's best for your students?"), and those that more fully elaborated teachers' definitions of reality (e.g., "How long does it take to learn to teach?" "Do you have any teacher leaders in your school? What do they do?"). Conducted by telephone, tape-recorded and then transcribed, the interviews ranged in length from a half hour to an hour. Trained members of the research staff conducted the interviews blind, that is, unaware of schools' social organization and, likewise, of the teachers within them. In all, we interviewed 74 teachers from 23 schools.

We conducted the interviews in such a way to encourage free expression. Some teachers, as usual, proved more open to the task than others, offering far more commentary than solicited. We promised teachers to take no more than an hour of their time. This meant that for a few particularly loquacious teachers, not all questions were asked. Moreover, not all questions were answered; some teachers refused outright, others evaded, while still others seemed to have in mind their own interview protocols despite persistent attempts to keep them on task.

We used an inductive approach to analyze interview data, first perusing relevant responses to each question in order to identify substantive categories. At least two members of the research staff then classified the responses independently. Classification proved highly reliable. Finally, we linked teacher responses within each category to their respective elementary school cultures.

SUMMARY

Many of the wondrous possibilities of schools as well as their awesome destruction make themselves known in this study of teachers' workplace. Building serially in an ever-widening understanding of schools' vast complexities, we test two major theoretical assumptions. The most central is that teachers' definition of their work—how it should be done, the way it is learned, what constitutes successful performance—is guided by their subjective construction of reality. As they seek to make sense of their school world in order to simplify, understand, predict, explain, and control events within it, their interpretations will be strongly influenced by the structure of their daily activity. Rather than being seen as relatively enduring qualities, teachers' beliefs, dispositions, identities, and resolves instead depend on the nature of contextual cues and communications they experience within the workplace itself.

A second conceptual theme is that uncertainty about the technology of teaching is the enemy of rational planning and action. Uncertainty undermines the purposive rationales and behaviors necessary to rally school faculties in single-minded pursuit; to request from and offer advice to colleagues; to continuously acquire new strategies and perfect old ones; to have faith not only in their capacity to teach but in students' ability to learn; to enjoy their work, to be motivated to achieve, and to be wholly committed to it.

That reality is seen as socially rather than objectively determined means that teachers' responses to events and situations cannot be understood without reference to their subjective interpretation of them. Hence we use two distinct types of data in this study. The quantitative data of teachers' workplace perceptions explicitly test our theoretical assumptions. We then use qualitative data garnered from teacher interviews to find interesting examples and plausible cases that both enrich and extend our practical understanding of how elementary schools work.

One methodological caveat warrants mention here, before we proceed to the study's substantive findings. We analyzed the quantitative (questionnaire) data using multiple regression, and its more complicated cousin, structural modeling. Both speak in the language of causality: variables "explain," "account for," and "predict" other variables. These are statistical explanations, not causal ones. At best such analysis lends support to a theoretical argument by indicating the strength of an association between variables, and in the case of structural modeling, the connection between variables as well. Similarly, sociologists who study the construction of meaning using qualitative data (in this case interviews) speak in the diction of causation. Phenomena "shape," "determine," and "construct" other phenomena. These are metatheoretical explanations, not causal ones. Nothing short of large-scale longitudinal or experimental studies with appropriate random assignment or matching of schools could speak unequivocally to the causal arguments we will make.

To conclude, what troubles the body of literature on effective schools, and what we seek to address, is the lack of plausible narrative, the absence of coherent motive that explains school success or failure. How do teachers form conceptions of their work? In what sort of workaday world do they find themselves resident? By looking at how schools are socially organized, we may begin to find some answers.

2

Shared School Goals

If there is any center to the mystery of schools' success, mediocrity, or failure, it lies deep within the structure of organizational goals: whether or not they exist, how they are defined and manifested, the extent to which they are mutually shared. Indeed, the hallmark of any successful organization is a shared sense among its members about what they are trying to accomplish (Peters & Waterman, 1982). Agreed-upon goals and ways to attain them enhance the organization's capacity for rational planning and action. There is a programmatic basis for directing behavior, for motivating behavior, for justifying behavior, and for evaluating behavior (Scott 1981).

For precisely this reason, schools' goal consensus or dissensus seems the fundamental place to begin our study, the foundation upon which subsequent analyses can build. But as most things go for elementary schools, there is neither consensus about goals of teaching nor, even more globally, agreement about the primary purposes of schooling (Metz 1978). Teachers, students, administrators, parents, politicians, and other interest groups all bring to bear a variety of perspectives and values which inevitably ensure that school goals will be multiple, shifting, and frequently disputed. Amidst this swirl of competing forces, we turn our attention to a unitary set of goals—student mastery of basic skills.

Some readers might quarrel with our singled-minded focus on basic skills mastery. Indeed, it can be reasonably if not decisively argued that other instructional priorities, such as problem-solving, critical thinking, or cooperative group behavior are of equal if not greater importance. With this observation we agree whole-heartedly. This does not imply, however, that in certain instances we would not choose one goal over another and have particularly good reason for doing so. Indeed, there are curious repetitive tides in the history of American education, a land given to sudden passing extremes of opinion, and one such tide swept us here. We conducted the study during a period when the issue of school quality—as measured solely in terms of students' basic skills mastery—had seized the attention and interest of policy makers nationwide, making the study's funding eminently more likely. Minimum competency testing became the legislative battle cry to regulate elementary schools' already professed goals, making outcome measures more readily available and random selection of a sample far less problematic.

Furthermore, our choice of goals seems appropriate enough when we compare the performance of Tennessee students to others nationwide. According to government statistics, Tennessee ranks third lowest nationally in high school graduation rates, eighth lowest in the proportion of high school graduates taking the American College Testing examination (ACT), and fifth lowest on ACT results (U.S. Department of Education 1985). Given that students from other primarily rural and impoverished states fare far better, we must look beyond Tennessee's locale and resources to explain these discouraging facts. As it turns out, students' ultimate educational attainment can be predicted with remarkable accuracy by the time they have reached the end of the third grade (see Pallis et al. 1987). The goals of elementary schools and how artfully teachers pursue them, therefore, tell us much about students' future academic possibilities.

More often than not the goals of elementary schools are disputed *within* the school's own membership (e.g., Metz 1978). Apart from coverage of basic skills, teachers may alternatively define their work as developing student initiative, tending to their affective needs, keeping them busy, encouraging friendly interpersonal behavior, instituting peace and quiet in classrooms and corridors, and so forth. Granted such diversity, the idea that teachers in any given school might serendipitously rally in single-minded purpose strains one's credulity at best. To complicate the issue still further, teachers themselves appear especially distanced from the goals of basic skills mastery: they seldom use objective test results to gauge their classroom effectiveness (Ashton & Webb 1986; Lortie 1975) and do not take kindly to outside policy interventions that reorient them in this direction (Darling-Hammond & Wise 1985; Rosenholtz 1987; Shannon 1986).

THEORETICAL FRAMEWORK

A strategic question facing most elementary schools, then, is how to increase consensus about the primacy of basic skills mastery without alienating most of their teachers. For one solution we refer back to communications that have to do with gathering and interpreting information related to teaching—communications through which teachers gain a sense of their work. The amount and type of information teachers gather in schools, the degree to which that information is consistent, and the ease with which teachers can interpret and integrate that information will affect their consensus about school goals.

Although many aspects of schools may influence the amount, type, and interpretability of information teachers receive, the factor of interest in our analysis is the subjective way teachers experience their everyday realities. That is, the way daily activities are structured in schools will in and of itself suggest how teaching goals should be defined and prioritized. Shared goals about teaching should develop most readily when the daily patterns of activities in which teachers engage, and the interpretations of their engagement in those activities are *congruent* with a unitary definition of teaching.

Further, in order for teachers in schools to hold the *same* definition of their work, such a definition must not only be logically plausible, but must also be the most salient interpretation possible. The picture painted for and by teachers must have *high resolution*. The more singular and unambiguous the picture teachers see, and the more consistent the information they both send and collect, the less apt they are to develop alternative teaching goals, and the more likely they are to persist in a manner consistent with the goals that they hold (Perrow 1970).

If, on the other hand, schools are organized in ways that allow multiple performance dimensions, multiple bases from which to define teaching goals and values will also exist. Varied standards of performance essentially grant teachers freedom to enhance their own self-esteem by selecting only those goals that suit them best. And if each perceives this choice as a legitimate component of the work of elementary schools, the probability of goal consensus diminishes.

Pivotal to the type, amount, consistency, and interpretability of information flowing to and from teachers is the nature of school leadership. Principals who involve teachers in generating information about the goals of teaching, in scanning and choosing the best alternatives, grant teachers a part in constructing school reality. Moreover, principals who facilitate networks among teachers to exchange ideas about the best way to reach school goals, who encourage teachers to accomplish school goals, and who themselves help teachers accomplish school goals, orient them to the school as a collective endeavor. These conditions increase the probability of shared schoolwide goals.

To identify school activities most likely to produce high goal consensus, we look to workplace conditions that generate the most visible performance information about how teaching should be done. What social organizational features of schools make it more or less likely that the interpretation process in which teachers engage will produce shared understandings about the importance of students' basic skills mastery?

The Social Organization of Shared Goals

School Goal-setting. Though goals of student learning may exist at the abstract level in most elementary schools, their application in classrooms is very much subject to teachers' discretion according to whatever circumstances they perceive. What are creative activities to one elementary school teacher may be classroom chaos to another. What is cheating in one classroom may be cooperation in the next. Because there is seldom agreement between teachers and principals about school outcomes that are sought, the managerial activities of principals are only marginally linked to the technical activities of teachers (Rosenholtz 1985; Metz 1978). Despite schools' espoused goals of student learning, for example, principals rarely use data on student achievement to evaluate teachers or to monitor student performance, even though such data are frequently available (Dornbusch & Scott 1975). Through these and other activities described next, principals unknowingly or intentionally grant teachers wide latitude to define those classroom goals they enact best.

There are some schools, by contrast, in which principals and teachers together set goals for students' basic skill mastery, agree about their primacy, and the procedures by which to carry them out (Rosenholtz 1985). Instructional goals, to emphasize the obvious, may be set by assessing student needs and then devising means that address them. Perhaps less obvious, goals may also be found without seeking, through serendipitous discovery of new priorities by organizational members (Thompson & McEwen 1958). Instructional goals, therefore, are neither static nor intractable. Schools may reformulate or reinterpret them as conditions within the workplace require it; with shifts in the school's clientele, perhaps, or as different student needs emerge, or through the discovery of new technical knowledge, bringing with it reappraisal of the way objectives are currently being met. Through all of this, the school's abstract goals of student learning remain intact; it is only their application that is subject to analysis and alteration (Thompson & McEwen 1958). In essence, goal-setting is a purposive, reiterative activity that orients teachers and principals engaged in this process to the school as a collective enterprise.

Teacher Recruitment and Selection. Another way to increase goal consensus is to recruit like-minded staff. In the most successful schools, principals, sometimes consulting faculty, recruit new teachers that share prevailing standards and values, with school goals the focal point around which hiring decisions are made (Rosenholtz 1985). Not only is the application of school goals to teacher selection a control mechanism to ensure faculty consensus and quality, it serves an important symbolic function as well. Schools that are clear about recruitment criteria underscore how teachers and principals collectively view their present school goals—what they stand for, what they care about, and what they ultimately aspire to become.

Just as principals and faculty may recruit new teachers who will add to the school's collective worth, applicants may try to join particular schools that will enhance their own careers. For prospective entrants, schools' recruitment criteria clarify the implications of their own group membership. Because their work juts out from a mass of mediocrity, schools that demonstrate high consensus about goals and well-deserved pride in meeting them experience greater ease of faculty recruitment (Spunk 1974).

The importance of careful selection procedures and their articulation with school goals cannot be overemphasized. If principals fail in their efforts to hire and keep good teachers—and there is ample evidence that most of them do (Kerr 1983; Wise et al. 1987)—they become mired in an endless array of difficulties that they are expected to solve: how to supervise large contingents of new recruits; how to insure the quality of instruction with frequent staff changes; how to socialize new teachers to the goals of the organization while minimizing the potential chaos of their individual preferences.

Teacher Socialization. Attracting and selecting outstanding teachers is one issue; working to ensure that they fit is quite another. Although hand-picked entrants may arrive inclined to embrace school goals, their ultimate commitment to them is in no small way determined by how successfully they are socialized. Thus organizational socialization refers to the process by which new teachers come to acquire the perspectives and goals of those within the organization. The currency of information newcomers collect, as we shall later see, comes directly from colleagues and principals who, by way of example, symbol, story, or advice, communicate the "correct" ideas, values, goals, and ways of thinking and behaving.

In schools with agreed-upon goals, principals and teachers socialize new recruits with a welcomeness that circumscribes their work to a unitary purpose—basic skills instruction. By eliminating competing bases for performance, newcomers are then more likely to internalize (i.e., accept as "real") those particular goals. Most schools, however, offer new entrants little direction in the details of practice. Newcomers must rely, in Lortie's (1975) terms, on sink or swim socialization—becoming a human litmus absorbing school impressions. They may, in this way, observe a number of varied perspectives, each seemingly legitimate elements of teachers' classroom worlds. In such instances newcomers face a large universe of possibilities from which to define their own views of their work. In other words, the numerous and scattered motifs found within most elementary schools convey symbolically that beyond the appearance of classroom decorum, recruits have the right to create their own performance realities; that schools, after all, are nothing more than collections of independent teachers, each marching to the step of a different pedagogical drum. And it is precisely this observation, of course, that undermines the development of shared instructional goals.

Teacher Evaluation. In most organizations, performance evaluations function to define tasks socially and symbolically and to specify relevant behaviors and outcomes. The lack of agreed-upon goals for teaching makes most schools organizational exceptions (Dornbusch & Scott 1975). Indeed, the absence of performance guidelines about what teachers are to emphasize in their work, the absence of clear criteria by which their performance is to be evaluated, and the frequency of evaluation itself, allows teachers leeway to define their performance standards and how they will gauge their success. Under these conditions of the workplace, goal dissensus is far more apt to develop (Natriello 1983; Rosenholtz 1985).

At the opposite end of the spectrum we find rare, iconoclastic schools where principals consistently monitor students' basic skill mastery and teachers' classroom efforts, give teachers clear, performance-based feedback, and perhaps of greatest importance, set evaluative criteria with teachers in accord with workaday goals (Natriello 1983; Rosenholtz 1985). That is, if evaluative criteria tend to be organized and applied around an explicitly valued dimension—a dimension that teachers themselves partake in shaping, internalization of goals should also take place. Under these workplace conditions we should see greater faculty agreement about teaching goals, beliefs, and values.

Teacher Isolation/Cohesiveness. Without the aforementioned structures, faculties fracture into atoms with entirely separate orbits, a melange of teaching definitions, goals, and indicators of success. Unbending in devotion to their individualistic preferences, teachers become isolated from colleagues—as connected pedagogically as commuters waiting briefly in a train station, each bound on a different route (e.g., Bishop 1977; Lortie 1975). In short, the more isolated the faculty, the more inevitable their pedagogical pluralism. And as we shall see in Chapter 3, where teachers perform their work independently, they show little concern for the professional needs of colleagues. The point to be emphasized here is *not* that teachers seldom talk, but rather that informal conversation rarely centers around a codified base of technical knowledge (see Bishop 1977; Glidewell et al. 1983; Little 1982).

At the same time, the less teachers talk professionally, the lower the faculty's cohesiveness. Cohesiveness is relationship oriented. It involves the affective attachment of people to the organizational community, with fulfillment derived directly from membership involvement. Interaction with organizational members is rewarding in itself, so that failing to conform to a group means a loss of relationships that may be important in the individual's life (Kanter 1968). Moreover, cohesiveness among faculty acts as social cement that strengthens the system of feedback to teachers and presses them to internalize goals. In sum, isolation and cohesiveness form a continuum that describes professional estrangement on the one end, and professional involvement on the other.

Managing Student Behavior. No less crucial to consensus on school purpose, and one of its primary adversaries, is the problem of student misconduct. Where student misbehavior in schools becomes conspicuously pronounced, classroom order often displaces learning as the definition of
teaching success. Competence in controlling students—sometimes using any
method—means that classroom lessons become oriented toward control
rather than learning (e.g., Blase 1986). Despite all this, however, there is an
absence of agreement on the nature of disciplinary standards, on the manner in which they should be enforced, on who should enforce them, and
even on the definition of what constitutes a disciplinary infraction (e.g.,
Metz 1978; Rosenholtz 1985).

Two points arise from this. First, disruptive students interfere with the
teaching process, and, in the broader sense, upset the running of the school.
That is, instruction is held captive in teachers' battles to uphold both their
classroom authority *and* their school reputations—reputations based, more
often than not, on their ability to maintain proper classroom control (see
Lortie 1975; Metz 1978). Second, while the work of teachers inevitably involves the skills to maintain some degree of classroom decorum, professional isolation from colleagues underscores their individual responsibility
to see that control is enforced. Especially in professionally isolated settings,
teachers tend not to involve themselves in incidents of student misconduct
outside the sphere of their own classrooms (Denscombe 1985). Thus teachers' inability to maintain classroom control represents a dual failure: the
failure to control their class and the failure to operate independently. In
both these ways the social organization of schools emphasizes classroom
control as the sole province of teachers' personal competence and authority,
a thoroughly individual enterprise.

Yet it is more than common knowledge that students are not always
willing partners in their classroom learning endeavors. Given that principals
and faculty in some schools set goals to overcome just such obstacles, it
comes as no surprise to find synchronized disciplinary policies and practices
there. Moreover, because standards are shared schoolwide as a communally
mounted endeavor, colleagues more readily assist each other in enforcing
them, and they do so without perjorative implication (e.g., Denscombe
1985). And it is precisely because principals and teachers enforce these rules
in preemptive, synchronized fashion that they can then attend to issues of
their school's instructional priorities (e.g., Metz 1978; Rosenholtz 1985).

School Demographic and Teacher Background Variables. Also considered
here and in subsequent quantitative analyses are several school demographic and teacher background variables. One is school SES. That low
SES schools experience the greatest difficulty in teaching basic skills may
underline its importance as a schoolwide goal. School size, a second demographic variable, may affect the ease of faculty and principal contact, and
thus teachers' opportunities for socialization, evaluation, cohesiveness,

and so forth. That is, the larger the school, the less opportunity teachers and principals may have to interact substantively.

Mean years teaching experience, a teacher background variable, may, on the one hand, increase faculty cohesiveness as well as participative opportunities such as setting school goals, developing rules for student conduct, and selecting and socializing new recruits. On the other hand, with increased experience, teachers may become more isolated professionally, as teaching beliefs and behaviors become firm and automatic and so less subject to change. Finally, we include the mean academic status of teachers' undergraduate institutions. This variable has been used in several studies at the individual level as a proxy for teachers' verbal ability (Murnane 1981) and, like verbal ability itself, relates significantly to students' basic skills mastery. We used this measure in the present analysis to examine whether schools that emphasize instructional goals tend to recruit the brightest candidates.

Summary. Consensus or dissensus about the goals of teaching, we have argued, is a direct function of the consistency and interpretability of information teachers gather and disperse in schools. Such information may come from a variety of social organizational sources and activities: goal-setting, recruitment, socialization, and evaluation; a faculty's isolation or cohesiveness; and the way student behavior is managed in the school. To the extent that each activity delimits what is important to emphasize in teaching and how one's success should be gauged, we should find greater consensus about the primary purpose of teaching and the goals within the school.

QUANTITATIVE MEASUREMENT AND FINDINGS

Operational Definitions

To test this conceptual model, operational definitions for each social organizational variable are first in order. Box 2.1 presents the scale measuring each concept, questionnaire items used to construct it, the scale's reliability as measured by Cronbach's Alpha Coefficient, and its range of item-to-scale correlations. To maximize variation, we constructed these scales with individual rather than school-level data.

Quantitative Findings

Statistical Procedures. Structural modeling can aid in the building and testing of various models of social behavior by forcing the researcher to make explicit substantive propositions about the interrelations between variables. The LISREL approach to structural modeling (Joreskog & Sorbom 1978), unlike multiple regression, allows one to deal with both reciprocal and non-

BOX 2.1   Construction of Scales

Shared Teaching Goals

1. At this school, we agree on the objectives we're trying to achieve with students.
2. If most teachers at this school feel that another teacher is not doing a good job, they will exert some pressure on him or her to improve.
3. I don't approve of the ways in which most of the other teachers in this school teach.*
4. My principal's values and philosophy of education are similar to my own.
5. Most teachers at this school have values and philosophies of education similar to my own.
6. Teachers at this school share a high level of commitment to student learning.

Alpha = .70; item-to-scale correlations = .19 to .32.

School Goal-setting

1. There are explicit guidelines in the school about the things teachers are to emphasize in their teaching.
2. Discussion about school goals and means of achieving them is a regular part of our school faculty or inservice meetings.
3. The principal of this school encourages teachers to talk with each other about instructional objectives.
4. At faculty meetings, we spend most of our time on the small stuff; we rarely get a chance to talk about the bigger issues in teaching and learning.*
5. There are a lot of irrelevant side conversations that go on at our faculty meetings.*
6. We have explicit goals for student achievement in this school.

Alpha = .73; item-to-scale correlations = .17 to .40.

Teacher Recruitment

1. Before I came to work in this school, the principal "checked me out," read my references, called people who know my work, and asked me about my ideas and plans for teaching.
2. Whenever there is an opening at my school, the principal takes charge in locating a good and competent person for the position.
3. Our principal consults with teachers here before hiring new personnel.

Alpha = .56; item-to-scale correlations = .30 to .44.

Teacher Evaluation

1. The standards by which my teaching is evaluated are clear and well specified.
2. My students' gains on achievement tests are a good way for others to judge my instructional effectiveness.
3. The methods used in evaluating my teaching are objective and fair.
4. Student gains on achievement tests are a good way for me to judge my instructional effectiveness.
5. I *know* what I'm being evaluated on in this school.
6. Evaluation of my teaching is based on hearsay and gossip.*
7. The principal spends time in my classroom observing my teaching.
8. When the principal comes into my classroom, the visit lasts longer than 10 minutes.
9. In this school, teachers participate in determining what they're going to be evaluated on.

Alpha = .73; item-to-scale correlations = .21 to .57.

Teacher Socialization

1. New teachers in this school know what our faculty is trying to accomplish and what will be expected of them as teachers.
2. When I started teaching at this school, the principal told me what the faculty wants to accomplish here.
3. The principal of this school spends time with any new teachers we may have, orients them and helps them feel welcome in the school.
4. The faculty makes new teachers feel very welcome at this school.

Alpha = .71; item-to-scale correlations = .26 to .62.

Isolation/Cohesiveness

1. Most of the other teachers in this school don't know what I do in my classroom or what my teaching goals are.*
2. Teachers in this school tend to be cliquish and catty.*
3. I do things that are apt to be accepted by only a few teachers at my school; the others don't agree or don't understand.*
4. I feel that what goes on in this school is my responsibility; I share responsibility for our school's successes and shortcomings.
5. Beyond saying hello, I regularly converse with:
   a. no other teachers
   b. one other teacher
   c. two other teachers
   d. three other teachers
   e. four or more other teachers

6. I can go for days in this school without talking to anyone about my teaching.*

7. I'm pretty much a "loner" in this school.*

Alpha = .74; item-to-scale correlations = .20 to .53.

Managing Student Behavior

1. There are explicit rules for student conduct at this school.

2. We have rules for student conduct here, but nobody follows them.*

3. Rules for student behavior are consistently enforced by teachers at this school, even for students who are not in their classes.

4. Teachers' rules for student conduct are always changing at this school.*

5. In this school, teachers participate in establishing rules for student conduct.

Alpha.77; item-to-scale correlations = .43 to .65.

*We recoded these items in calculating scale scores.

reciprocal models, as well as the relationships between independent and intervening variables, apart from their effects on the dependent variable. That is, instead of independent variables expressed solely in terms of the size of their effect on dependent variables, LISREL allows one to specify *both* the direction and strength of relationships between independent, intervening, and dependent variables. Moreover, whereas regression analysis measures the prediction of dependent variables from one or more independent variables without error, path analysis estimates these relationships with or without error.

LISREL uses a correlation matrix and sample size as data input. The overall intent of LISREL is to reconstruct its path estimates as closely as possible by imposing one's conceptual model on the data. The program provides two methods for evaluating the "goodness of fit" of a theoretical framework to the data: the chi-square test for overall goodness of fit (maximum size 1.0) and the critical ratios formed by the LISREL path coefficient, divided by the standard error of that coefficient. The chi-square test allows one to test whether the conceptual framework actually accounts for the data or simply represents chance correlations. The closer the chi-square to the degrees of freedom, the smaller the error (residual difference) between the initial and the reconstructed coefficients. In general, chi-square values that are three times the degrees of freedom indicate a poor fit of the model to the data. In the second method of testing the fit, one scrutinizes each path coefficient to capture the most parsimonious statistical explanation for the model. If the critical ratio is large, the variable is necessary to the model; if small, it is probably unnecessary. Some investigators require that the path coefficients equal at least two times their standard error, while others accept the .05 or .10 level of significance. The present study uses .10, mindful that small samples generally call for lower probability levels.

The correlations, means, and standard deviations for the social organizational, demographic, and teacher background variables taken either from the teacher questionnaire or districts' archival records appear in Table 2.1. Although each social organizational variable moderately to strongly correlates with the others, no school demographic variable bears any relationship to shared school goals. School SES, however, correlated weakly with other social organizational factors. Specifically, the higher the school's SES, the more likely new teachers will be recruited and socialized, but the less schools engage in setting instructional goals. The status of teachers' undergraduate degrees is moderately correlated with teacher recruitment. That is, to the extent that recruitment takes place, teachers from higher status universities are those most likely to be hired. Finally, in examining the correlations between school demographic and teacher background variables, we observe with interest that teachers' undergraduate status is strongly and negatively correlated with school SES. The lower the school's SES, the less likely faculties from higher status universities will be teaching there.

Retaining only those variables of statistical significance, we generated a structural model between variables using LISREL. The path diagram depicting "causal" links between variables appears in Figure 2.1. The LISREL analysis shows the model's goodness of fit index at an acceptable level—.955. Its chi-square, with 13 degrees of freedom, equals 14.75, a .32 probability level. The average residual size (error term) equals .03. Path coefficients are shown on the lines connecting variables, with arrows indicating the direction of their relationship. Percentages in parentheses express the unexplained or residual variance for each variable. We note first that among all variables, school SES makes no significant contribution to the model. Its strong skewness in the direction of low SES schools accounts in large measure for its lack of significance. We discuss each remaining variable in terms of its direct or indirect effect on shared goals.

Direct Effects. Comparing path coefficients, we find that far and away the strongest predictor of shared goals is teacher socialization, the extent of newcomers' mediated entry into the school. To the degree that principals and colleagues orient newcomers, make them feel welcome to the school, and communicate what will be expected of them and how their purposes fit with those held by others, they seem to etch the substance and shape of school goals into novices' own definitions of teaching. Further, principals and teachers who socialize new entrants in this way may revitalize their *own* aspirations for the school.

Teacher evaluation makes the second largest contribution in accounting

TABLE 2.1. Correlation Coefficients, Means (M), and Standard Deviations (SD) for Variables Examined with the Dependent Variable Shared Values

Variables	2	3	4	5	6	7	8	9	10	11	M	SD
1. Goal-setting	.67	.46	.74	.84	.60	.79	.18	.11	−.07	.01	14.45	2.25
2. Evaluation		.55	.58	.64	.39	.71	−.01	.09	−.00	.13	20.21	2.80
3. Recruitment			.48	.56	.34	.54	−.19	.18	.18	.38	5.93	1.40
4. Managing student behavior				.74	.60	.76	.08	.03	.03	.00	13.38	2.18
5. Socialization					.68	.86	.17	.03	.06	.07	10.18	1.64
6. Isolation/cohesiveness						.69	−.05	−.09	.03	.13	22.28	2.01
7. Shared goals							.03	.05	−.12	.16	14.27	1.44
8. School SES								−.27	−.18	−.16	.41	.22
9. School size									.00	.07	19.49	8.13
10. Teaching experience										−.06	12.73	3.00
11. Undergraduate status											2.61	1.01

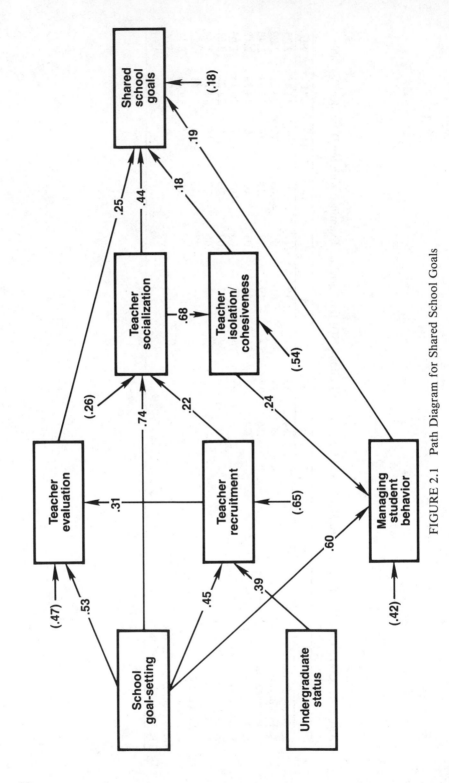

FIGURE 2.1 Path Diagram for Shared School Goals

26

for shared school goals. Teachers who believe that evaluation criteria are important, central to their work, applied frequently, and capable of being influenced by their own effort report greater commitment to school goals. To a lesser extent, faculty isolation/cohesiveness and collectively enforced standards for student behavior also account for differences in schools' goal consensus. Isolated, teachers tend to be thrown back on their own resources and pushed toward norms of self-reliance. Cohesive, teachers tend to see themselves more as equal partners in the school enterprise, share greater responsibility for school outcomes, and exert collegial pressure on those who deviate from them. For its part, the extent to which student conduct is choreographed schoolwide seems a necessary prerequisite for goal consensus, as teachers and principals remove those obstacles that stand in the way of instructional goals. Together these four variables combine to account for 82% of the variance in shared school goals.

Indirect Effects. Examining Figure 2.1, we can also comment on the social organizational antecedents of each direct effect. Goal-setting and teacher recruitment, while showing no direct effect on goal consensus, are implicated in nearly all direct paths. For instance, 35% of the difference in recruitment is accounted for by two factors: goal-setting and the status of teachers' undergraduate degrees. That goal-setting shows significant effects supports the idea that principals and teachers with clear aspirations for student learning are apt to select new recruits with the tightest fit.

The influence of teachers' undergraduate status poses at least two interpretations. When viewed as a proxy for verbal ability, on the one hand, schools may actively seek recruits that show the greatest intellectual prowess. On the other hand, an institutional effect may exist: candidates may be selected on the basis of their preservice education, which may be qualitatively better in higher than in lower status schools. Indeed, the variation in status of Tennessee's undergraduate institutions looms enormously large (College Blue Book 1985). Only three universities offer an Ed.D. or Ph.D. in education, and seven more an M.A. degree. The remaining 30 are secular, racially segregated, or otherwise small colleges with less than 3000 students that offer teacher certification at the Bachelor's level, some with only a skeletal crew of education faculty (e.g., two members). At the farthest end of the continuum are 7 institutions granting two-year Associate Teacher Certificates, from which small rural districts confronting severe teacher shortages sometimes desperately, illegally, and therefore surreptitiously, recruit.

Despite such variation, however, there is a dearth of sound empirical support that preservice education makes a difference in teacher effectiveness (Ashton, Crocker, & Olejnik 1987; Griffin et al. 1983). One explanation offered by Lanier and Little (1986) is that professors from prestigious universities consume themselves with research, working more with graduate than undergraduate students. In any case, researchers repeatedly conclude that whatever the short-term effects of their preservice courses, experienced teachers appear to bear few of the hallmarks of their preservice training (Denscombe 1985; Koehler 1985). Although the research evidence for either of these interpretations is far from conclusive, this much in our data is certainly true: not every elementary school starts from the same vantage point of collective faculty qualifications with respect to their preservice education, their academic prowess, or, as we shall see in Chapters 4 and 6, their ability to help students learn.

Figure 2.1 also reveals two antecedents of teacher socialization that together account for 74% of its variance. The stronger of the two, goal-setting, suggests that as entrants are socialized, they take on school goals in part because their colleagues and principal emphasize clear instructional aspirations for the school. The role of recruitment follows similar tendencies; the greater the effort to locate the best fitting teachers, the more effort is expended to induct them properly. Similarly, 53% of the variance in teacher evaluation is explained by goal-setting and, albeit of lesser strength, teacher selection. Thus principals' and teachers' clarity of purpose seems also to encourage clear and frequent evaluation. Apparently principals tend to take greater care in evaluating teachers where they expend more energy selecting them.

Faculty isolation or cohesiveness is affected directly by only one variable in the model—teacher socialization—although through socialization, goal-setting, and recruitment each contribute indirectly. Thus socialized newcomers tend to internalize school goals in part because of collective pressure wielded by colleagues who march in compatible cadence knowing exactly what they are about professionally. As Figure 2.1 also reveals, the stronger teachers' cohesiveness and goal clarity, the more they appear to orchestrate student conduct at the school level. In fact, 58% of the difference in collectively enforced standards for student behavior is accounted for by these two variables alone. The implications here cannot be missed: with greater sense of purpose and school belongingness, faculties work more closely to ensure appropriate student conduct. This, in the end, may strengthen their commitment to the instructional goals of the school.

THE SOCIAL CONSTRUCT OF SHARED GOALS

People assign meanings to situations and to the actions of others and react in terms of their interpretation of those meanings. The logic of those meanings may be understood, our theoretical perspective holds, through organizational members' communications. That is, to understand what members regard as rational, one must understand what is taken for granted within the social organization in which their shared rationality is located. The information people exchange through conversation enters into the commonplace—the meanings that organizational members regard as natural when attending to their daily affairs (Berger & Luckmann 1966). Communications can thus be understood as a mirror to the rest of the social organization; a representation of ways of life within it.

Patently inductive, our approach assumes that what is important in teachers' working lives will make itself known by its frequency of appearance or its salience in interactions. Only after such categories appear can one legitimately begin to construct deductive hypotheses about teachers' consciousness and behavior in different contextual settings. To the extent that social organizations differ, then, teachers should have their own ways of looking at things and at people and their own ways of dealing with them. At the same time, the communications in which teachers engage should provide a tacit understanding of the school's social organization itself. The interviews we conducted with teachers allow us to explore both these premises. We back into these analyses slowly by first examining the fit between our quantitative and qualitative data.

Analysis and Findings of Qualitative Data

We followed identical procedures in each chapter to analyze interview data. First, using quantitative data, we computed z-scores for each social organizational variable on a samplewide basis. For each school, we then averaged z-scores on those variables *directly related to, and including, the dependent measure* (in the present case, shared goals, teacher evaluation, managing student behavior, teacher socialization, and teacher isolation/cohesiveness). Where social organizational variables averaged approximately one standard deviation or more *above* their respective means, schools received a high value for that analysis. Where social organizational variables averaged approximately one standard deviation or more *below* their respective means, schools received a low value. Schools assigned a moderate value were those where social organizational variables averaged close to their respective means.

Overall, the trichotomy of values samplewide was strikingly consistent. Of the 23 schools from which we interviewed teachers, 15 held the same value: 4 all high, 5 all medium, and 6 all low. That is, schools assigned a low value on goal consensus were also low on collaboration, instructional certainty, commitment, and so forth. Of the remaining schools, 4 were more medium than high or low, 2 more high than medium, and 2 more low than medium. In no case did schools span both extremes. It is in these latter 8 schools that we find fluctuations in the number of teachers interviewed for each analysis.

In the present case, and with reference to the overall sample of 78 schools, 17 held high goal consensus. We interviewed 21 teachers from 6 of these schools. From 9 of the 17 schools with low goal consensus, we sampled 28 teachers. Among the 44 schools with moderate goal consensus, we talked with 25 teachers from 8 schools.

In one question we asked teachers, "What do you usually talk about with your colleagues?" If our thinking is correct, that conversation reflects the commonsense view of its members, and alternatively, that members form commonsense notions through their workaday worlds, we should find that teachers from varied social organizations talk about entirely different things. Results of the analysis by the schools' level of goal consensus appear in Table 2.2

Curriculum and Instruction. Approximately one sixth of the teachers in moderate consensus schools and one fifth of the teachers in low consensus schools mentioned conversation about the substance of teaching—curriculum and instruction. In striking contrast, more than half of those sampled from high consensus schools talk about these things:

> We talk about the new ideas someone has tried, how they worked or didn't work. We make an effort to do something different on a regular basis. One [idea] that works for one teacher may not work for another. We try to figure out why that's so.

> I guess mostly academics. We talk about teaching in new ways. Someone will try something new and tell the rest of us about it if it's successful. It seems like we're always experimenting.

> The progress of the students, any problems they are having. Getting advice from each other, especially from teachers who may have had them in the past. If there was some instructional technique that worked better for them, we tell each other about it.

As these data indicate, social organizations that screen out some aspects of teaching and magnify other parts successfully direct teacher attention to what the nature of the commonplace should be. Thus, because teachers share common goals about the importance of students' learning, they talk about the ways this best can occur. The essential point to recognize is the normative agreements that are at the very heart of the school enterprise. Norms are those beliefs to which teachers appeal for their ultimate rationales of action. In high consensus settings, teachers' talk reflects a conception of the desirable, explicitly defined and mutually shared, which seems to direct and unify behavior, just as the funnel of an hourglass forms the sand and sends it all in the same direction. That is, talk at once produces and is a product of norms that underlie most aspects of behavior in the school: behavior aimed at one end, one result. High consensus schools represent a solidity, a bringing together, a balance that binds all elements into one entity, from which the removal of a single part may jeopardize the whole. But in lower consensus schools, there is little within the social organization to consolidate common means and ends. Here teachers mingle and separate yet remain utterly distinct. Talk about curriculum and instruction occurs far less frequently because there are neither consistent nor explicit

TABLE 2.2. Teacher Talk

| Level of goal consensus | No time to talk | WHAT DO YOU USUALLY TALK ABOUT WITH YOUR COLLEAGUES?* | | | | N |
		Social plans and activities	Complaints about work conditions	Complaints about student behavior	Curriculum and instruction	
High	8%	4%	33%	4%	54%	24
Moderate	11%	19%	22%	32%	16%	37
Low	20%	11%	33%	28%	19%	45

*Teachers sometimes offered multiple responses to this question. Percentages therefore reflect the number of times each category was mentioned.

structures to guide them in their thinking. In fact, norms of self-reliance, as we shall see in Chapter 3, centrifugally pull teachers away from such substantive conversation.

Student Behavior Problems. It is not only teachers' right but their presumed obligation to keep students engaged in some legitimate curricular activity. We have also acceded the complexity of this task in the absence of preemptory and synchronized action, where principals and teachers wrestle and diverge in many disparate directions. It is not unexpected, therefore, that far more often teachers in lower rather than higher consensus schools discussed the foibles of individual students. Conversation about student conduct prevailed in about one fourth of teachers' responses from both moderate and low consensus schools:

> We discuss a child that one of us is having problems with. Discipline problems, usually. It helps to be able to discuss it with someone else. It may not always give you an answer to the problem. [Does it help you to get support from other teachers?] Yes. A lot of times we just get sympathy from each other if we have a bad class.

> We discuss children's backgrounds a great deal and reasons for their behavior. Sometimes there are problems with a child's background that are responsible for the problems at school. And I feel that sometimes by explaining a background to another teacher, the teacher is more supportive of the child. Now I know this happened last year. I had a child last year who was doing poorly. I explained his background to his third grade teacher and, although he still didn't do good work, at the end of the year she plans to give him a certificate for effort.

> Discipline. Just the fact that we have no control any more, no leverage, other than sitting them in the corner or the reward system or ignoring them. That works up to a point, but they've been rewarded so much that they expect any good behavior to be rewarded.

Again we observe through inductive stance that conversation meshes with the governing structures of the school enterprise. In low consensus schools, where there may be little common intent to deal with student misbehavior, some pupils become major school problems and a natural basis for teachers' dark communion. As subsequent chapters will make patently clear, anger and frustration has taken seed in them, for it defines boundaries, escalates frictions, and sets laboring teachers against principals, parents, and students. Contrary to this, in high consensus schools, with intentional striving to institutionalize appropriate conduct, only one teacher mentioned conversation about student behavior, and the substance of that conversation took an entirely different and substantially more positive bent:

> Students and behavior. This year we had a little girl who was very tall and self-conscious about her height. She walked stooped over a lot. Several of the teachers and myself worked on ways to get her out of her shell and we worked with

her mother, too. Now at the end of the year she is walking more straight up and proud of herself.

The cooperative efforts within this teacher's school underscore its faculty cohesiveness—a group of colleagues banded together in common purpose. In high consensus schools, teachers affirm this point again and again:

We're like a family of teachers, rather than one person.

The best thing [about this school] is the capability of everyone working together.

Everyone at this school cares that we all do our best and teachers help each other to do that.

Without ongoing, communal efforts, the definitions of school problems themselves vary widely, and strategic solutions, as we shall see in Chapter 5, are apt to be drawn solely from one's internal resourcefulness. One teacher from a low consensus school makes this point clear in her depiction of students' cafeteria behavior:

Student discipline mostly. But there are some things that happen here that we wouldn't let happen at my other school. [Such as what?] At one time, when students left, they were noisy—running down the hall. So we all tried to get them under control. We held up stop signs if they were too noisy in the cafeteria, we had railroad tracks that they had to walk on, and there were more teachers supervising. [But in your current situation this doesn't happen?] They [students] aren't as controlled. Some teachers just want to eat. They don't want to be bothered with it. What some teachers see as a problem, other teachers think is okay.

This teacher's frame of reference, her consciousness of different and better possibilities, is held fast by memory flooding back in such pungent ways as to allow her reentry to a former school experience. That is, the taken-for-granted workplace remains just that unless people experience a different sort of reality in their past. Thus schoolwide student misconduct might have been less problematic had this teacher not enjoyed a better set of circumstances elsewhere. Furthermore, student misbehavior in this school appears to be individually defined in the sense that what passes for appropriate behavior in one teacher's view may not pass the same test in another's. Teachers here tend to be wary of collective thinking and resolute about their individual preferences. Yet ironically, norms of self-reliance often impede the struggle for teaching success by failing to secure the cooperation of students for the whole faculty. Precisely why this may occur is the subject of Chapter 3.

Working Conditions. We found no difference between schools of high and low consensus in the extent to which teachers complained about their working conditions, reflecting, at least to some extent, the State's meager funding of elementary education, and the representativeness of our sample state-wide:

> About the school. It's an old building and the heat and cold are completely out of whack. There's no air conditioning and we have the old furnace. On the northwest side of the building it's very cold. It takes a long while for it to warm up and in the summer, when you're getting ready for school, it's very, very hot.

> The overcrowding in our school. It's too small. It has no air conditioning. It's one of the oldest schools in the system. Paint is peeling off the walls in the corridors.

> The physical conditions of the school. There are always puddles in the bathroom because the toilet leaks. Many things don't function well because the custodians can't fix them. And if we need special repairmen, we never get them. [Why not?] There's no money.

These data mirror several national surveys of teachers' dissatisfaction with the physical conditions of work (e.g., Educational Research Service 1985). What is contextually remarkable about these complaints, however, is that despite poor working conditions, teachers in high consensus schools appear nonetheless to carry on with the business of teaching, whereas those in moderate and low consensus schools seem to find diversions from work lurking all about.

Social Conversation. One such diversion clearly more evident in moderately low than in high consensus schools is social conversation, mentioned by about a fifth of the teachers sampled:

> Well, the thing we've been talking about the most is that the assistant principal had to have some eye surgery done. You know, the kind of surgery you have done to correct your vision. Anway, he had the whole surgical procedure on videotape and we saw that. [Is this a typical kind of conversation?] Yes. We try to stay away from academic talk; we need some relief from it, especially after a hard day.

> Mostly we talk about what we're doing socially. It helps to relieve the tension of the day to get your mind on something else.

> As far as education is concerned, I don't know. Usually what it comes down to is that you get women together and chat. I don't think that's unusual. [What kinds of things do you talk about?] Nothing special. Stuff like where you bought your sweater, what you did over the weekend. I don't think anybody really does talk academics that much. We all want a break from the education atmosphere. When you have to work so hard all day, you need a chance to cool your heels. We never talk about lesson plans or objectives, if that's what you mean.

In these teachers' comments we observe a particularly good example of taken-for-granted reality. Teachers had no qualms about confessing that it is neither commonplace nor desirable to discuss instructional matters with colleagues, that the need for these brief mental holidays is similar in all schools. Lurking beneath the surface of these beliefs—but probably not at the conscious level—may be norms of self-reliance, far more prevalent in lower consensus schools. This seems to be part of the reason that teachers talk and complain but show little enthusiasm for open, serious dialogue about curriculum and instruction. Since teachers are at liberty to go their own ways, to protect this right they must be willing to let colleagues do likewise. The many deleterious consequences of these norms and the professional isolation they spawn is a matter we explore in subsequent chapters.

No Talk. Finally from Table 2.2, teachers reporting no conversation with colleagues at all was inversely related to the level of schools' goal consensus. Only two teachers made mention of this in high consensus schools, compared to one fifth of the responses from low consensus schools:

> We really do not have much interaction. The only time we can talk is before or after lunch. This is a problem. You may only express your ideas to one or two people that you see, but there may be some people who feel the same way; who may be frustrated by the same things.

> I often go for a long time without ever even talking to another teacher. So I would have to say that I haven't talked about anything much with faculty members—certainly nothing earth-shattering.

> There's not a lot of time for socializing. Also, the teachers' lounge isn't exactly conducive to sitting and talking. We have a tacky lounge. There are broken chairs. It's pretty dirty. It's dark. There's a coke machine, but it's so gloomy and cluttered. You just don't want to sit in there. There's not even a couch.

Most revealing about these responses is the fact that almost all other teachers reported talking (albeit sometimes only briefly) to their colleagues before or after school, while passing in the corridors, or during lunch, whether or not they enjoyed a planning period, regardless of their school's level of goal consensus, and the physical conditions of their workplace. The idea that schools with low goal consensus may generate their own levels of professional isolation is again important to recognize here.

Teacher Socialization. Nowhere in teachers' responses are the contextual effects of their talk more evident than as they regard novices to the school. In high consensus schools, colleagues, in explaining their conversations, often expressed an awareness of newcomers' needs that openly exposed the norms of their schools:

> New teachers need to be able to discuss situations with older teachers who have been there several years.

> They [new teachers] need to know there is someone that they can go to for advice.

If you need help, ask! Don't just blunder your way along. You can save yourself a lot of grief if you ask soon enough when you have a problem.

Three second-year teachers, also from entirely different schools, make the success of these socialization practices abundantly clear:

Mostly we talk about problems we are having with teaching. There are some really great teachers at this school and they have all sorts of ways to handle difficult problems; last year it seemed that all I did was pump these teachers for ideas—but they seemed to enjoy helping me. [In what ways did they communicate that they enjoyed helping you?] They would always ask, "Did you try this and that?" And, "What happened?" They took a real interest in me, and that made me feel good, too.

Oh, we talk, for instance, about special materials we make and how they work with children. When I came to this school I expected to teach kindergarten and there weren't enough students. I had worked all summer making materials for the year and at the last minute I was given a sixth grade. What an adjustment! [How did you make it through the year?] Well, people on the faculty—other teachers—pitched in and helped. One teacher gave me a bunch of material on synonyms and antonyms, another gave me math materials. I went to many people with teaching problems. [Do you think that "pitching in" is a regular occurrence at your school?] Oh yes. We all work together here.

Mostly we talk about teaching. They [other teachers] spent all their time [last year] trying to make sure I understood everything I was doing, so that children at our grade level wouldn't fall behind for the fifth grade teachers, and also, I guess I felt like they really wanted me to be successful. They were always there when I needed some help or whenever they thought I needed some help. It made me feel that I had something important to do for the children and the other fourth grade teachers.

In high consensus schools, socialization appeared aimed at helping beginners distinguish specious ideas from sound ones; at grounding their perspectives in the school's traditions of challenge and change; at asking not only "What did I do wrong?" but also at asking "What can I do right?" And as these latter comments reveal, beginners, filled with shining and fragile dreams, were easy prey for a cohesive faculty, who etched indelible confirmatory memories of their first workplace reality.

In low consensus schools, newcomers and their colleagues described the more common sink or swim socialization—an informal experience of the sort that, like a battle, results in many effects, helter-skelter: in aborted dreams, lasting pain, ill will, and most important of all, fugitive glories. One experienced teacher related such an instance for a first year colleague in her isolated school:

There seems to be a lot of dissatisfaction among the faculty members with the principal. They seem to complain quite a bit. They feel that the principal doesn't always back them up on discipline or some decision that he's made. [Does that kind of talk disturb you?] Sometimes yes. I'm spending less time with teachers because of that. But mostly I feel sorry for the beginning teachers. With all the griping and gossiping going on they don't get any support or help from anyone. It's sad to see an excited beginner struggle and struggle and finally turn sour.

Reports of professional isolation in low consensus schools also came from newcomers themselves; a transfer teacher with little experience, and two disillusioned novices relayed:

> I couldn't answer you there. This is my first year in this school. I have stuck pretty much to myself. I'm really not on the grapevine so I just don't know. I'm just not really involved in this school. [Did others help you learn school procedures?] No. I more or less figured those things out for myself.

> Oh, student discipline, that sort of thing. [Does anyone at your school help you?] No, nobody's even asked me how I'm doing. [Do you talk to others about *your* classroom problems?] I'd be too embarrassed. I don't know anyone very well yet, and I'd be afraid it'd get back to the principal that I couldn't control my class.

> Teachers here talk about children in a very negative way. And they don't really talk to you unless you go along with their ideas. If you talk about how this kid or that kid is a pain in the neck, they welcome you with open arms.

The last teacher finds herself in something of a dilemma: she clearly resents the faculty's belittlement of students as the only permissible way in which to discuss them, and yet she recognizes that a breach in their tradition carries serious and far-reaching consequences. If newcomers do not accept prevailing norms and values of the faculty, they may find themselves isolated socially, deprived of any sense of group belongingness. In the next comments a transfer teacher with four years of previous experience stresses this very point; then another teacher unapologetically describes the ostracism of a colleague who clearly does not fit within her low consensus school:

> I can't think of anything. [Do you talk to other teachers?] Well, you can't always get the help you need. [Do you ever get help when you have problems?] At my old school I got help from my principal. I'm pretty much of a newcomer to this school and I still feel like an outsider. Four years is not really new, but I still feel that way.

> Sometimes we discuss problem students and problem teachers. We have a couple of bad ones [teachers] now; one uses up all her sick leave. She has a poor reputation with the rest of the teachers. She doesn't *look* like a teacher. [What do you mean?] Well, she wears tight clothing and lots of makeup. Her attitude is poor. She doesn't fit in with the rest of the teachers. [How well does she perform in the classroom?] Oh, her achievement test scores show that her kids learn a lot. We think maybe she is teaching to the test. But the kids in junior high come back to see her all the time. [How long has she taught in your school?] Four years, I think.

This teacher, outrageous though successful, did not enjoy the approval of her colleagues, who seem to have removed themselves from their work and find no pleasure in it. Indeed, teachers in isolated workplaces, as we shall see in Chapter 3, are not rewarded for their successes but rather are punished. Against this backdrop it is plain that questions of "teacher fit" carry substantial consequences. A teacher's effectiveness is not an objective, uniform, or unvarying judgment. It depends heavily on the specific situation into which the teacher is placed, the expectations and behavior of one's colleagues, and the goodness of fit between the teacher's own behavior and the norms of the school. The same individual who fits poorly into one situation and is judged to be unsuccessful in it, may fit superbly and successfully into another. And these dramatic differences may in part be explained by school practices of recruitment and socialization.

Thus we see with some precision the experiential differences newcomers face as they enter schools of contrasting circumstance. In high consensus schools, on the one hand, idealistic novices seem to encounter a community of professionals whose basic thrust is helping students learn. Through the flow of recurrent daily activity, observation, and conversation, newcomers learn that their own professional aspirations coincide with the majority of others; that their enthusiasm has its place and is real, something to be brought to life and actually touched; and that their own development is part and parcel of community growth. Equally important, they may find moral obligation to contribute reciprocally to their school's collective enterprise.

In low consensus schools, on the other hand, newcomers receive their textbook manuals, pencils, and class rosters along with the same parsimonious introduction that is accorded them by principals and colleagues about the school and what is done there. They, too, may observe and converse for a time. But beneath the customary civility that accompanies such conversation, they hear strident messages: messages that it is all right to talk about students as long as those conversations barely penetrate the surface; that one's professional reputation hinges precariously on keeping students in line; that teaching, after all, is about the confidential interactions that transpire between students and individual teachers. For neophytes, idealistically committed to developing the potential of each of their student charges, there are conflicts: conflicts between treating students humanistically and making them toe an overly punitive line; between not really knowing what to do and keeping inadequacies concealed; between earning colleagues' friendship and respect by joining their demeaning banter about students that, at the same time, belies novices' best professional intentions. Just how these conflicts are resolved is addressed in the next three chapters.

SUMMARY

In this chapter we postulated that teachers in elementary schools vary in their degree of goal consensus and that those differences are strongly associated with the social organization of their schools. Since daily experience and interpretations of reality tend to be congruent, we argued, those school features presenting the most consistent and visible definition of work in teachers' everyday experience would come to be internalized. We found strong support for this conceptualization in our quantitative analysis. To the degree that the school's social organization pointed teachers in a unidimensional direction, they appeared to adopt a singular gauge of their own teaching success. And to the extent that principals interacted with teachers to shape their school reality, to construct school traditions (e.g., to define instructional goals, to select and socialize new recruits, to determine policies of student behavior, and to develop evaluative criteria), goals about the importance of students' basic skills mastery came to be commonly shared.

We also argued in this chapter that articulated speech was one of the most patterned and therefore revealing forms of school culture, disclosing teachers' uniformity of goals, beliefs, and values. In this regard our qualitative data articulated well with quantitative data. Indeed, in the qualitative data we found plausible cases and repeated examples to buttress our conceptual underpinnings. Here we observed three things: (1) that teachers talk in accordance with the social organization in which they are members; (2) that knowledge through conversation is one way by which moral action (i.e., norms) is educated; and (3) that whatever the nature of "reality" may be, what teachers take to be real is, at least in part, socially constructed.

In low consensus schools, teachers took their pedagogical explorations in entirely different directions. Because of their unprogrammatic activity, these schools were not colonies but stranded hinterlands or closed-off emperies. Confronted by instructional libertarianism and provided with nothing to counterbalance it, new entrants were cut adrift to discover and define their own ways. In this way norms of self-reliance became moral imperatives—collectively arrived at, collectively shared, and collectively enforced.

When teachers conversed in either moderate or low consensus schools, they stressed students' failings instead of their triumphs perhaps to avenge themselves of the daylong strain imposed upon them. In high consensus schools, by contrast, shared goals, beliefs, and values led teachers through their talk to a more ennobling vision that placed teaching issues and children's interests in the forefront, and that bound them, including newcomers, to pursue that same vision. One outcome of such unified, collective thinking—teacher collaboration—is the subject we address next.

3

Teacher Collaboration

It has long been established that given a problem-solving task, a task novel to all concerned, some groups accomplish a good deal more than others (e.g., Johnson & Johnson 1975). Although various explanations have been offered for differential productivity, we argue here that when collaborative norms undergird achievement-oriented groups, they bring new ideas, fresh ways of looking at things, and a stock of collective knowledge that is more fruitful than any one person's working alone.

However, teachers' willingness to work together in solving instructional problems is not an immutable fact of everyday life, as we saw in Chapter 2. In the present chapter we explore schools' social organization that encourage or dissuade faculty collaboration, defined here as their requests for and offers of collegial advice and assistance. Not only are we attentive to teacher perceptions of work as a shared or an individual endeavor; also foremost in this chapter is teachers' certainty about a technical culture and their instructional practice and therefore possible threats to their self-esteem. With these and other organizational constraints or opportunities, we examine teachers' meaning of sharing, of collegial leadership, and the manner in which teachers' consciousness of appropriate collegial relations takes shape.

THEORETICAL FRAMEWORK

Threats to Self-Esteem

Whether or not teachers seek or offer help depends to no small extent on the perceived consequences of that aid. If help-seeking is potentially embarrassing or stigmatizing, if it may prove threatening to people's sense of self-worth, they will avoid self-disclosure and through various maneuvers maintain their sense of control (Amato & Saunders 1985). In a like manner, if help should be requested, and if some question should arise about how capably people can render it, if they might be found wanting or deficient, then rather than suffer any public or private embarrassment, they, too, will forego aid on behalf of another to protect their self-esteem and to maintain their sense of control (Aderman & Berkowitz 1985; Berkowitz 1970).

To forestall self-threatening possibilities that may arise in the offer or request of assistance, then, people seek ways to avoid it. The search can take many guises: avoiding self-directed public attention, withdrawing from the situation, or refusing outright to participate. People can also avoid self-disclosure by establishing that reasons for poor performance are beyond their control—the task is too difficult; that it involves such uncertainty that no person could reasonably expect to succeed; or that others are behaving precisely the same way as one's self (Snyder & Wicklund 1981).

Contextual and Normative Factors

People's willingness to request or offer help may also depend on certain normative factors. If work is perceived as too uncertain, if it is clearly apt to challenge one's esteem, people often develop alternative definitions of performance success. We saw some of this in Chapter 2. In schools with low goal consensus, teachers forged varied conceptions of their work that seemed then to call for norms of self-reliance. Within that social organization, teachers' conversations focused on experience-swapping about student misbehavior or on poor working conditions, their conversations adhering to the social conventions around them. Of equal relevance, teachers in low consensus schools tended to devalue work-related talk whereas the opposite was true in high consensus schools. Colleagues' complaint-driven conversations and their non-performance-based relations might thus be understood as redefinitions of workplace success.

And if teachers confronting thoughts of inadequacy recast the definition of work in terms of social relations with peers, protecting the status of those relations seems paramount. Thus offers of assistance to colleagues (who may also experience self-doubt) threaten one's professional standing by implying that the donor of advice is more competent than the recipient. Further, once the definition of work is recast in nonproductive terms, teachers who lay claim to classroom triumphs may suffer severe social censure from colleagues for appearing boastful and conceited (e.g., Tetlock 1981). Counterpointing this are achievement-oriented groups where pride in one's accomplishments is socially supported and encouraged by colleagues (e.g., Crittenden & Wiley 1985).

When people define work as inherently difficult, helping behavior occurs because it is both necessary and legitimate to seek and offer assistance. That is, to the extent that people believe that anyone, even the most capable person, might need help in a similar situation, it becomes unnecessary to question their own adequacy. But in settings where people believe that few others are in need of help, the inference of low ability is more likely to be drawn (Fisher et al. 1981).

All of this implies that a specific social organization may make one social identity more adaptive than another. It suggests, therefore, that beliefs which constrain requests for and offers of assistance can be overridden—and reality recast—in at least two normative ways: by workplace conditions that emphasize achievement-oriented identities, and by workplace conditions that emphasize that performance success requires mutual advice and assistance. In the discussion that follows we identify the social organization of schools under which these alternative definitions of appropriate teacher behavior are most apt to occur.

The Social Organization of Collaboration

Teachers' Certainty about a Technical Culture and Their Instructional Capability. Where goals are ambiguous, where socialization and evaluation lend no clear direction, and where there is no common sense of purpose, teachers feel uncertain about a technical culture and their own instructional practice (Azumi & Madhere 1983; Glidewell et al. 1983). And with teacher uncertainty comes the need to avoid situations that threaten to disclose it. Indeed, under conditions of high uncertainty, colleagues are most apt to interpret requests for help as clear evidence of performance inadequacy (Glidewell et al. 1983).

But in schools where teachers receive clear performance feedback based on mutual goals, they may suffer far less instructional uncertainty (Ashton & Webb 1986; Azumi & Madhere 1983). And the less threatening their workplace circumstances, the more readily teachers will ask for or offer advice. Because of the inherent difficulty of the work, teachers tend to converse about management and instructional procedures and outcomes, instead of workplace complaints and non-performance-related conversation.

In all likelihood, of course, there is a reciprocal relationship between teachers' certainty about a technical culture and instructional practice and their mutual, collaborative exchange. We leave exploration of this hypothesis, as well as the social organization of teacher certainty itself, to Chapter 5.

Shared Goals. Whether or not teachers exchange mutual help depends in large part on a harmony of interests within the school. In cohesive settings, the reader will recall, teachers commit themselves to the goals of student learning and the agreed upon means to achieve them. In these types of schools there is much greater reason for faculty collaboration. Communal goals, problems, and values offer common substance from which to share; and because teachers commit themselves to helping students master basic skills, collaboration may be viewed as a moral imperative to bring such mastery about.

Isolated settings compel teachers in the opposite direction—toward norms of self-reliance. Under these circumstances, requests and offers of assistance seem far less apt to occur. For one thing, where teachers seldom discuss substantive issues, each may perceive that they alone suffer classroom problems; that few others have similar needs. For another, given their singular orientations, teachers may share little substantive interest upon which to render mutual help. Finally, unsolicited aid *by definition* circumscribes a particular course of aid that violates school norms of self-reliance. In fact, in settings where strong norms of self-reliance inhere, unsolicited help typically elicits responses that derogate both the donor and the advice (Fisher et al. 1981).

Involvement in Decision-making. Norms of collaboration don't simply just happen. They do not spring spontaneously out of teachers' mutual respect and concern for each other. Rather, principals seem to structure them in the workplace by offering ongoing invitations for substantive decision-making and faculty interaction. At some schools, time is set aside for meetings among faculty where joint planning, problem-solving, and decision-making occur. At other schools, principals build interaction opportunities into decision-making about inservice programs, or formally establish subgroups of faculty charged with particular technical decisions and responsibilities (Rosenholtz 1985). In other words, faculty members' involvement in decision-making about the technical matters of teaching appears to be one organizational vehicle that lends substance to their performance-based interaction. Even so, it is highly improbable that principals can forge collaborative relations simply by inviting teachers to work together professionally.

Instead, norms of collaboration may evolve directly from faculty decision-making in at least four ways. First, in making technical decisions— in reasoning, formulating, debating and discovering—teachers may become sensitized to their own situations so that their needs become defined as "problems" for which possible solutions might be found. Second, teachers may discover the relevance and usefulness of colleagues' special skills and competencies, partaking of the pleasures of other people's work as well as their own. Under both these conditions, helping behaviors have been found to increase sharply (Gross et al. 1979). Finally, decision-making opportunities may develop the awareness that no teacher is immune to classroom problems and therefore that all teachers stand to benefit from the mutual exchange of ideas. To overcome difficulties inherent in the practice of teaching, mutual assistance may come to be understood as a necessary and legitimate prerequisite to successful teaching.

Team Teaching. Team teaching, an organizational arrangement in which two or more teachers share responsibility for the instruction of a particular group of students, may also influence the extent of their helping behaviors. Cohen (1981), in her extensive review of the literature, found team teaching was a vehicle for greater instructional interaction, as teachers discussed and challenged each other's ideas about students, grouping arrangements, the curriculum, and classroom management. Unlike isolated settings, work arrangements and communications in team teaching related directly to the nature of instruction; teachers held greater decision-making rights, collaborated more with principals about those decisions, and markedly increased their own exchange of advice and assistance.

School Demographic Variables. Two school demographic variables may also affect teacher collaboration. School size might influence faculty members' ease of contact and thus their opportunity for substantive dialogue. Moreover, the smaller the school, the greater teachers' opportunity to learn about their colleagues' unique talents and strengths, and the more willingly they may render mutual help. School SES may also be implicated. In lower SES urban schools, teachers often complain that their custodial function far outweighs their educative function. And if teachers concentrate more on classroom order than on students' mastery of basic skills, their instructional certainty will diminish (Rosenholtz 1985) along with their willingness to collaborate, as a distinct and critical performance deficit comes more clearly into view.

Summary. To conclude, we propose that several workplace conditions influence the extent to which teachers render mutual advice and assistance. First, teachers' certainty about a technical culture and their own instructional practice should avert threats to their self-esteem, spawning greater levels of mutual assistance among faculty. Second, shared teaching goals— the fact that teachers feel part of a community endeavor—should serve as a normative imperative for help-seeking and offering. Third, involvement in schools' technical decisions may offer substance, interaction opportunities, recognition of common teaching problems and needs, and colleagues' unique competence in solving them, thereby enhancing teacher collaboration. Fourth, team-teaching may encourage the rendering of mutual assistance, given the organizational need to coordinate, plan, and evaluate classroom instruction with colleagues. Finally, both school size and SES may also influence teacher collaboration to the extent that they permit faculty to engage in substantive interaction.

QUANTITATIVE MEASUREMENT AND FINDINGS

Operational Definitions

To test the hypothesis that teacher collaboration rests at least in part on the specific social organizational conditions described above, four new variables require introduction: teachers' certainty about a technical culture and their instructional practice, participation in decision-making, teacher collaboration, and team teaching. The questionnaire items used in the construction of each new scale, their Cronbach Alpha Coefficients, and their item-to-scale correlations appear in Box 3.1.

Quantitative Findings

Table 3.1 presents the intercorrelations between social organizational and school demographic variables, their means, and standard deviations. With the exception of school SES and size, each variable is moderately related to the dependent variable. School size correlates weakly with teacher collaboration, but school SES shows no relationship. Teachers from high SES schools appear no more likely to collaborate with colleagues than those from low SES schools. Eliminating school SES from consideration, we next turned to multiple regression to test the independent effects of each variable.

The results, presented in Table 3.2, reveal that the extent to which teachers share instructional goals, involve themselves in technical decision-making, feel less uncertain about their technical culture and instructional practice, and work as part of a teaching team combines to explain 60% of the variance in teacher collaboration. Contrary to expectations, school size shows no appreciable effects.

Comparing standardized beta weights, we find that teachers' certainty about a technical culture and their instructional practice is one of the most powerful predictors of collaboration, a finding that lends support to the notion of threatened self-esteem. To the extent that teachers lack technical knowledge and control of their ability to help students learn, they are less apt to ask for assistance. Uncertainty also tends to undermine teachers' willingness to offer assistance to those experiencing difficulty. If offering or requesting aid threatens to disclose some kind of professional inadequacy, it appears that teachers, like other people, simply avoid it.

That shared teaching goals make a similarly robust and independent contribution to teacher collaboration also supports our conceptual model. A lack of awareness that others are experiencing similar difficulty, or, alter-

BOX 3.1   Construction of Scales

Collaboration

1. Other teachers at this school seek my advice about professional issues and problems.
2. I don't offer advice to others about their teaching unless I am asked for it.*
3. If another teacher asks me for advice, it implies that I am more competent than he or she is.*
4. Other teachers at this school come to me for help or advice when they need it.
5. I give help and support to other teachers when they are having problems in their teaching.
6. I can get good help or advice from other teachers at my school when I have a teaching problem.
7. I regularly share teaching ideas or materials with:
   a. no other teachers
   b. one other teacher
   c. two other teachers
   d. three other teachers
   e. four or more other teachers

Alpha = .63; item-to-scale correlations = .14 to .45.

*Team Teaching***

1. Do you share teaching responsibilities with other teachers in this school (e.g., team teaching)?
2. I like to share teaching responsibilities (e.g., team teaching) with other teachers here.

Teachers' Certainty about a Technical Culture and Instructional Practice

1. I feel as though I am not making any academic progress with my students.*
2. It's hard to know how I'm doing in my teaching.*
3. I am uncertain about how to teach some of the students in my class.*
4. I feel that I am making a significant difference in the lives of my students.
5. Children are so private and complex I never know if I am getting through to them.*
6. I don't know how to make academic progress with some of my students.*
7. I feel good about my teaching style and strategies; I think they are successful.
8. I am pleased with the progress my students make.
9. Expertise on good teaching exists in the profession of education.

10. There is a body of knowledge out there that can really help teachers improve their teaching.

11. Good teaching is a gift; you can't really learn it from anybody else.

Alpha = .70; item-to-scale correlations = .27 to .48.

Involvement in Decision-making

1. In this school, teachers participate in selecting instructional texts and materials.

2. In this school, teachers participate in determining the type and content of inservices we have.

3. Teachers participate in determining appropriate instructional methods and techniques in this school.

4. My principal participates in instructionally related decision-making along with the teachers.

5. I am encouraged to modify the curriculum to meet my own students' needs.

Alpha = .69; item-to-scale correlations = .36 to .56.

*We recorded these items in calculating scale scores.
**Scale reliabilities can be computed only with three or more items.

TABLE 3.1. Correlation Coefficients, Means (M), and Standard Deviations (SD) for Variables Examined with the Dependent Variable Teacher Collaboration

Variables	2	3	4	5	6	7	M	SD
1. Collaboration	.56	.49	.50	.50	−.01	.17	20.49	1.56
2. Teacher certainty		.02	.55	.39	−.17	.20	27.94	1.98
3. Team teaching			.39	.50	.04	.26	4.17	.33
4. Shared goals				.68	.03	.05	14.27	1.44
5. Decision-making					.01	.17	16.19	2.14
6. School SES						−.27	.41	.22
7. School size							19.49	8.13

TABLE 3.2. Regression Analysis of Teacher Collaboration

Variable	Beta	R^2	F
Decision-making	.19	.27	4.32*
Certainty about a technical culture and instructional practice	.34	.45	17.26**
Shared teaching goals	.37	.56	18.78**
Team teaching	.29	.60	10.13**
Multiple R	.80		

*p .05.
**p .001.

natively, conformance to norms of self-reliance, reduces the extent to which teachers engage in reciprocated help. But to the extent that faculty share responsibility for specific teaching outcomes—outcomes that may elude teachers unless they work together—they tend to both seek from, and offer counsel to, each other.

Team teaching also makes a significant difference in teachers' willingness to collaborate. Whether two or more teachers delegate subject matter within a team, or together share teaching responsibilities, they negotiate instruction for students, make work-related decisions, face common teaching problems, and, if the team is to survive, solve them with mutual help.

Finally, although to a lesser extent, involvement in decision-making independently and significantly predicts teacher collaboration. This finding supports the argument that collective decision-making may provide a substantive forum for faculty interaction, information about colleagues' particular teaching strengths, recognition of common teaching problems, including the need for common expectations, and an awareness that teaching perplexities may not be altogether intractable.

Having identified some of the social organizational arrangements that may explain *why* teachers seek or offer advice and assistance still leaves wholly unresolved a number of related questions: How are collaborative networks initially forged? How are they sustained? How do social organizations within schools influence teachers' consciousness of appropriate collegial relations? To explore each of these questions, we turn next to interview data from teachers working under widely varying circumstances.

THE SOCIAL CONSTRUCT OF TEACHER COLLABORATION

Using mean z-scores computed on those five social organizational variables directly involved in teacher collaboration (decision-making, teacher certainty, shared goals, team teaching, and collaboration), we trichotomized the interview sample into high, moderate, and low levels. Schools that offered the greatest impetus for mutual helping behaviors, here called *collaborative* settings, were those in which the five variables averaged approximately one standard deviation or more *above* sample means. From the total of 78 schools, 13 were identified as collaborative. We interviewed 18 randomly selected teachers from 6 of these schools. Schools that offer the lowest impetus for helping behaviors, we termed *isolated* settings; those in which the five contextual variables averaged approximately one standard deviation *below* sample means. From 7 of the 15 schools classified in this group we interviewed 22 randomly selected teachers. Schools that offered a moderate impetus for collaboration, labelled *moderately isolated* schools, were those whose contextual conditions averaged close to their respective means, a level characterizing 50 schools in our sample. From 10 of these we interviewed 33 randomly selected teachers.

Teacher Sharing

To explore whether the social organization of schools influences the nature of collegial relations, we asked, "Do you share things with other teachers? What sorts of things do you share?" If definitions of "good" collegial relations are situationally negotiated, and if qualitative and quantitative data converge, we should discern differences in both the frequency of collegial sharing, as well as the *types* of sharing in which teachers permit themselves to engage—differences that correspond to the degree of collaboration in schools. Teacher responses, classified by their schools' level of collaboration, appear in Table 3.3.

Consistent with predictions, in collaborative settings, all but one teacher reports they engage in mutual sharing with colleagues: either exchanging instructionally related materials and ideas, and/or mutual problem-solving and planning. Typical responses from three schools below underscore the importance of teacher consensus about school goals:

> We share what we need to do or how to make our work better. Sometimes someone will have a way to do things better. Somebody will have a way to do something a little differently—like once I was having a difficult time teaching a little boy the short e sound and a first grade teacher gave me some suggestions. [What did you do with the suggestions?] Well, I borrowed her materials, changed it around a little and tried it out—it worked pretty well.

> There is a cooperative spirit here. No one seems to be trying to be on top here. We're not competing with each other. Rather, we're working together for the good of the children. We prefer to work together rather than compete. I think that teachers here will do anything for their kids. Also, the teachers here are not just colleagues, in a lot of instances we're also friends.

> Well, we work as a team in each grade level. Our school does an exceptional job of helping each other. Other teachers are always willing to help. There is a great deal of mutual concern and people are not standoffish. If there is a problem we talk to each other and try to help. An example might be, "I've tried this with this child. If you've had a similar problem, what you did might help." You just relate the problems you're having to other teachers.

For these teachers, instruction seems a natural subject for reflection: they set goals to improve instruction, grapple with and share teaching problems, make suggestions to overcome instructional hurdles, and show mutual concern for their collective teaching performance. When the number of choices teachers have increases, an entirely new range of possibilities opens up, as colleagues expose each other to a world linked to vast new realities. The data also disclose that teachers tend to hold few inhibitions about soliciting and offering help. Their sense of confidence in a technical culture seems so strong that it proclaims itself as a basis for faculty collaboration:

TABLE 3.3. Teacher Sharing

Level of collaboration in school	DO YOU SHARE THINGS WITH OTHER TEACHERS?*				
	None	Experience swapping	Instructional materials and ideas	Instructional problem-solving and planning	N
Collaborative	3%	0%	47%	50%	32
Moderately isolated	51%	26%	46%	20%	35
Isolated	56%	33%	30%	0%	27

*Teachers frequently offered multiple responses to this question. Percentages therefore reflect the number of times each category was mentioned.

You just have to ask other teachers if you want to share.

People who enjoy teaching are more open to criticisms and suggestions.

If a person is secure in her teaching, she won't be obsessed with hoarding ideas and keeping things to herself.

I think that most teachers do share unless they have a personality problem.

Not only do teachers appear to talk spontaneously about technical ideas or problems; they implicitly convey that it's a taken-for-granted, natural thing to do.

With its arrangement by schools' levels of collaboration, Table 3.3 discloses a reality of a different sort experienced by teachers in moderately isolated and isolated settings. While more than half of the teachers exchange instructional materials in moderately isolated schools, only 7 of the 34 engage in problem-solving. In isolated schools, only about a fourth of the teachers exchange instructional materials and ideas, but no one reported instructional problem-solving and planning with colleagues. These data, as above, support the notion of threatened self-esteem. Like the oyster that neutralizes an irritating grain of sand by coating it with layers of pearl, isolated teachers seem to coat their irritating self-doubts and inadequacies with comforting layers of self-deception. Some typical comments from various isolated schools:

Teachers here see it as their job to do what they're doing, and yours to do what you're doing.

I think everyone has their own ideas of what they should do.

Teachers here hoard their ideas. They don't want anybody else to know what they're doing.

I am *very* hesitant about the idea of going to another teacher. That suggestion makes me feel very uncomfortable—like I'm stepping on their toes.

Teaching seems very much more a singular possession here—not the school community's, but the individual's own to dispose of. School life may not be real or right living under the tyranny of a possible invader or observer, and the fact that teachers concealed their treasures or treasons went without saying.

Instead of advice and assistance, teachers articulated several alternative types of sharing. The first was experience-swapping, noted by over a fourth of the teachers from moderately isolated schools and a third of those from isolated settings. Illustrative are these remarks from two isolated schools:

Problems with student discipline. Student behavior is quite a serious problem for us and we're not sure what to do about it. So mostly we just complain to each other. Kids from the same family get into trouble year after year.

Well, we share things about children. We have one boy in particular. He is really backwards and is always saying something funny. You know, we don't talk about him in a bad sense; we just talk about the things that he says and does.

An ill-conceived consequence of experience-swapping is brought to light by teachers from two other isolated schools, but with former experiences elsewhere:

> We usually share things about the children in a negative sense. They'll [the other teachers] tell me what one of my children had done in a lower grade. It doesn't help me in dealing with the children, but it helps me in knowing that this isn't the first year they behaved badly. [Do you feel then that you get support from your colleagues?] I don't know if you can call it support, but sympathy. [Does that make you feel better?] Yes, but I think I need a little more substantial help.

> We share things about our classes. My class this particular year has been particularly rough. There's been a lot of sympathy from other teachers. They agree that it's an unusual group of kids. I'm not saying that it's any one person's fault, but there's not a feeling of teamwork in the school. The teachers don't really give me any input as to how to handle the problem.

Although active participants in defining and reaffirming their present school reality, these latter two teachers acknowledge its negative implications, garnered perhaps through prior school experience: that the product of experience-swapping is sympathy and support instead of helpful assistance.

These data parallel the same differences between cohesive and isolated faculties found in Chapter 2. On the one hand, the definition of sharing in collaborative settings pivots upon teachers' daily patterns of goal-directed activity. Bolstered by the notion that instructional success is in fact possible to achieve, these teachers impute a meaning to "sharing" that involves communal efforts to bring such learning about. In more isolated settings, on the other hand, uncertainty about a technical culture and instructional practice looms large indeed, particularly given teachers' melange of competing goals, values, and beliefs. As we shall see in Chapter 5, particularly when faculty complaints suggest that no one is expected to succeed, teachers feel less certain that their own classroom success is possible. Ironically, consoling conversation becomes the one secure thread that binds these otherwise divided faculties. Such knowingness may sustain the widespread reality that teachers early in their careers suffered from a bout of vast idealism; and yet they cannot confirm this illusion unless they keep swapping their stories.

We confront a self-fulfilling paradox here. The definition of sharing in collaborative settings may lead colleagues to behave in ways that reduce their uncertainty by requesting and offering advice about instructional problems, thereby building a technical culture. But the definition of sharing in more isolated settings may lead teachers to behave in ways that tend to confirm that instructional ambiguities inhere in the nature of teaching, and that they can do little to reduce them. If our account is correct, the consequences will be far-reaching—both in and outside of the classroom. These propositions will be elaborated more fully in Chapter 5.

Teachers in more isolated settings offer several additional definitions of sharing. The first involved noninstructional duties. For example, four teachers report sharing recess and study hall responsibilities, while three others share supervisory responsibilities during lunch ("I take the lunch duty one week and the other teacher takes it the next week"). Three teachers shared suggestions about clerical duties and how to accomplish them more efficiently. And then there were several others who cover in some way for each other:

> Not with teachers I'm not close to, but with colleagues I am close to. If they get behind, if they've been ill, if they find themselves in a bind, I'm always there to cover for them and vice versa.

Another definition of sharing rendered by five teachers involves the exchange of students who posed particular instructional or behavioral difficulties:

> I worked with the gifted and I was out [of school] for a half day each week and there was a substitute teacher. I had several [students with] behavior problems and they would work all week to decide what they could do to the substitute on Tuesday afternoon. I decided that I should put them in another classroom to do their work. The other teachers were very gracious and they each took one.

> Well, I teamed this year. It was wonderful because if I got frustrated with a child, she [the teammate] would take her and vice versa.

Again, in these latter definitions, the substance of sharing focuses not on ways to reduce ambiguities in the complicated nature of teaching, but instead on better ways to cope with its uncertainties.

One last finding presented in Table 3.3 deserves attention. Almost half of the teachers from moderately isolated schools, and over half of those from isolated schools, report no time whatsoever to share things with colleagues. Teachers invoke a variety of reasons to explain:

> No. There's no time for sharing. The only time teachers are ever together is lunch time, and we have to eat with the kids. We eat at our own table but they're so noisy you really can't hear anybody else.

> Quite frankly there isn't a lot of time for talking. And even if we did have the time, there isn't a place where we can go and talk.

> There's no opportunity to talk with other teachers. I mean we could, but I couldn't get my work done and visit because we have an hour break, and we have before school and after school and it takes all my time.

For all the promises of "choice," norms of self-reliance are nearly perfect in their emptiness, used to protect teachers from outside and possibly negative self-scrutiny. The irony of this account of teacher isolation becomes clearer with the knowledge that in collaborative settings, all but one teacher reported that their opportunities for sharing were at precisely those times spurned by teachers in more isolated settings, namely, before, during, and after school. For example, although the information was not formally solicited, teachers in collaborative settings often report a departure time of 5:00, while teachers in isolated schools often report leaving school at 3:00.

The denial of opportunities for interaction is perhaps the most theoretically interesting response to the question of sharing because it most audibly exemplifies a defensive maneuver to avoid self-threatening circumstances. That is, communicative distance, whether physical or social, reduces the opportunity to cast precisely those aspersions that teachers seek most earnestly to avoid. Avoiding substantive interaction may in fact be an attempt to shortcut teachers' dreadful deteriorating processes; to abort their inevitable trajectory; to elude a painful professional death. So it appears that they leap toward the curtain of oblivion before the final act is through.

Origins of Helping Behaviors

Having established that alternative definitions of sharing vary with the contextual arrangements of schools, our next task is to examine how these definitions of "appropriate" collegial behavior may actually be brought about. Because prior research points largely to principal intervention, we asked our subsample of teachers, "Is your principal a good problem-solver?" Our purpose here was two-fold: (1) to determine whether principals' leadership behavior was essential to teacher collaboration, and (2) to determine whether goal-directed principals structured the workplace with frequent opportunities for faculty collaboration.

Related to the first purpose, principals might well foster collaboration among teachers through their own helping behavior. Here we reasoned that principals who both solicit from and offer advice to teachers as an everyday fact of school life should encourage such behaviors among colleagues. There is, in fact, substantial support from both experimental and naturalistic studies that the presence of helping "models," a substantially different reality from isolated settings, increases the subsequent helping behavior of observers (Staub 1981).

Turning first to overall responses to the question of principal problem-solving, in collaborative settings, 87% of the respondents answered "yes"—that their principal was a good problem-solver—and the remainder "no." In moderately isolated settings, 31% responded yes, 25% sometimes, and 44% no. Finally, in isolated settings, 29% answered affirmatively, 6% equivocated, and 65% responded negatively. The more collaborative the school, the more teachers perceived principals as good problem-solvers.

What makes this tally most provocative, however, is that teachers' definitions of principals' problem-solving skills varied dramatically by their social organizational circumstance.

We discerned several distinct characteristics of principals' "problem-solving" behavior, and in some of them we recognize their role as evaluator. The first is the extent to which principals pose threats to teachers' self-esteem. In collaborative schools, 8 out of 18 teachers who make reference to their self-esteem express the idea that help-rendering by principals poses little threat. As a result, they seem not at all hesitant to ask them for help:

> [From a second year teacher:] Yes. He never makes you feel like you're inadequate—for me, he just made me feel like there was a lot to learn and he was there to see that I learned just as well as I could.

> Yes, I think he is. He can be critical of you but not make you feel bad about it. He's not hesitant to help me. He's critical in areas where I'm having problems but he does not make me look bad. I feel like I can go to him no matter how small the problem.

> Yes, he's kind and professional. He tries to help you when you're having problems. I feel that he really knows what I'm talking about when I ask for help—he doesn't make me feel like there's anything wrong with *me*.

The freedom to disclose teaching problems in collaborative settings strikingly counterpointed the compulsion to conceal them in isolated settings. Over a third of the teachers here were quick to acknowledge that their principal was a scolding presence, a direct threat to their sense of self-worth:

> No. He always makes me fear him. He watches everything you do. If you make a mistake he will always call it back to you. You can't take children to him because he always makes you feel like you are there because you can't handle the problem yourself.

> No. She's mean. She comes into my room and reprimands me in front of my students. She does that to everyone. The principal says teachers won't listen unless they are watched. It's gotten to the point where I can't handle it any more.

> No. She is very unprofessional. She screams at children. She screams at teachers. You don't go up to a teacher and say, "Are you in charge here?" or "Are these children following your directions?"

The decline of trust in light of principals' excessively harsh tactics here is not unexpected, and helping-seeking on any grounds received only limited mention in response to this question. All of this was made more dire because at the same time that teachers consumed themselves with self-defensive posturing, principals seemed to pass through these same loops of fear about their own performance. Thus when teachers did ask for or offer advice, they often perceived that it threatened their principal's self-esteem and sense of control:

> The principal likes to have control of everything. He wants to say "Yes, this will be done," and "No, this will not be done." I think it's a fear of a lack of control. If teachers are making decisions about students then he is not in control. He's insecure enough that he needs to have complete control. He doesn't want teachers to be making decisions that he thinks he should be making.

> When there's a problem, if you don't totally agree with the principal's decision, you're labelled as a rebel, and accused of not trying to fit in, of being a trouble-maker. He labels us. He thinks we are a threat. I think he is intimidated. He makes you very hesitant to make a comment. There is a lot of retaliation by the principal.

> No, I don't think so. His viewpoint is too authoritarian. He has to be above the teachers in all instances. He won't allow input into solving a problem; he doesn't value input from teachers. He is mainly dictatorial. He will try and figure out the problem himself, and then he will tell us what to do.

With too little certainty and too little tolerance for ambiguity, principals, like teachers, may draw in, making a circle around themselves to avoid any circumstance that may call their performance into question. It is therefore unsurprising that they react aversively to teacher-initiated requests for or offers of advice. Most principals of isolated schools, when confronted by teachers' myriad classroom problems, appeared to use only one method to carry on their workaday lives—total bland pretense that nothing is ever wrong:

> My principal doesn't support us. The children are very, very loud in the cafeteria. I have to wear two hearing aids now. When I go into the cafeteria I am always tempted to turn off my hearing aids except that I do like to talk with my colleagues. About three years ago, all the teachers in the school did a year long inservice project. This came about when a professor from the university came out and asked everybody to work with him. We talked about the things we thought should be improved in our school and discipline was one thing. At that time, we had a teacher whose husband was a traffic engineer with the city and he said he would provide us with a traffic light and set it up so that if the noise level became too high in the cafeteria the yellow light would go on and this was a signal to the children to talk more softly. If the red light came on they had to be silent for the rest of the day. If the green light was on, then everything was okay. Our principal would not permit us to have that. When he was talking and the university professor was present, he agreed to it; but as soon as the man left, the teacher put the requisition on his desk and he just never signed it. He never gave any explanation. I did tell him that I thought the noise level in the cafeteria was harmful to the children's ears and he just looked at me and said, "The noise doesn't bother me." And I was tempted to say, "It wouldn't bother me either if I ate in my office."

The difference between isolated and collaborative schools in principals' willingness to confront classroom or school problems is made even more apparent by the contrasting experiences of one 13-year veteran:

> Before I came to this school I was in a very effective school. Here the principal doesn't recognize the teachers as professionals and as adults. He doesn't seem to take part in the process very much; he doesn't give pats on the back. He doesn't make himself part of what's going on in classrooms. He doesn't really know individual children; he certainly doesn't know individual teachers, and I don't think he really has any idea of what goes on in individual classrooms. He doesn't keep track of projects too well. This principal doesn't make it a point to be in the classrooms. I think he thinks that the administration should be in the office. He doesn't make it his business to contact kids or teachers. At the other school I was in, things were terrific. The principal was constantly in and out of classrooms. She wouldn't ridicule ideas and she encouraged teachers to try new things out and work together. Here our principal doesn't go along with new kinds of ideas. Those things just won't go over well so you just don't try them.

The point this teacher makes patently clear is that principals' efforts in solving problems vary with their instructional certainty and their belief in a technical culture ("He doesn't make it his business to contact kids or teachers" versus "The principal was constantly in and out of classrooms") and likewise, their need for personal control ("Here our principal doesn't go along with new ideas" versus "She encouraged us to try new ideas"). Principals from collaborative schools seem to set themselves apart from others by their everyday accessibility and involvement in classroom affairs. And perhaps because they ubiquitously monitor instructional matters, they find greater opportunity to render technical assistance. In this regard, teachers from various collaborative settings repeatedly stress the benefits that accrue from their principal's advice and help:

> Yes. He is in each classroom at least once a day. He will bring you materials he thinks might help you. Sometimes he will come in and say "May I show them something?" Then he will teach a part of a lesson. It is very helpful, not obtrusive.

> Yes. He will help you with anything. He is always there and will sit in on talks with parents and students when you need him. If he is on the phone when I need him he will get off right away. I think I could depend on him for anything. I go to him for everything. He is great at solving problems.

> I would say that he is. Sometimes he will give you ideas for how to handle the situation. [Could you give me an example of a situation he helped you resolve?] Well, I was having trouble with one student in my class. She was a transfer student. She could read well, but she had no phonics. He [the principal] suggested things that I could do to help her with phonics. He is always there to help you when you need it.

Teachers in more isolated schools describe a different sort of reality. More common to moderately isolated than isolated settings, teachers stress that while their principals might tackle school or classroom problems, seldom do they resolve them:

> The principal is moody. You never know how he'll take something. Sometimes he takes suggestions like we're criticizing him. He is very unpredictable; you never know what he'll do next. He takes a lot of different approaches to the same problem. That inconsistency doesn't always work too well. But I've never worked with another principal so I really can't compare.

> No he isn't. I had the biggest problem I've ever had with a kid all year last Friday. The principal talked with the parent and said the mother could help the situation, could handle it better than he could. But the problem's still not resolved.

> My principal is not really a good problem-solver. I can't think where he *is* a problem solver. Like, we're having a lot of trouble with kids on the bus. I often work in the workroom that's near the principal's office. Often he'll drag me in to witness a paddling. It seems like we're always paddling the same kids. Therefore, I don't think we're solving any problems. [Do you ever say anything to the principal?] No, I've never really said anything. Sometimes paddling seems to him to be the only way. In response to your question, should I tell the principal things? Is it my place to do that?

This latter teacher's questioning of the interviewer suggests an unanticipated need for redefinition of the boundaries being drawn. It did not occur to her to question her principal's policy, a policy she found inevitable and unshakeable, because both parties seemed to agree on where policy-making should and did reside. Teachers' lack of involvement in isolated schools, at least as revealed in this one teacher's queries, is part of their taken-for-granted reality. As we shall see later, in collaborative settings, principals decisively empower teachers to solve both school and classroom problems. As a result, teachers become aware of the importance of their input and feedback to principals.

But we are getting ahead of ourselves. Most frequently, teachers in isolated settings complain that their principals simply abdicate responsibility for handling or solving either school or classroom problems:

> No. My class this particular year has had an excessive number of academic and social problems. I think the children were very poorly placed. I've looked into their files and have found all sorts of notes saying things like, "Don't put these students together. It will lead to a lot of behavior problems." This is the time of the year when questions about retaining students come up. I feel badly that some students just haven't gotten it together, but I have big questions as to what I should do with them. I have asked the principal for his input into this situation. I have found that the principal is no help at all. He won't help unless it involves a problem with an official policy. He is always looking for an official policy to figure out how to deal with a problem.

No he isn't. He doesn't know how to communicate with parents. He doesn't know how to treat teachers or students. He just sits in his office all day long and shuffles papers around. He ignores any problems so we have to solve them ourselves in the best way we know how. So some problems just keep on getting worse.

I would have to say no. The reason is that he sets up the school so that problems occur and then he backs away from solving them. [Could you say more about that?] He stays in his office most of the time so that he doesn't know what's going on in and out of classrooms. We have some real rowdy kids here, and they play around in the bathrooms and corridors during school time. So it's up to the teacher to make sure that her kids are not doing that when she gives them passes. If the principal was more visible to kids, maybe that sort of stuff wouldn't happen.

These grievances about principals' problem-solving behavior—their infrequent communications with teachers, their indecisiveness or unwillingness to attempt to resolve school or classroom problems, and their refusal to solicit or accept faculty advice and suggestions—may be interpreted in at least two ways. As we saw in Chapter 2, principals, like faculty members, may view control of problem students as the sole providence of each teacher. Failure to perform this function well may mean a loss of respect for teachers, suggesting that they cannot succeed instructionally. And given such an overwhelming deficit, there may be little point in trying to help them. This idea receives greater elaboration in Chapter 4.

Alternatively, principals' noninvolvement with school or classroom problems may again reveal tactical maneuvers to evade questions about their own professional competence. Setting problems outside one's workaday life is itself a way of dealing with them, a form of beleaguerment in its own right. The irony, of course, is that principals who deploy such tactics to protect their sense of self-worth—and assume themselves immune to question—do not stave off others' judgments of their inability to lead. Ultimately it seems that faculties will not consent to look up to principals who are not themselves looking up to something higher than their ordinary selves. The image teachers conjure here is one of a rudderless ship drifting endlessly from problem to problem. And despite their survival, most teachers tend to question whether their principal should remain at the helm. At the same time, principals' tactical maneuvers of self-defense may insulate them safely from the turbulence of any outside storm.

In collaborative settings, where principals' problem-solving involves substantive help and advice, few threats to self-esteem and accompanying defensive tactics are apparent. Seeming to feel more certain about a technical culture and their own professional competence, principals not only help resolve school or classroom problems, they also mobilize faculty resources toward this same end:

He seems to recognize people's strengths and weaknesses and is great at pulling teachers together to help one another. If he can't help you, he'll admit it. He's not afraid to admit when he doesn't know something but he knows—most of the time—which teacher can solve the problem.

She always encourages us to go to other teachers for advice. I can remember the first staff meeting we had. She said, "If you don't know—ask." Nobody had ever said that to me before. That made me feel good about going to someone, if I had to ask. I felt comfortable.

The principal puts stronger and weaker teachers together to team teach. Often that is conducive to sharing ideas. New teachers are automatically given team teachers in our school. I think it helps them to get started. I know that if I hadn't had a team teacher to help me out, I would have had an even harder time.

It is exactly at this point that we see how principals may establish collaborative norms. They make helping behaviors salient, necessary, and dominant features of school life. Their interventions include specifying relevant behaviors (e.g., "If you don't know—ask") and structuring specific helping relationships between needy and more highly skilled teachers. Norms of collaboration become a portent, a symbol, a landmark in the new pedagogical journey of teachers' workaday worlds. Furthermore, that principals may challenge well-trodden policies is to legitimate that teachers, too, can share in shaping the reality of their school; in the birth of new selves, new professional lives, new or redeemed talents.

Several experimental studies elaborate the notion that the genesis of collaborative behavior resides in this sort of intervention (Berkowitz 1970). Where group members' helping behavior can advance all members toward specific goals, each feels that others depend on him or her. People's helping behavior is further strengthened by telling them that their colleagues' chances of attaining a valued goal depends upon their own performance in the situation. Thus, where principals encourage helping relationships, that is, where teachers perceive that colleagues depend on them for greater instructional success, they tend to work harder to help their colleagues succeed.

In addition to encouraging helping behavior in collaborative settings, it seems that principals trust teachers' creative instincts as much—if not more—than their own. They therefore tend to relinquish their need for control and share technical responsibilities with them:

The principal assigns certain teachers to be responsible for that grade level for a month. Everybody takes their turn. They take care of any problem that may come up in that grade. We also have committees that discuss ideas. They present ideas to the faculty and if it's something we can do, we do it. If not, we move on to the next thing.

The principal encourages us to work together. We have planning time together and we have unit meetings to work out teaching problems. Everyone takes a turn as lead teacher. I think that's much better than being left to deal with things by yourself. It's very helpful.

In these two schools, as in others, principals make leadership a responsibility for every teacher—much like jury duty—a schoolwide system of local assemblies directed toward the deliberation of teaching. The symbolic impact of these actions can hardly be missed: they assure the presence of a technical culture and the situation in which teachers take responsibility for their school reality by engaging in activities by which that very reality is forged. Here teachers may have the unaccustomed but altogether pleasant sense of having been active in shaping the norms of the school, a powerful scaffolding for future expectations.

Certainly some teachers would be anxious, apprehensive, ill at ease. Then there were those who congratulated themselves on having found a new sense of purpose, a new reality. After some years of drifting, of idle ebb and flow, there seemed to be a current:

Our new principal [of three years] expects us to work together as a team. A few teachers are definitely not willing to. But most teachers, after they have tried solving a problem with the principal and other teachers, are all for it. It's better this way than it used to be, working all alone.

In a world at once of risk and opportunity, principals' purposive behavior assumes the consummate, essential postures: helpful but not threatening, directive but not overbearing, facilitative but not laissez-faire, acting with all their organizational resources against a perhaps initially resistant but ultimately alterable reality. In essence, great principals redefine and stretch the limits of the possible.

In isolated settings, teachers' opportunities for decision-making—their discretion, judgment, and choice—seem subverted by principals' ego-defensive maneuvers. Teachers portray principal control of decision-making as a series of selfish power plays over which they are sufficiently indignant:

No. He has to be in charge of everything. He doesn't want to listen to teachers' side of things. If there's a problem he'll decide what to do and then tell everyone else. He doesn't like to hear teachers' ideas on how to solve problems. I think he's afraid of losing control.

No, I don't think so. I think his viewpoint of his own role is too authoritarian. He won't allow input to solve a problem. He has to be above the teachers in all instances, so he doesn't welcome input from teachers. He is mainly dictatorial. For example, we have no carpeting and there is a lot of echoing in the hallway. Last year I suggested that in order to cut down on noise they ought to think about putting up bulletin boards in the hallways. The principal completely ignored the suggestion. He said that most people *envied* the tiles in the hallway, that he wasn't going to cover them up with bulletin boards. Here a teacher can make their own classroom nice but they can't do anything with the common areas.

No. For example the phone company is "adopting" us. I had some ideas about things that I thought they could do. I told the principal and he said, "No, those aren't good ideas." And that's as far as it will go.

Where principals reject teachers' ideas for school improvement, it is the threat of the very look it has, its veering from their control, its deviationism, that seems most to be feared. And as carriers of perniciousness, principals undermine teachers' participatory spirits, leaving them discouraged, defeated in spirit, and low in imaginative thought. Reality, teachers may then conclude, is that the nature of school life is completely intractable.

It is clearly not the case, of course, that increasing teachers' involvement in decision-making represents a loss of principal control. On the contrary, it can be used to guide critical managerial decisions, helping principals to choose the most appropriate course of action, to select among multiple alternatives. If principals seek out, rather than impose or ignore, possible solutions, the problem touches them and they it. Only with such understanding is a positive resolution and a belief in a technical culture likely. Principals' discretion to hoard or delegate authority, and the subsequent benefits that teachers accrue or forego are, as always, made most apparent to those who have taught in both isolated and collaborative settings. We hear the next teachers describe brief rainbow episodes in the long, iron-gray histories of their elementary school lives:

I know I have sounded very negative about my principal. He's not a complete jerk. He has several good points. But you have to realize that I have come from Camelot. You must realize that that school was wonderful—everything that was done there was focused on the children. The principal totally inspired us. We were never told to be positive; it was just catching. The principal was the key figure in the school. Even in Wonderland there were teachers who didn't like each other. The principal was able to disarm them, to make them see positive things about each other. I think a really effective principal can minimize problems in any situation, and turn teachers toward helping children.

The situation I am in now is so different from my old school. That was a good school, and had teachers who could work together. The interests of the children always came first. At my last school, every opinion was considered. Teachers were treated, in general, as more professional. Now I have no input as to what goes on. That probably has to do with our present leadership problem. Things I think should be brought up with the entire faculty are not. Information is distorted. It's as if the principal doesn't want us to know everything.

These teachers' sudden exposure to a different and less sanguine reality knocked the figurative ground from under their once assured selves and left them helpless to face new and disturbing challenges. In their new realities, principals brooked no compromise with ambiguity and uncertainty. At the same time, the entrapments of their threatened self-esteem have all the makings of a self-fulfilling prophesy: Uncertain principals demonstrate greater need for control, which prevents the very collaborative activities necessary to bolster their professional knowledge. And in their departure from reasonableness, their self-defensive behavior, is an exasperating act as often as it is pitiable. These consequences will be further unraveled in Chapter 6; at present the key thing to note is that principals who make teaching solutions impossible may unknowingly make teacher isolation and uncertainty inevitable.

Less uncertain principals seem to empower and join with teachers in school improvement, thereby enhancing their professional confidence. The obvious benefit that accrues to principals who share power and authority over matters related to teaching is that by delegating some of the many technical demands of their work, they have many more resources with which to pursue the instructional improvement of their schools.

Teacher Leaders

Although principals may initially define school reality as collaborative, its momentum most likely will flag without ongoing teacher support. That is, teacher collaboration is unlikely to stand in the shadow of one powerful actor alone. Instead, norms of collaboration tend to maintain themselves through daily activities led by those who possess such inclinations. To explore the hypothesis that empowered teachers furthered their own helping behaviors, we asked, "Do you have teacher leaders in your school? If so, what do they do?" Teachers' answers, analyzed by schools' level of collaboration, appear in Table 3.4. Perhaps the most striking and obvious feature of the data is that teachers hold markedly different conceptions of collegial leadership under different school social organizations.

Teacher Leaders in Collaborative Schools. Of the 30 responses from teachers in collaborative schools, 27 laid claim to teacher leaders, and their roles were defined by their performance-related interactions with colleagues. Although teachers responded with multiple characteristics that tended to overlap, we identified at least three distinct dimensions of collegial leadership. First, teacher leaders revealed to others new ways of doing things:

> They set a good example for how to work with children. They are willing to take responsibility when volunteers are asked for. They will try new things. They share more than their part of the bargain when they work on projects with other teachers. They put the child's welfare before anything else.

> They have initiated new programs. They are receptive to suggestions and exhibit leadership. They are active and eager to volunteer. They're usually very involved with curriculum planning and various school committees.

TABLE 3.4. Teacher Leaders

DO YOU HAVE TEACHER LEADERS IN YOUR SCHOOL? WHAT DO THEY DO?*

School level of aid-related behavior	No teacher leaders in our school	Faculty union representative; keeps us informed	Listens to teachers' problems	Initiates new programs, tries new ideas	Motivates teachers with enthusiasm	Helps teachers solve problems	N
Collaborative	0%	7%	3%	43%	20%	27%	30
Moderately isolated	12%	21%	21%	21%	12%	12%	33
Isolated	12%	37%	37%	17%	0%	0%	24

*Teachers frequently offered multiple responses to this question. Percentages therefore reflect the number of times each category was mentioned.

The principal gives me certain responsibilities. I developed and run a school committee for problems that come up. I help train new teachers. I don't lecture them because I resent that and I'm sure they would too. I organize a lot of inservice meetings and I give some of them in the school.

Second, teacher leaders suggested and inspired ideas and discourse, drawing others upward to higher places:

They have enthusiasm. They have initiative. Their enthusiasm rubs off on other people. They'll try anything, adapt it, get people interested.

They are more professional. More interested in furthering their education and trying to grow and change and be willing to change and adapt and try new things. They have a positive outlook. They think that their co-workers can do things, and they look for the best points in students. They support other teachers, and respect the people they work with, believe that they can do their job, and that they are capable and willing to work and work together.

We have several people at this school who are great teachers and who go out of their way to share their good ideas with everyone else. It seems like they're always coming up with something new and get everyone else excited about it. It makes coming into the faculty room fun, when people are excited about something that worked.

Finally, teacher leaders helped others with problems that seemed insolubly interlocked:

My principal says I am one. He says I have to keep on my toes because people look up to me here. I guess it's because I've been there. I have experience. Teachers come to me for advice and I'm more than willing to help. It's not like I have all this knowledge and am going to hoard it. Also, I don't mind trying new things. Like the new computers we have. I decided I was going to teach them. Our librarian wrote the unit and so I took it and just followed what it said. I didn't have to have any special training or anything. And it worked.

One person who has training in many different areas has helped the group become more cohesive. She says, "Let's sit and talk about this and see what we can do." She is well trained in the profession, has high goals, and is empathic and concerned with the people she works with. She wants us to meet those goals.

Teacher leaders seem to position themselves on the cutting edge of the pedagogical frontier; they like to plunge, go for broke, boldly explore the realm of possibilities, and take action in the spirit of exigency rather than waiting for any problem to present itself. That feat, however, requires new and sudden insights, active learning, belief in a technical culture, and long, successful practice. The beatitude of helping other teachers with a leap of intuition and knowledge is a form of inspiration, an elixir that can permanently stymie the recipient's self-doubt with a high, hopeful spirit. Not only does the derring-do of teacher leaders hold at bay the tyranny of instructional uncertainty; they make clear through their actions how collegial behavior is appropriately defined. That is, they enunciate the ideal—a stable, evolving, reciprocal relationship between colleagues. Under these everyday workplace conditions, teachers may come to perceive that advice is frequently required to master instructional goals, that mutual assistance is often needed, and that teachers should avail themselves of collegial resources whenever possible.

Teacher Leaders in Moderately Isolated Schools. Of the 33 responses from moderately isolated settings, 15 teachers imbued collegial leaders with these same characteristics—a surprisingly large ratio. Yet as in any intra-organizational comparisons, no matter how outwardly similar, there is always some variance in people's perceptions of work, in how they define their workplace reality. Moderately impoverished schools illustrate this axiom particularly well where more than one modal characteristic described teacher leaders. Among those interviewed, 24 teachers also identified collegial leadership by their union roles or by their involvement in other noninstructional enterprises.

Teacher Leaders in Isolated Schools. In isolated settings, only one sixth of the teachers identified collegial leadership by their instructional pursuits. Instead, 23 out of 24 responses equated collegial leadership with union involvement or with other noninstructional transactions:

> A lot of them are really active in the union—the educational association. They go to a lot of meetings, and distribute a lot of materials that take up their time. That makes them leaders in that they know what's going on, and they bring back all that information to us. They are very comfortable speaking before a group.

> They're very active in our district teacher organization, the county organization, and the PTA. They bring back information to us so that we can find out what the teacher association is doing for teachers in the county. Several that I know are strong leaders within their churches. They are very outspoken and direct about the way they approach things.

> One in particular has been TEA [Tennessee Education Association] president, so she has lots of leadership qualities. She helps us see things that we may let slide as teachers; some things that are going on at the state level, for instance. I think teachers are very guilty of thinking that if something isn't happening to them they won't worry about it. I think this is a big fault of the teaching profession now, that we won't stick together. She has a lot of experience and just about everything she says is true.

Teacher leaders were also characterized by their empathic mothering, as people who understood colleagues' problems and soothed them, as if with a childhood lullaby. Here teachers came to exorcize their own doubts and enmities and to seek a lifting of the pall, if only for a moment:

I think a leader is a listener. I'm almost like a mother to other teachers. I listen to their problems. Sometimes they're personal; sometimes they're discipline problems. I've taught longer than any of them. I think experience is a big part of that.

We have two of them. They'll listen to your problems and make you feel you're all right. They seem to know what you're going through. They're sympathetic and kind.

They make you feel better when you have a problem. It's just great to know that they're there when you need them. You can talk or cry on their shoulder or yell about it too. They have lots of experience.

Finally, some teachers responded that there were no teacher leaders in their schools. This finding can be understood as self-defensive posturing, where teachers protect their own classroom turf without any interference from, or interaction with others. Indeed, in data presented earlier, those who reported no faculty sharing and no time to talk with others were some of the same individuals who found no teacher leaders present in their schools.

Taken together, then, these data illustrate how teachers' consciousness about the nature of work may be contoured by the contextual circumstances in which they are embedded. Collective commitment to student learning in collaborative settings directs the definition of leadership toward those colleagues who instruct as well as they inspire, awakening all sorts of teaching possibilities in others. By contrast, lacking shared visions about school purpose and possibilities, and professionally remote from others, teachers in isolated settings are not made privy to colleagues' specialized knowledge. Collegial leaders are defined not by their extent of involvement in instructional matters, but, instead, by the only formal and visible avenues to follow: either they are active union representatives or a haven for temporarily ravaged souls.

A slight yet penetrating glimpse into the manner by which these definitions may come to be known is revealed by one teacher's description of collegial leadership in an isolated school:

We do have teachers that are on the Negotiation Board and several that are active in the local teachers' association, but we really don't have any academic leaders. [Do you think it's unusual that you don't have strong academic leaders?] No. The principal only hires people who tend to fit in.

The suggestion offered here—that this principal has done a good job of screening academically talented teachers out of his school—again circles back to principal uncertainty and threatened self-esteem. Strong, pedagogically minded teachers may undermine this principal's authority and control, threatening to challenge some deficiency in his leadership. He therefore engages in still another self-defensive strategy: hiring only those teachers who docilely conform to his present school reality. In Chapter 7, we will see more of this strategy put to use.

In sum, teacher leaders in isolated schools—if they exist—seem to earn their esteem by engaging in noninstructional activities, either by their political representation of colleagues, or by their confessional intimacy—the solace of understanding. Although these leadership qualities pose no threat to colleagues' self-esteem, neither do they appear to resolve recurrent teaching problems.

SUMMARY

In this chapter heavy emphasis has been placed on teachers' uncertainty about a technical culture and instructional practice and on self-defensive posturing by both teachers and principals. Without common goals, as we saw in Chapter 2, teachers' instructional paths lead them in entirely disparate directions, each teacher compelled by her or his own pedagogical interests, each protected by school norms of self-reliance. While uncertainty is endemic to teaching, even under the best of circumstances, norms of self-reliance in isolated schools leave teachers even more uncertain about a technical culture and instructional practice. Ironically, as teachers contemplate the enormous challenges before them and how or whether they should confront them, perhaps the best weapon they could wield against uncertainty lies in colleagues, particularly teacher leaders, within their own schools.

In this way norms of self-reliance and teacher uncertainty both function as double-edged swords. Self-reliance inhibits teachers' knowledge that others suffer common instructional problems, and teachers become turf-minded, unable and unwilling to impinge territorily on the domain of others' classroom practice. Akin to turf-consciousness, teacher uncertainty constructs the unwitting perception that if others suffer few instructional problems, there is personal shame in admitting one's own. Lest teachers confront their own professional inadequacies, or, worse still, inflict personal insult on colleagues by challenging their sense of competence, collegial interaction avoids help-seeking or help-offering, so that although teachers remain professionally aloof, they are not socially estranged. So it seems that isolated teachers suffer more from incompleteness than from loneliness.

Instructionally uncertain principals may also become turf-minded, unable to help teachers solve classroom problems, and unwilling to relinquish control in order that colleagues may render mutual assistance. By contrast, more certain principals seem able to galvanize their faculties in specific, goal-directed endeavors, increasing teachers' clarity about what to pursue. Principals' feedback mechanisms, the opportunities they create for faculty collaboration, and their ability to share authority by empowering faculties to make work-enhancing decisions may cause teachers far less suffering in the face of uncertainty. Armed with greater certainty, a shared sense of school purpose, and the trust and value accorded them by principals, teachers are more likely to share their expertise with others and to seek out their advice. One area that is affected by the consequences of these varied social organizations, which we will explore next, is the realm of teachers' and students' learning opportunities.

4

Teacher Learning

It has become axiomatic in the sociological literature that for organizations to remain viable and productive, they must adapt to ever-changing needs, find solutions to problems and uncertainties, and develop and implement new knowledge, skills, and ideas (Perrow 1979). In short, successful organizations must have the capacity for regulation and self-renewal. Organizational renewal results in large measure from contextual variables—those processes and structures set in place for purposive experimentation, change, and continuous growth. It requires a problem-solving orientation by its members undertaken reiteratively and on a collaborative basis. Finally, it reflects the view that even for organizations that are performing adequately or superbly, as conditions change, there is need for still further improvement.

The present chapter weaves together earlier threads of schools' social organization to explore self-renewing schools; that is, we will examine *teachers' opportunities for learning,* defined here as the extent to which the social organization of schools poses restraints or opportunities for professional development. To what degree do teachers' learning opportunities depend on prevailing structures, norms, and patterns of interaction? What formal and informal mechanisms shape teachers' beliefs about the definition of what good teaching is, accentuate the importance of ongoing learning, define the standards by which teachers measure their growth, and therefore signal the need to develop new teaching skills or perfect old ones?

How do opportunities for teacher learning affect students' basic skills mastery? Our analysis begins by specifying how five previously introduced variables suggest answers to these questions.

The Social Organization of Teachers' Learning Opportunities

Goal-setting. If schools are to be uplifted in their performance, aiming their sights ever higher, information exchange among principals and teachers is an essential, dominant variable, since school renewal depends on its ability to detect and respond to subtle changes, new problems, and growing needs (Scott 1981). Goal-setting of this sort seems essential to teachers' learning for two reasons. On the symbolic level, new goals underscore norms of school renewal—that teachers are expected to learn on a continuous basis. On the practical level, teachers' growth and development depend to no small extent on a recognized need for new skills. The absence of clear guidelines about what teachers are to emphasize leaves many uncertain about how well they are doing (Ashton & Webb 1986; Rosenholtz 1985), and offers few means by which to either identify improvement needs or redirect energies to correct them. Without school goals, therefore, teachers may point their efforts toward improvement—if they make them—in entirely disparate directions.

Teacher Evaluation. Performance ambiguity springs at least as much from principals' lack of clarity about how teachers should be monitored and evaluated. Most principals, uncertain that they can render needed help, or alternatively, that their actions will produce positive effects, not surprisingly muster little effort to resolve this uncertainty for teachers, either in the frequency or the usefulness of their evaluation efforts (Natriello 1983, 1984).

In stark contrast to schools where uncertainty on the part of teachers arises from infrequent, unclear supervision (if, indeed, any supervision at all), principals of self-renewing schools, guided both by the belief that teachers can learn and by explicit learning goals, regularly monitor classroom affairs and student learning. The most useful evaluation systems place emphasis on improving both individual and collective teaching practices within the school. Teachers and principals decide what to evaluate, how to evaluate, and what one should do with the results. Consequently, each system sharpens awareness of the process of instruction within teachers' classroom practice, accelerates remedial help by principals and teacher leaders, and permits situation-specific rather than standardized assistance to be rendered (Gersten et al. 1986; Rosenholtz 1985; Wise et al. 1985). As a result, teachers try harder to improve (Natriello 1984) and better their classroom performance (Gersten et al. 1986).

Involvement in Decision-making. Teachers' involvement in decision-making, as we saw in Chapter 3, lends substance and structure to their collaboration and presumably, the implementation of school goals. But the process of decision-making may itself be instructive. As colleagues sift and winnow strategies, ideas, and materials, and cull from them those most likely to enhance the quality of their classroom instruction, they also deliberate, evaluate, suggest, and modify their own classroom practices. These activities may clarify teachers' instructional method and purpose, thereby enhancing their opportunities for learning, as decisions become conscious and well-reasoned choices rather than arbitrary or automatic reactions.

Teacher Collaboration. Chapter 3 detailed the professionally orphaned life most teachers lead lest they reveal pedagogical shortcomings to themselves or others. With norms of self-reliance militating against requests for, and offers of, assistance, teachers' opportunities for growth in isolated settings are limited almost entirely to trial-and-error learning.

A number of problems arise for teachers who rely almost exclusively on trial-and-error (Lortie 1975). Their opportunities for learning are circumscribed by their own ability to discern problems, develop alternative solutions, choose among them, and assess the outcome. Further, the absence of shared goals in isolated settings limits opportunities to learn any pre-existing body of practical knowledge. Without such knowledge, teachers are less able to perceive and interpret daily events and critical transactions that might be easily understood if they had access to already developed technical culture. Isolated teachers, then, must construct for themselves an individual conception of teaching excellence and a manner in which to attain it.

Collaborative settings, on the other hand, stress norms of continuous school- and self-renewal. Here it is assumed that improvement in teaching is a collective rather than individual enterprise, and that analysis, evaluation, and experimentation in concert with colleagues are conditions under which teachers improve instructionally (Little 1982).

Nowhere are the effects of collaboration on teachers' work orientations more apparent than in studies of idealistic beginners, since no other teachers are more vulnerable and more given to pressures for group conformity. Beginners in isolated settings soon abandon their initial humanistic notions about tending to students' individual needs in favor of a routine technical culture characterized by a more custodial view, where order is stressed over learning, and where students are treated more impersonally, punitively, and distrustfully (Ashton & Webb 1986; Bishop 1977; Denscombe 1985). This transformation of meaning in isolated settings is rendered almost palpable by the strong normative arm of self-reliance, pressing the need to maintain adequate classroom control—a skill that gauges the initial aptitude of beginners, as well as their future teaching potential (Bishop 1977; Denscombe 1985). Beginners in collaborative settings, by contrast, sustain their initial humanistic views about caring and tending to the individual needs of students—a nonroutine technical culture—and strive to collect a portfolio of strategies to meet them. The emphasis here on learning opportunities, including essential strategies in classroom management, may imbue new teachers with sufficient support and practical knowledge to avoid custodial orientations (e.g., Ashton & Webb 1986; Bishop 1977; Denscombe 1985). Nor, it appears in collaborative settings, do veterans deem novices hopelessly inadequate by any initial problems in maintaining classroom control (Denscombe 1985). It is simply a matter of management skills that they will acquire with help from others.

Shared Teaching Goals. As we have seen in Chapter 3, low consensus among faculty and principals about what should be emphasized in teaching brings little direction to, and even less purpose for, teacher collaboration. The other side of the same coin is that repeated exposure to collaborative exchange awakens teachers' consciousness that learning is a continuous process. Thus if continuous self-renewal is defined, communicated, and experienced as a taken-for-granted fact of everyday life, teachers negotiate and build a mutually acceptable definition of reality—that continuous self-renewal is both the legitimate and preferred orientation for them to hold.

School Demographic and Teacher Background Characteristics. Several school demographic and teacher background variables may also affect schools' capacity for self-renewal. In Chapter 3 we argued that both school SES and size warrant considerable attention. Similarly, teacher–pupil ratio may affect teachers' learning if they feel overburdened and professionally constrained (Eberts et al. 1986). In such situations their incentives or opportunities for professional development may be lowered substantially.

Two teacher background characteristics may also be relevant. Given the curvilinear or negative relationship between teachers' experience and their effectiveness (Katzman 1971; Sizemore et al. 1986), teachers' mean years of experience may influence their level of learning. On the one hand, schools containing large contingents of older teachers may experience difficulty in locating internal sources of professional self-renewal. On the other hand, the contagious enthusiasm of beginning teachers may revitalize veterans' excitement about learning new things, should there exist a sufficiently critical mass. Teachers' educational attainment may also apply to the extent that new technical knowledge brings learning opportunities for others into the school.

Summary. In sum, we propose that several workplace conditions are strongly implicated in teachers' learning opportunities and their school's self-renewal. Goal-setting may permit specific targets and directions for teacher improvement. In monitoring teacher progress toward improvement via clear and frequent evaluations, principals may supply continuing insight and help. Commonly held goals that teachers take part in shaping may define their continuous improvement as a moral imperative of the school. Both collaboration and technical decision-making, to the extent that they encourage critical examination of teaching practice, may provide opportunities to learn new ways. School SES, school size, and pupil–teacher ratio may negatively affect school learning opportunities if teachers feel overburdened and professionally constrained. Finally, mean teaching experience and teachers' mean educational attainment may influence their flexibility in changing old patterns for new ones, as more current technical knowledge passes their way. In the next section we test the usefulness of this model in explaining teachers' learning opportunities.

QUANTITATIVE MEASUREMENT AND FINDINGS

Operational Definitions

Only one new variable requires introduction to test our hypotheses. The items used in our operational measure of teachers' learning opportunities appear in Box 4.1.

Quantitative Findings

Means, standard deviations, and correlation coefficients for all variables appear in Table 4.1.

It is noteworthy, first, that all social organizational variables show moderate to strong correlations with teachers' learning opportunities, and

---

BOX 4.1   Construction of Scales

Teachers' Learning Opportunities

1. At this school, I have many opportunities to learn new things.
2. When teachers are not doing a good job, our principal works with them to improve instruction.
3. My principal provides suggestions or support staff to help me become the best possible teacher.
4. Evaluation of my teaching is *not* used to help me improve.*
5. New ideas presented at inservices are discussed afterwards by teachers in this school.
6. I receive informal evaluations of my teaching performance from other teachers.
7. My principal encourages me to try out new ideas.
8. Other teachers encourage me to try out new ideas.

Alpha = .78; item-to-scale correlations = .32 to .63.

*We recorded this item to calculate scale scores.

TABLE 4.1. Correlation Coefficients, Means (M), and Standard Deviations (SD) for Variables Examined with the Dependent Variable Teacher Learning

Variables	2	3	4	5	6	7	8	9	10	M	SD
1. Learning opportunities	.83	.74	.74	.60	.07	.06	−.00	.16	−.07	17.38	2.67
2. Goal-setting		.67	.75	.50	.18	.11	.15	−.07	.03	14.45	2.25
3. Evaluation			.73	.38	−.01	.09	.00	.13	−.06	20.21	2.80
4. Decision-making				.50	.01	.13	.10	.16	−.07	16.19	2.10
5. Collaboration					−.01	.17	−.30	.02	−.09	18.40	1.56
6. School SES						−.27	−.06	−2.3	−.22	.41	.22
7. School size							.00	.12	−.22	19.49	8.13
8. Teaching experience								.28	−.25	12.73	3.00
9. Educational attainment									.10	2.40	.54
10. Pupil–teacher ratio										24.52	2.63

second, that no demographic or teacher background variable bears any significant relationship to the dependent variable. This means that teachers' opportunities for professional development relate *less* to external factors over which schools have little control, and *more* to internal conditions subject to policy manipulation and change by its members.

Deleting nonsignificant variables, we generated a structural model (using LISREL) that describes the relationship between independent, intervening, and dependent variables. Figure 4.1 depicts these latter results for significant parameters only. Once again we locate the path coefficients and their direction of influence on the lines connecting variables. Numbers in parentheses indicate unexplained or residual variance. The model represents a significant fit—.989. Its chi-square, with 4 degrees of freedom, equals 2.71, a .61 level of probability. The average residual size equals .02.

Direct Effects. Turning first to direct effects, the analysis reveals quite dramatically that four organizational factors combine to explain 79% of the variance in teachers' learning opportunities—the support, encouragement, and technical knowledge offered by colleagues and principal to enhance teaching strategies. Comparing LISREL path coefficients, school goal-setting activities exert the strongest influence. To the extent that principals and teachers establish, talk about, and institutionalize the same instructional goals, teachers know which way to aim their own improvement efforts. Goal-setting may also be a time for stock-taking—for reviewing the growth and accomplishments of the school and of individuals within it, and for laying future improvement plans, always in the direction of student progress. To the degree that the school lacks any unified purpose, on the contrary, teachers gain leeway in having their own instructional preferences about them, and in deciding whether or not improvement is even warranted.

Teacher evaluation follows next in the strength of its independent contribution to learning opportunities. To the extent that principals embed their evaluation system in teachers' own improvement goals, set and use objective, clear guidelines (including achievement test results) to monitor student and teacher progress, regularly observe the actual classroom performance of teachers, and spend considerable time in classrooms doing so, they are better able to supply situation-specific feedback and assistance. The other side of the argument, as we shall later see, is that principals who impose evaluation criteria without direct teacher involvement invite resentment of even the most routine feedback. This is particularly true when evaluation criteria are not perceived by teachers as legitimate, fair, and helpful indicators of their classroom performance (Dornbusch & Scott 1975; Natriello 1983; Rosenholtz 1987). Worse still, when principals view evaluation of teachers as a discretionary activity and choose to either perform it perfunctorily or entirely forego it, the results clearly impede individual and school renewal.

The extent to which teachers share instructional goals also contributes

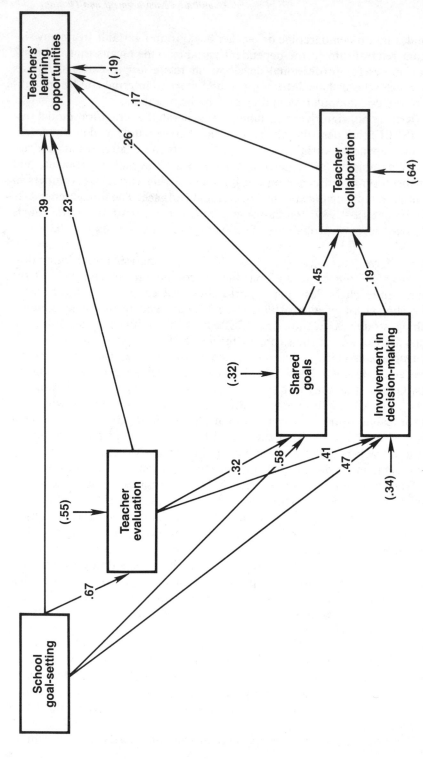

FIGURE 4.1 Path Diagram for Learning Opportunities

independently to their opportunities for learning. The most carefully constructed and articulated school improvement effort will flounder if the objects of that improvement—in this case teachers—do not accept its importance, define it as legitimate, believe it possible to accomplish, and share in its development. Shared goals about teaching render legitimacy, value, and support, or, if need be, collective pressure to conform to school norms. They assure that individuals' improvement efforts are pointed in a mutually supportive and consistent direction, and they offer a stalwart base from which to launch collegial or administrative assistance, should the need arise.

Teacher collaboration is the final predictor of teachers' learning opportunities, independent of all others. Learning may be the direct outcome of collaboration, as teachers request from, and offer colleagues, new ideas, strategies, and techniques. But quite apart from the rendering of technical assistance, collaboration may indirectly influence learning through the leadership of teachers within the school. Teacher leaders' enthusiasm for experimentation, as we saw in Chapter 3, has a contagious quality. The pedagogical appeal of such energetic locomotion seems almost irresistible in inducing others to share, to experiment, and to grow.

Indirect Effects. Contrary to our predictions, teacher involvement in technical decision-making bears no direct influence on their opportunities to learn. Instead of clarifying teaching techniques, procedures, and materials as predicted, in the present data, decision-making serves indirectly to enhance teacher learning only to the extent that it may stimulate colleagues to collaborate. We need not tarry further on the indirect influence of other social organization variables, such as teacher socialization, as they have been sufficiently elaborated in Chapter 2.

In sum, the extent of school goal-setting, evaluation, shared values, and collaboration represent the workplace conditions most conducive to teachers' learning opportunities and their schools' self-renewal. How these workplace conditions in turn shape teachers' cognitions about their learning and the learning of their colleagues is the subject we address next.

THE SOCIAL CONSTRUCT OF TEACHER LEARNING

Temporal Views of Teacher Learning

To emphasize the point that schools' social organization is the reality-definer of everyday life, we turn again to our interview data to explore teacher learning. The central theme of our qualitative analysis concerns how teachers learn the interpretation that allows them to feel competent in teaching basic skills and that encourages continuous self-renewal. In one question we asked, "How long does it take to learn to teach?" If our thinking about reality construction is correct, teachers in settings that offer protracted opportunities to grow and develop should provide a *sustained* view of teacher learning—one that is infinite and boundless—while teachers in settings that offer only limited opportunities should provide a *terminal* view of teacher learning—one that is finite and bounded.

Averaging school z-scores computed on the five social organizational variables directly related to and including teachers' learning opportunities (i.e., goal-setting, evaluation, shared goals, collaboration, and learning opportunities), we trichotomized the school sample into high, moderate, or low levels. *Learning-enriched schools* were those in which the five organizational factors averaged approximately one standard deviation or more *above* their respective means. From the total sample, 13 were classified this way. We interviewed 20 teachers from 6 of these schools. *Learning-impoverished schools* were those in which the five organizational variables averaged approximately one standard deviation or more *below* their respective means. From 8 of the 16 schools classified in this group we interviewed 24 teachers. *Moderately impoverished schools* were those whose five organizational conditions averaged close to their respective means, a level characterizing 50 schools in our sample. From 9 of these schools we interviewed 28 teachers.

Learning-enriched Schools. Consistent with expectations, in learning-enriched schools, 80% of the teachers responded, first, that their own learning is cumulative and developmental, and, second, that learning to teach is a lifelong pursuit.

> You never quit learning.

> I'm still learning.

> I think you learn every year.

> It's a continuous process.

Teachers hold a sustained view of their learning for two closely related reasons. Some stress the contextual nature of their work—that dealing sensitively with different student populations, situations, and settings brings the demand for a variety of skills and classroom strategies. We hear this viewpoint expressed first from a 21-year veteran, followed by a teacher with 8 years' experience:

> You always keep learning. You never stop. Every child is different and a challenge, so you have to keep learning in order to help each one. We have upper-middle and lower-SES students in our school. That makes a very wide range. We need different ways to deal with those differences in background.

> You never stop learning. Our school has many different levels achievement-wise. And students also differ culturally. It's important to learn how to teach something in as many ways as possible to reach all these students. I'm always on the search for new ideas.

Others emphasize sustained learning as a way to expand their professional portfolios of successful ideas and strategies to better meet the challenge of students' individual and diverse intellectual needs. Two teachers, each with over 10 years' experience, put it this way:

> I think it takes your whole career, really. Even today, I may find a great idea, or even another teacher may use a great idea, and it may not work for me. If it doesn't work, then I'm going to have to try something else. Different students respond to different things. I just keep trying until I do find some activity that will get them to respond.

> I think it takes your whole lifetime and then some. There is so much to learn. Every child that I teach is unique, so that I must have special ways of teaching each one. What works wonderfully for one child may not with another. There is no recipe for good teaching.

Explicit in these veterans' responses is the idea that there is no one best instructional or managerial system that can be applied in all contexts, to all students, for all learning objectives. Teachers do not see their effectiveness as routine or unvarying—instead it depends heavily on the specific situation, teaching objective, and child. The same strategy that succeeds in one context may fail miserably in another. Their view calls for a full repertoire of teaching techniques, generalized knowledge about their application, and the acquired sense to know when those strategies should be applied—a nonroutine technical culture. It follows logically, then, that maximizing the fit between teaching method and student need requires continuous learning, refinement, and adaptation of different instructional and managerial strategies. In addition, these comments imply *prima facie* that teaching is something more than the doing; that teachers need to know something other than prescriptions for practice; and that learning is not finished business once one acquires the appropriate certification and credentials.

Learning-impoverished Schools. Teachers' responses from moderately impoverished settings present an altogether different picture, and hold only a modestly positive edge over impoverished schools. Here only 17% express a sustained view of learning. Instead, most emphasize a terminal view, perceiving that one acquires teaching skills after a finite and surprisingly few number of years. Averaging numerical responses, teachers in their view learn to teach after 4.5 years. This number takes on special significance in light of the curvilinear or negative relationship between teacher experience and student learning—that five years is the demarcation for teacher growth—as well as the initial encroachment of teacher burnout in schools (Farber 1984; Rosenholtz & Simpson in press).

Those in learning-impoverished schools offer an even more terminal view of learning. Teachers here estimate that learning to teach would require an average of only 2.3 years. A teacher with 9 years' experience, followed by a 12-year veteran, explains:

> I learned by my third year. How to handle kids so they pay attention, what you're going to teach them and how, takes a little time. You also need to be familiar with the textbooks you use. Without them you'd be lost.

> I'd say two years. The first year you're so nervous and everything is so new. You're trying to shuffle through the new paperwork, all the new books, feeling your way. The second year you start to relax, and you really start to teach. I think that after that second year you have the confidence that you know how to teach. The first year you make so many mistakes.

In settings offering limited professional growth, learning to teach apparently means arriving at a fixed destination through the vehicle of experience. Teaching skills are at once predetermined and inflexible: if teachers become familiar with textbooks and curriculum, paperwork, and other routine operating procedures, they seem to have learned their craft:

> What you've got to learn is your curriculum and all the basic procedures.

> It will take two or three years to get the hang of it.

> You have to learn your curriculum, student discipline and the rules of the district and school. You have to feel comfortable with your textbooks.

This suggests one of the paradoxes of experience. Does the teacher have ten years of experience or one year of experience repeated ten times over?

The belief that successful teaching does not entail more than a rudimentary command of routine classroom practices conjures a view of large student batch processing, where the same techniques can be applied over and over to essentially the same raw material. We hear this task conception espoused by veterans and novices alike:

> [From a 13-year veteran:] There are a ton of guidelines for new teachers to consult. They can check in the manuals if they don't know what they are supposed to do. There are instructions for how to deal with grades, parent–teacher conferences, and math or reading checklists. There are lots of checklists, but they [the manuals] tell you what to do with them. Therefore, it's hard *not* to do your job.

> [From a second-year teacher:] It's hard at the beginning. There's so much to learn. But there are guides to follow in how to teach just about everything. If you follow them, the job becomes easier and easier. I'd say that probably one more year and I'll have everything together.

Missing in more learning-impoverished settings is the sense of teaching as a complex undertaking that requires an ever-expanding repertoire of strategies, that takes into account differing student needs based on contextual or population differences, and that matches particular teaching strategies with different requirements or purposes. Most conspicuously absent from teachers' consciousness is the primacy of tending to individual students' learning.

Organizational theorists may again be of some help in contrasting routine and nonroutine technical cultures a bit more precisely. As Scott (1981) explains, differing task conceptions—how people view their work and the technical culture enabling them to perform it—are associated with preferred work structures. Teachers who view their work as more complex will try to maximize their professional repertoires to carry it out. Teachers who view their work as more routine will prefer standardized instruction that can be applied uniformly to all students.

Different task conceptions and preferred work structures are exactly what we find in our data: Teachers from learning-enriched schools stress the need for curricular diversity, whereas teachers from learning-impoverished settings emphasize curricular uniformity. In learning-enriched settings, teachers stress curricular complexity, whereas in learning-impoverished settings, teachers emphasize curricular simplicity. In this way, social organizations establish and maintain a self-fulfilling prophecy: *The more impoverished the school's opportunities to learn, the less about teaching there is to learn, and the less time teachers require to learn it.*

Teaching Excellence and Its Sources

We asked a second interview question to further probe teachers' consciousness of their learning: "What do you think you do especially well in teaching and how did you learn to do that?" Opportunities to excel, we reasoned, were in large measure a function of workplace exposure, practice, and feedback. In other words, like children, teachers may learn best what they have the greatest opportunities to learn. If the social organization of schools indeed suggests either a narrow or a more expansive interpretation of teachers' work, *what* one learns to do well, and *how* one learns to do it, will, at least to some extent, be governed by workplace opportunities and constraints. We again tabulated and categorized teacher responses by school levels of learning opportunities.

Teachers' Professional Accomplishments. First we consider what teachers say they do well. As Table 4.2 indicates, almost all teachers in learning-enriched schools report excelling in some area of academic content—an expressly narrow view of classroom success. More than half, for example, target reading instruction as their primary professional accomplishment. In moderately impoverished settings, less than a third of the sample identifies reading instruction as their greatest strength and in learning-impoverished schools only a fifth do so.

Hence the more learning-enriched the school, the more its social organization narrows teachers' identification of what they do best—teaching basic skills. The more learning-impoverished the school, the more vast the universe from which to choose one's major accomplishments. In the loose vagaries of an uncompelled and nondirected social organization, teachers' curricular emphases tend to be matters of personal choice, for example,

TABLE 4.2. Teaching Skills and Their Sources

Level of schools' learning opportunities	What do you think you do especially well in teaching?*	HOW DID YOU LEARN TO DO THAT?*				
		Other teachers	Preservice training	Inservices, workshops, outside courses	Experience	Innate quality or gift that can't be learned
Learning-enriched (n = 20)	55% teaching reading 25% teaching math 10% teaching science 30% motivating or relating to students	65%	0%	15%	10%	15%
Moderately impoverished (n = 26)	31% teaching reading 19% teaching math 23% individualizing and personalizing instruction 38% motivating or relating to students	0%	14%	38%	38%	19%
Learning-impoverished (n = 28)	11% classroom discipline 21% teaching reading 39% motivating or relating to students 29% classroom discipline 7% using visual aids 29% creative arts, activities	0%	14%	4%	32%	50%

*Teachers often offered multiple responses to these questions. Percentages therefore reflect the number of times each category was mentioned.

motivating students ("I love and enjoy students"; "I give my children a feeling of self-worth"; "I have an understanding relationship with children"); personalizing their instruction ("Making things relevant to my students"; "Teaching to their strengths"); engaging in creative activities (storytelling, dramatics, music, art); and disciplining students ("Running a tight ship"; "Keeping students in line"). Furthermore, for nonacademic endeavors such as music and art, or raising children's self-esteem, there exist myriad routes to define one's success because such goals do not easily lend themselves to ojective performance evaluation.

Using the number of different teaching accomplishments as a measure of organizational latitude, Table 4.2 reveals that teachers in learning-enriched schools identify only two distinct categories of individual merit: motivating students and helping them acquire basic skills. In schools with moderate learning opportunities, teachers identify four distinct categories of individual merit: the two named above, personalizing instruction, and classroom discipline. Teachers in learning-impoverished schools identify six distinct categories of individual merit: the four named above, creative activities, and using visual aids (e.g., "Use of the overhead projector"). That the number of different teaching accomplishments relates inversely to schools' learning opportunities underscores with particular emphasis the effects of shared school goals. At the two extremes, social organizations function either as centripetal forces pulling teachers to pursue common purpose, or as centrifugal forces allowing teachers to pursue individual interests. In the former, teachers celebrate common achievements; in the latter, teachers celebrate successful endeavors alone.

A final observation is in order before we move on to sources of teaching accomplishment. Earlier we saw that mastery of student discipline was cited as a major achievement only by teachers in more learning-impoverished schools. Is it then unimportant to those in learning-enriched schools? We tested this notion by comparing z-scores between schools on the extent to which student behavior is managed at the school level. In learning-enriched settings, as one might suspect, almost all z-scores of student behavior are about one standard deviation or more above the mean, indicating that student management is orchestrated and performed by teachers and principals working in concert. And because maintaining an orderly classroom is more a communal than an individual undertaking, it is less apt to be singularly prized. In more learning-impoverished schools, z-scores of student behavior fall around or substantially below the mean, indicating that students' orderly conduct is less a harmonious blending of collective deeds and more a cacophony of discordant perspectives. Some teachers perceive success while others see failure. And it is precisely these performance comparisons that allow some to celebrate student control as their greatest teaching triumph. We might ponder as well if the student control ideology characterizing more isolated settings might account for the different accomplishments teachers come most highly to prize.

Sources of Professional Accomplishment. Data concerning the sources of teaching accomplishment, also presented in Table 4.2, provide still greater insight into the social organization as a reality-definer. In learning-enriched schools, where students' basic skills mastery is the dominant teaching achievement, the majority of the teachers cite colleagues as their major source of renewal, a finding that meshes clearly with quantitative data. An individual idea may have a haze around it, like a street lamp in the rain, but given a hairsbreadth twist by a colleague, it might open up entirely new vistas in teachers' pedagogical repertoires.

In moderately impoverished schools, perhaps because colleagues less typically share common interests, and because classroom goals may not co-incide, teachers pursue instructional mastery outside their organizational settings. This makes sense in light of threats to self-esteem: the greater the communicative distance, the more teachers protect themselves from any damaging scrutiny. Hence teachers forego the value of inherited wisdom; collaboration is not cited as the vehicle for perfecting one's accomplishments. The majority of teachers instead report learning through a melange of resources external to the school, such as inservice programs, workshops, courses, and their own trial-and-error.

In learning-impoverished settings, which offer the greatest latitude in selecting teaching goals, and where the majority of teaching achievements themselves reside in personal resources (i.e., motivating or relating to students, creative activities), most teachers believe that their major accomplishments are not at all learned. Instead they are "gifts" or "innate" properties that individuals bring with them to the practice of teaching (e.g., "It's in your blood"; "It comes second nature to me"; "It's just in me"). Creative gifts, of course, do not exempt teachers from the struggle with instructional uncertainty or from the constructive sharing of that struggle with co-workers. Thus we might view this response as the ultimate manifestation of threatened self-esteem. If accomplished teaching cannot be learned, there is precious little basis for social comparison, and far fewer challenges to one's sense of self-worth.

If the majority of teachers in the most learning-impoverished settings perceive their greatest talents as innate properties that cannot be learned, it follows that there is little reason to collaborate and little reason (perhaps other than incremental pay raises) to pursue outside resources to further one's talents. Therefore, teachers use neither colleagues, nor workshops, nor outside courses. The minority of teachers in these schools who cite classroom discipline, basic skills, and use of visual aids as major accomplishments do report deriving benefit from either preservice training or trial-and-error learning. But creative activities and relating to students (the latter category cutting across all levels of schools' learning opportunities) are perceived as acquired neither through external means nor cumulative experience—instead they may depend exclusively on teachers' internal, individual resources.

Assuming for the moment that teachers' task conceptions are determined by what they do best, we see clear logic in why the majority of learning-impoverished teachers believe their greatest talents are innate rather than learned. Unencumbered by a social organization that centrepitally pulls them to value, emphasize, and share common goals, they may tend to discover what they most enjoy doing and define those activities as tasks most essential to the practice of teaching.

The Learning Problems of Colleagues

That the majority of teachers in learning-enriched schools believe that they acquire and develop their best professional skills, whereas the majority of teachers in learning-impoverished schools believe they are instinctive carries profound implications for school renewal. Specifically, it suggests a consciousness in the latter setting that teacher learning itself may not be possible. We explored this idea indirectly by asking, "What happens at your school if there is a teacher everyone knows is not doing well?" If, on the one hand, schools sustain the reality that good teachers are born rather than made, colleagues and principals should respond to unsuccessful teaching with little intervention. If, on the other hand, schools sustain the reality that good teachers are made rather than born, colleagues and principals should respond to unsuccessful teaching with appropriate instructional or managerial help. We must also be mindful that teachers' willingness to help and be helped depend in part on threats to their self-esteem.

Improving in Learning-enriched Settings. In learning-enriched schools, teachers revealed a consciousness not dissimilar to that predicted above:

> Teachers always pitch in. We cover for the teacher when she has behavior problems and we sort of take control of her class when we go on field trips. And of course we try to be helpful in the faculty room by giving suggestions. [Do your suggestions help the teacher improve?] Sometimes yes and sometimes no. [Can you give me an example?] Well, there was a beginning teacher who had trouble handling her class—they were so loud you could hear them down the hall. One of the teachers came in and took over the class to show her what could be done. This first year teacher improved a lot after that. [What about tenured teachers? Do they get help when they are having trouble?] We [the faculty] try. The principal encourages us to try. But he does the most to help them. He spends a lot of time in those classrooms.

> Most of us pitch in to help, including our principal. We offer advice, materials, and any other kind of assistance the teacher may need. We don't hesitate at all to do these things. We want every teacher to teach as well as she can; that makes for a better school and far fewer problems.

> We have a couple of teachers like that. One of them is having problems and she comes to me for help. She'll ask me about instructional decisions. The

principal asked several of the teachers to help her. She's young and the principal also has conferences with her. There's another teacher having problems who's set in her ways. You can't change her mind about anything. We have tried, but she's very old and getting ready to retire. Anybody younger is automatically suspect. The principal has also tried, but he's younger and so I think that's inhibiting. The principal has called other teachers in and said, "She is not the same quality as the rest of the teachers . . . You need to pick up the slack for her."

Each of these school faculties approaches troubled colleagues with similar remedial tactics. First, improvement attempts are initiated both by principal and teachers. Second, while colleagues perceive that professional renewal is painstaking, uphill work with older teachers (perhaps because of threatened self-esteem), they do not consider them terminal. This underscores the implicit assumption that teacher learning, even with those who most need intensive assistance, is possible. Finally, several of the faculty become involved in remedial efforts; it is a group rather than a solo endeavor. For both donors and recipients of help, this reaffirms professional self-renewal as a communal rather than solitary happening.

Teachers in learning-enriched schools also understand that no matter what they do, some things can't be changed; that still others can be changed if they try. They devote most of their energies, therefore, to teachers they can do something about. Thus, when progress with problematic teachers is not apparent, colleagues pool their resources in a collective interest to diminish any negative effects that poorer teachers may have on children in the school—they "pick up the slack" or "cover for the teacher." That is, colleagues counter threats to the success of the school with swift, corrective action:

> Well we [teachers] tried, but we got negative feedback [from the teacher]. We saw that children were being damaged. The discipline got out of hand and if you don't have discipline, you can't teach school. It got to the point that when they [students] went to the restroom, someone [another teacher] would have to stop what they were doing and try to calm them down. We didn't want our kids to think that they could get away with acting like that.

Notice how the character of this school emphasizes unified disciplinary action. In this example, teachers share responsibility to still the raucous behavior of a colleague's wayward class. That responsibility for school success lies in cohesive rather than fragmentary action again underscores the effects of shared goals and teachers' ownership of them. One twelve-year veteran from a learning-enriched setting succinctly offsets the place of shared goals in providing specific substance and direction for teacher learning:

> The principal assigned a certain teacher for the new teacher who came in, so she could go to someone for help. [Do you ever find yourself being assigned a new teacher?] Yes. I let them know that I'm there if they need me. If I see that

a certain person is struggling, I won't lord it over them, but I'll let them know that *there are certain policies that we go by that help.*

In addition to noting that improvement benefits rest fundamentally on shared understandings about teaching, this teacher's consciousness of her role as colleague, particularly when combined with views presented above, evidences strong norms of collaboration, and few threats to self-esteem. Collaborative norms become even more apparent when experienced colleagues describe their performance-related interaction with beginning teachers. Recalling from earlier analysis the pivotal role of shared goals in teachers' collaborative efforts, and what veterans choose to emphasize in socializing newcomers, this finding takes on clearer meaning. Beginners socialized to accept collaborative norms as the appropriate way in which one learns to teach, and who see these norms manifest all about, more readily believe that success would be theirs if their passion for learning takes hold; their schools are an authentic account, a dazzling gateway of possibilities, a rendering of the actual. One teacher from a learning-enriched school explained her first year this way:

> Well, I was having some difficulty last year. And everyone pitched in and helped me. My principal took lots of time with me, explaining things, and made sure I got a chance to talk to other teachers. [Did you mainly get help with the curriculum?] No. It wasn't so much with teaching materials, though everyone was really generous with those. It was more with teaching problems: how to handle children who didn't know their multiplication tables; how to involve this child or that child; what to do when kids didn't do their homework. Last year it seemed that all I did was pump these teachers for ideas—but they seemed to enjoy helping me. [In what ways did they show that they enjoyed helping you?] They would ask, "Did you try this and that? And what happened?" They took real interest in me. I felt like they really wanted me to be successful.

This teacher describes a setting in which colleagues and principal unofficially work together to support growth and to provide in a communal way for new teachers. And here, as in views expressed earlier, we find principals to be the indisputable linchpin in helping poorly performing teachers to improve. In fact, 85% of the teachers from learning-enriched schools report constructive principal involvement with troubled teachers: through frequent and clear evaluation; their own suggestions and advice; and their mobilization of other resources, particularly the school's teacher leaders. Through these actions principals communicate no small degree of certainty that ineffective teachers *can* be helped to improve. Nowhere is this more poignantly illustrated than in the next account of a struggling teacher under two successive principals. Again the informant teaches in a learning-enriched school:

> We have a teacher like that. Some parents wouldn't allow their children to go into that classroom. If our old principal knew that parents would raise flack, then those kids weren't ever put into that teacher's classroom. Only low-income children went into that classroom. But our new principal stopped that practice

four years ago. And the problem has worked its way out to a degree. The new principal put this teacher on a probation system. Everybody tries to help her; give suggestions where we can, give her materials, and try to include her in our planning activities. I would say there is more teamwork now. That has helped.

The change in this faculty's character seems to have worked like penicillin, clearing away the chronic anemia, the spasms of fear, summoning new vitality and strength. And in this instance we gain additional insight into ways principals rally faculty in common purpose and establish norms of continuous improvement: they direct helpful attention not only to needy teachers, but, perhaps more crucially, to the previously uninvolved faculty. These principals seem to find ways to turn adversarial relations among colleagues into fruitful coalitions. Their tactics are not to ferret out and penalize ineffectiveness, but rather to devise ingenious ways of putting new information and experiences within the reach of those teachers in order to improve the quality of their work.

Moreover, if substantial collegial interaction revolves around teacher improvement, then the norm of self-renewal for *all* teachers becomes a highly salient fact of everyday life. Building a collaborative scaffolding for the school's social organization redefines not only the nature of appropriate collegial behavior, but also what is possible to achieve. When teachers' work is revealed as one of expanded possibilities, norms of self-reliance are reduced to the status of only one conscious choice; escape from these norms becomes still another. In the more isolated school that has passed away here, no thoughts of remorse are apparent in its members, as they doff their cloaks of self-deception. Indeed, in learning-enriched schools, 85% of the teachers report constructive collegial involvement with poorly performing colleagues.

The Pivotal Role of Colleagues. As implied above, colleagues take on special ability to mediate individual performance. Although principals may initially have the power to define teachers' performance levels and set them remedially on course, colleagues' collective involvement in that effort makes principal evaluations about performance perceived more convincingly as fact than opinion.

Further, colleagues' perceptions are critical because they are the major source of external self-definition other than the principal. If colleagues differ from principals, granting teachers alternative performance information, they can see in their performance what they wish to see—the view that casts them in the most favorable light. We find two veterans of learning-impoverished schools, each with over twenty years' experience, in exactly these circumstances:

> Our principal did an evaluation on me last year and gave me several comments. I didn't agree with a single thing he said. I think he is dead wrong about my teaching. My colleagues do, too.

I was evaluated this year. The reading supervisor gave me confidence that what I was doing was good and in fact it seemed that she thought I was doing a better than average job. So I've felt especially good this year about my teaching. But then a parent wanted to have his child removed from my classroom because I did not know how to teach reading. The principal agreed. [How did that make you feel?] I felt that he [the principal] was not supportive of me.

In these teachers' schools, no strong tide of feedback insisted that they accept the reality of their poor performance. Indeed, both teachers took acrid exception to their principal's negative performance evaluation because alternative sources granted them wider latitude from which to interpret their performance. They then selected from competing perceptions the most self-enhancing stance. That teachers can resist negative evaluations with impunity illustrates the importance of colleagues in negotiated meaning, as well as teachers' tendency to manipulate cues within a social context to their own presentational advantage.

In schools where principal and colleagues reach high consensus about teachers' improvement needs and take collective measures to bring that improvement about, teachers can prevail less on counterdefinitions of their circumstance. Having fewer degrees of freedom, ineffective teachers may be pressured to accept the validity of those negative designations, as a powerful collective perception is brought to bear. That is, social pressure regularly visited on those performing poorly tends to diminish the possibility of an overly positive self-presentation. And the more singular and unambiguous the tide of feedback flowing to teachers, the less likely they will develop alternative interpretations of their classroom performance.

Consensus between principals and colleagues about the need for remedial action is, of course, highest in learning-enriched schools. Thus, consistent performance evaluation by principals and colleagues tends to tighten the system of feedback and presses teachers toward betterment. The more consistent and strong the message of improvement needs presented to troubled teachers, the more compelling the reason for the reality of those needs to be internalized, and the more readily colleagues' suggestions and advice may be accepted and, perhaps, eventually solicited.

Improving in Learning-impoverished Settings. Next we consider the possibilities for teacher improvement in more learning-impoverished schools. Responses to the question, "What happens at your school if there is a teacher everyone knows is not doing well?", as the reader might anticipate, portrayed a markedly different reality of school life:

I really don't know. I know that there are teachers who are not good at this school. I think that the principal is aware of the situation but he doesn't seem to be able to do much about it. [Why is that?] Those bad teachers are tenured, so there's not much he can do, unless, of course, they're *real* bad. But, I mean, they have to be just rotten before you can get rid of them. [Do other teachers try to help in your school when they know that a teacher is not doing a good job?] No, it's pretty much just the principal who deals with it. [What would be your reaction if you knew a teacher wasn't doing well and the principal wasn't dealing with it?] I wouldn't dare step in unless I were friends with that person.

Basically nothing is done. Everybody just tends to ignore it. [Do others try to help?] I don't know of anyone ever being helped. [What is your feeling about making suggestions to those teachers?] That's a very hard thing to do. Basically I think that it's the principal who has to take the responsibility—to have the guts—to get rid of ineffective teachers. It's the principal who needs to step in. I can't deny that I would feel very defensive if another teacher came in and told me what to do.

In more learning-impoverished schools, the large majority of teachers believe that dealing with inadequate teaching is the exclusive responsibility of their principal. Almost all acknowledge their principal's awareness of the "problem," and, by their accounts, principals do remarkably little to remedy it. At the heart of principal inaction may again lie uncertainty about instructional practice. Where principals believe little improvement is possible, or, alternatively, where the requisite assistance exceeds principals' range, they may simply take evasive rather than helpful measures. With principals as unwitting transmitters of self-reliant norms, the lesson about teacher learning is not lost on faculty within the school: nothing can be done. In fact, teachers' consciousness about the futility of improvement in learning-impoverished schools leads the two quoted above to pronounce that the function of principals is not to *help* those in trouble but instead to *get rid of them.* Troublesome teachers are a burden, a weight, a problem separate from other colleagues, and something to be ended.

But what of struggling teachers themselves in more learning-impoverished settings? Do they, like their counterparts in learning-enriched settings, come to realize their own improvement needs? Several typical teacher responses are instructive in this regard:

To my knowledge, they are not even told. There is one teacher who doesn't do much of anything. Sometimes I wonder why she even goes on teaching; I don't understand. It kind of bothers me, but it's not my place to go to the principal. And he seems to know what the situation is.

Nothing. We try to ignore it the best we can. [Does the principal help this teacher?] He has to walk softly in the situation. Our principal is a nice man. He's a minister at the same time as he's a principal. He tries to walk easy, not get too involved.

We have had one teacher like that. He should have been helped when the problem started, but he wasn't. He never got any help to solve his problems. His evaluations were all good and he was never told that he was having a problem.

In these comments we sense teachers' remoteness from both troubled colleagues, and interchangeably, the welfare of the school—a thick cloak of indifference that they seem seldom to cast off. Here contrasting opportunities for teacher learning again become graphically clear. In learning-enriched settings, principals and colleagues tend to press teachers about their improvement needs, provide guidance along the way, and measure progress made through frequent observation. But if the consensus held in impoverished settings is that poorly performing teachers cannot be helped, refusal to impart bad news is a powerful motive for principal or faculty inertia. And if struggling teachers receive little feedback and guidance from principals or colleagues, they may be unable to recognize their teaching inadequacies, to realize the need for assistance, and to redirect their energies toward improvement. Two teachers from learning-impoverished schools lucidly illustrate these consequences:

> We are evaluated every three years. This was my year to be evaluated. Now, he did come into my classroom to observe me teach a lesson. He was complimentary of my lesson and he said that he had seen things there that he had never seen before. However, on the evaluation, there were places he could mark if the person had done minimum requirements. There was a place underneath for comments. Under each thing he checked that I had completed the minimum and made no comments and I felt that this was damning me with faint praise. And I had done a good job.

> My principal evaluates teachers every three years according to central office policy. He comes in twice during the year for this, and he checks your lesson plans before he observes you. [Does he check your lesson plans any other time?] Not really. [Are his observations helpful?] Well, if he likes you they are. If he doesn't they aren't. [Does he help the teacher in trouble you just described to me?] No, he doesn't talk much to her.

In learning-impoverished schools, only 29% of the teachers view their principals as engaged constructively in helping ineffective teachers improve. If colleagues believe that dealing with teacher inadequacy is the exclusive domain of principals, and if threats to principals' self-esteem dissuade their own remedial intervention, the lesson to be learned is straightforward: since troubled teachers cannot improve, there is little point in helping them.

And colleagues from more learning-impoverished settings learn this lesson particularly well. Only 25% of the teachers from moderately impoverished schools and, even more strikingly, only 8% of the teachers from learning-impoverished schools report constructive involvement with colleagues experiencing difficulty. They respond neither by taking helpful measures nor by claiming responsibility for the task:

> You can only do your own job; you can't do everyone else's.

> I'm responsible for running my classroom. I expect no help and so I'm not responsible to give any.

> I worked with one. She asked me for all my teaching materials and she never produced anything in return. I just told her, no, I did not wish to work with her.

Given teachers' interpretive freedom where colleagues and principals give little (if any) support, feedback, or guidance, it is not surprising that ineffective teachers show little visible improvement. At the same time, professional and social isolation helps buffer these same teachers from knowledge of their pedagogical problems by avoiding the gossip that so engages others. And the absence of improvement over time then tends to circle back to confirm colleagues' and principals' beliefs that no remediation is in fact possible. The paradox, of course, is that no intervention can possibly succeed unless it is first attempted.

Even when principals do offer suggestions to help teachers improve, they face an unenviable predicament. Without the reinforcement of colleagues who press teachers to accept reality about the need for improvement, the attempt may not succeed. Good intentions and deeds are rarely enough where circumstances allow for wide interpretive latitude to discount or altogether ignore principals' advice. Attesting to this evanescence of power and influence are veterans from two learning-impoverished schools. It is plain from their comments below that their task conceptions, in contrast to that of their principals, maintain their sense of control and their feelings of professional self-worth, while presumably having the opposite effect on their supervisors:

> If the principal sees a weakness he goes in and evaluates the teacher. There are certain things he emphasizes—he doesn't like any noise or sounds in the classroom. He has worked with me on that because my room isn't as quiet as he would like it. [How did you feel about that?] Well, I didn't agree—there are times when children need to be loud. But I try to make it nice when he comes in. [Here the teacher laughs.]

> My principal does do evaluations every three years, and my turn was last year. Now he did compliment me on my room, on my bulletin boards. But he criticized the way I taught the reading lesson. He thought some children weren't understanding the assignment I had given and so afterwards they were goofing around during seatwork. I know these kids and they always goof around, no matter what the assignment is and how well they understand it.

The importance of collegial involvement in helping teachers realize their improvement needs, then, cannot be overemphasized. If principals fail in their efforts to enlist teachers' help, to give themselves plausibility, and to define school renewal as a mutual, ongoing enterprise, they may become trapped in an unending cycle of teachers' unwillingness or inability to acknowledge the reality of their performance deficits and to deal with them straightforwardly. Even with the best of intentions to help them improve, principals' intervention may only stir denial and resentment, distancing the source of teacher improvement from its primary target of change.

Collegial Talk about Troubled Teachers. As implied above, another potential embarrassment awaits troubled teachers who receive no collegial support or assistance: they become isolates in the social system of the school, victims of collegial banter and ridicule. As colleagues talk about them collusively, comments of sympathy, compassion, and comfort appear to find no utterance here:

> Everyone talks about them. We gossip about them all the time; we tell each other the things we hear about those teachers. We don't dare offer them help, though.

> In this school there are two in particular who aren't doing well. All the other teachers talk about how they're not doing well. They are not really given any help. One of them quit and went to another system. There was really no advice given to them to improve.

> Maybe they get helped by someone, but the majority of teachers don't really like having a bad teacher in the school. You know, one bad apple can spoil the barrel. There is a lot of resentment toward them. They are discussed a lot.

For conversants themselves, such disparaging talk has all the makings of a superb paradox. It reinforces the improbability of teacher change while at the same time legitimating nonintervention by colleagues. One would think that the principle of living in glass houses and not throwing stones would ward teachers off, but it does not seem to occur to them that they are asking for trouble of precisely the same kind—the most intimate sort of anguish—that could one day be theirs. That is, their vulnerability admonishes those engaged in such talk to hide their classroom problems lest they, in the future, fall victim to the same unbridled ridicule. The net effect tends both to diminish professional conversation and to reduce teachers' willingness to seek constructive help (e.g., Glidewell et al. 1983). Because teachers view requests for advice or assistance in these settings more as signs of incipient incompetence than as eagerness to learn, in times of trouble colleagues seldom ask.

Fortunately, all is not so bleak. Quite to the contrary, there was no comparable evidence of collegial reproof regarding ineffective teaching in learning-enriched schools. In fact, internalized norms of collaboration actually militate *against* such reproof in some schools. Faculty did not abuse weaker colleagues in order to catch some self-esteem, some sense of dignity, some sense of fitting into a larger scheme of things. They seemed already to have that. Their own opinion, as we saw in Chapter 3, was that some colleagues were at a zenith of force, inspiration, and dedication, surpassing anything others had yet to accomplish. Offered one teacher, whose positive explanation about helping unskilled colleagues we have already heard, "We don't talk *about* teachers here—we talk *to* them." In answer to our original question a second teacher said:

> We never talk about our fellow colleagues behind their backs, so I can't tell you. We have a great working relationship; we try to be professional and not talk about those having problems. [Who tells the person, then, if they're having problems?] We try to help the person if we can. That's the way our faculty is—we try to help.

A third teacher with 41 years of varied experience in several different settings offered this observation on the reality of collegial disenfranchisement in schools other than her own:

> One thing that bothers me is professionalism. I think teachers should hang together more. I think they should be more professional like doctors. They should collaborate more with each other. [Is there anything else about doctors that makes you feel they're more professional than teachers?] Well, you just don't hear many doctors gossiping about each other. I don't think teachers support their profession when they do that.

As in Chapter 3, teachers regard less able colleagues as deserving of help because they are not held entirely responsible for their performance misfortunes (i.e., skills are acquired rather than born). Further, help may be more propitious in learning-enriched settings because it eventually makes less skilled teachers more self-renewing; that is, because their learning is perceived as developmental, poorly performing colleagues may become self-sufficient in the future, contributing more constructively to the school.

Nowhere, then, is the contextual nature of teaching more vivid than in the contrasting treatment of troubled colleagues: teachers from learning-enriched settings seem to take collective and individual responsibility for the quality of their schools and for those who work within them, whereas teachers from more learning-impoverished settings appear to attend solely and unapologetically to themselves.

Sources of Professional Renewal

Contextual differences in teachers' consciousness about their learning surface in another interview question about their sources of professional renewal—"Where do your new teaching ideas come from?" Results tabulated and categorized by the school's level of learning opportunities appear in Table 4.3.

Turning first to the origin of new ideas, we see that under learning-enriched conditions, colleagues seem to take the forefront in teachers' professional renewal, ever present when most wanted. In moderately impoverished settings, only about half the teachers mentioned colleagues, and in learning-impoverished schools, colleagues receive mention by less than a third of the teachers. The most striking difference, however, lies in teachers' use of their own talents and creativity. Learning-enriched schools might be viewed as a kind of trampoline for the individual imagination, for a healthy utilization of human potentialities. Unhampered by school pathologies, teachers are capable of blooming out into the mind. But since nothing can be perfectly anticipated, all experiments are subject to error or even failure. Healthy schools seem to withstand these high fevers of experimentation, flexible enough to embrace all promising ideas with confidence that teachers will come back even stronger.

TABLE 4.3. Sources of New Teaching Ideas

Level of schools' learning opportunities	WHERE DO YOUR NEW TEACHING IDEAS COME FROM?*				
	Other teachers	Teaching magazines	Professional conferences	Inservices, workshops, outside courses	Own problem solving, creativity
Learning-enriched ($n = 20$)	90%	60%	45%	50%	72%
Moderately impoverished ($n = 26$)	54%	65%	4%	54%	4%
Learning-impoverished ($n = 28$)	32%	50%	0%	39%	4%

*Teachers frequently offered multiple answers to this question. Percentages therefore reflect the number of times each item was mentioned.

That problem-solving, creativity, and faculty collaboration become the most prevalent sources of teacher renewal captures part of the synergism in these schools: the comments of one colleague may prompt quick and sometimes innovative responses by another, which leads a third to see a synthesis between the ideas of the first two, and so forth. In this way enthusiasm for classroom experimentation gathers momentum and direction cumulatively, like a train rushing downhill without obstacle. But more impoverished schools, at least in this small sample, seem to replace the incentive for imaginative thought with the routine sequences of a computer program. Here principals, parents, and colleagues sap teachers' mental strength as much as students who are importunate. The fact is that—whatever the source of that mysterious human property we call creativity—many teachers in learning-impoverished settings seem to have just about come to the end of theirs.

Almost half the teachers in learning-enriched schools report gathering new ideas through professional conferences; specifically, national or regional meetings of the International Reading Association and the National Education Association, whereas these same meetings received no appreciable mention in more learning-impoverished settings. Reading professional magazines such as *Instructor* and *Learning* and attending inservices, courses, and workshops as sources of professional renewal did not differ substantially between learning-enriched and moderately impoverished schools. But in learning-impoverished schools, we see a marked decline in the use of each of these resources, indicating the grip of a terrible inertia.

Interpreting these findings, we see a consistent tendency for teachers from more learning-impoverished settings to use primarily those resources that schools or districts make locally available, such as magazines or inservices, or those that can be readily accessed externally, such as workshops and courses. Teachers' tendencies in learning-enriched settings, by contrast, are to use both commonly available resources as well as those that require substantially greater expenditure of their time and psychic energy—attending instructional conferences, problem-solving, and thinking privately and aloud with colleagues in the direction of self and school improvement.

There are at least three plausible explanations for these findings. The school's social organization may shape teachers' consciousness and behavior to the extent that the more varied and enriched the setting, the more teachers within them vary and enrich their own professional growth. An alternative possibility rests on earlier findings that in learning-impoverished schools, teachers tend to define their professional growth as terminal, culminating in the mastery of routine practices that are applied uniformly, and more unimaginatively with each successive year. Their counterparts in learning-enriched settings tend to define professional growth as sustained, where new skills and practices may be filed into an ever-expanding portfolio that pliantly accommodates diverse student needs as contextual differences arise. And as awareness of student diversity and need heightens experientially in learning-enriched settings, more varied practices may be demanded and therefore culled from a wider range of sources—the essential ingredients of a flourishing technical culture. Finally, that the majority of teachers from impoverished settings tend to believe that their skills are largely instinctive implies that few learning resources can actually augment their "natural" ability. But because teachers in learning-enriched schools tend to believe their skills are largely acquired, they can therefore develop, perfect, and add to their fund of new skills by expending more time and effort. In any case, we can tentatively identify conditions under which teachers aspire to learn as a life-long pursuit.

LEARNING OPPORTUNITIES AND STUDENT ACHIEVEMENT

We have argued that learning-enriched schools accentuate the development and mastery of teaching techniques and strategies that, when applied with proper knowledge and care, meet with student success; and that there are organizational signals beckoning for greater professional growth to better meet the challenge of students whose learning requirements still exceed teachers' collective grasp. To the extent that continuous school renewal exists, then, it should be manifest directly in students' basic skills mastery.

Testing this latter proposition was no easy undertaking, however. In Tennessee, which had no state-level requirements for standardized testing in basic skills, districts had the liberty to select any test, to administer it at any grade, at any time, or to decide to forego it completely. A quarter of the districts we initially contacted fell into one or more of these categories. Therefore we whittled our sample, mindful of critical district characteristics, and a representative sample, to include only those districts that annually administered standardized tests in reading and math. With the exception of one small district with four schools, others tested at the beginning of each academic year. Much to our chagrin, however, the districts sampled used three different standardized tests: the California, the Metropolitan, or the Stanford—achievement tests in no way comparable statistically.

To calibrate tests, we used the *Title I Evaluation and Reporting System User's Guide* (TIERS) that essentially standardizes either percentiles or grade level equivalencies of different achievement tests into z-scores for reading and math. TIERS, however, uses far more inclusive distribution points than any of the tests named previously. This means that we sacrificed variance in favor of attenuating effects. We focus attention on one student cohort's performance between second and fourth grade—part of the same period that we collected other school and district data.

In addition to second grade reading or math scores, we controlled for other school demographic variables and teacher qualities in our regression analyses: school SES, pupil–teacher ratio, school size, teachers' mean educational attainment (measured by the highest degree held), teachers' mean years of experience, and teachers' mean undergraduate status. The correlation coefficients, means, and standard deviations of these variables, including teachers' learning opportunities, appear in Table 4.4. Mean undergraduate status moderately correlates with students' reading and math achievement in both second and fourth grades. The mean level of teaching experience *negatively* relates to reading achievement, and school size correlates significantly with math. Pupil–teacher ratio, to our surprise, correlates only weakly with second grade reading and math.

Eliminating variables of no significance, we hierarchically regressed fourth grade reading or math scores on each variable, entering learning opportunities last in each equation. These results for significant coefficients appear in Table 4.5.

First we consider students' reading achievement. Controlling for second grade reading, we find that both teachers' mean experience and school SES *negatively* predict students' reading in grade 4. That is, the more experienced the faculty or the lower the school's SES, the less apt children are to progress in reading. Indeed, on the latter point, one of the clearest findings from educational research is that the socioeconomic background of students, and the learning resources they have available at home, powerfully affect student achievement (Epstein 1987; Good & Brophy 1987). The inverse relationship between teachers' mean experience and their teaching effectiveness, although less known, is also a consistent finding in the literature (Eberts, Kehoe & Stone 1984; Katzman 1971; Sizemore et al. 1986). After a time, the emptiness of teachers' professional growth tends to become a numb ache felt in students' learning opportunities. The lack of significant findings for any other variable may be substantive, or alternatively, the result of an insufficiently small sample size.

Even after controlling for the effects of teacher experience and school SES, teachers' learning opportunities, as revealed in the comparison of beta weights, holds far greater impact on students' reading gains. The greater the opportunities for teachers to learn, the higher their students' reading performance. When combined, entry level achievement, teacher experience, school SES, and teacher learning account for 64% of the variance of students' fourth-grade reading results.

Turning next to students' achievement in math, and after controlling for the effects of prior knowledge at grade two, no school demographic or teacher background variable influences student gains. Instead, teachers' learning opportunities monolithically predicts math achievement. Again, the greater teachers' opportunities for learning, the greater students' learning of basic math skills. Second-grade math scores combine with teacher learning to explain 61% of the variance in fourth-grade math achievement.

The finding that school SES is unrelated to fourth grade math achievement, of course, runs counter to available knowledge. There are several possible explanations. The sample is heavily skewed in the direction of

TABLE 4.4. Correlation Coefficients, Means (M), and Standard Deviations (SD) for Variable Examined with the Dependent Variable Teacher Learning

	2	3	4	5	6	7	8	9	10	M	SD
1. School SES	-.27	-.22	-.37	-.29	-.22	-.18	-.18	-.61	.07	.41	.22
2. School size		.18	.02	.02	.10	.22	-.00	.07	.06	19.49	8.13
3. Pupil–teacher ratio			.12	-.01	.14	-.02	-.25	.19	-.07	24.47	2.69
4. Reading, grade 2				.44	.66	.24	-.02	.45	-.05	51.96	6.78
5. Reading, grade 4					.27	.47	-.16	.40	.46	54.62	6.66
6. Math, grade 2						.59	-.04	.51	.11	52.87	9.95
7. Math, grade 4							-.03	.40	.44	53.62	10.78
8. Years teaching experience								-.01	-.01	12.73	3.00
9. Undergraduate status									.18	1.13	.03
10. Learning opportunities										17.38	2.67

TABLE 4.5. Multiple Regression Analysis of Learning Opportunities on Reading and Math Gains

A. *Reading, Grade 4*	Variable	Beta	F	R^2
	Reading, grade 2	.58	57.51**	.38
	Teaching experience	−.14	3.61*	.40
	School SES	−.14	3.31*	.41
	Learning opportunities	.48	47.00**	.64
	Multiple $R = .80$			
B. *Math, Grade 4*	Math, grade 2	.65	79.95**	.46
	Learning opportunities	.39	29.21**	.61
	Multiple $R = .78$			

$*p < .08$.
$**p < .001$.

lower SES rural schools, reducing variability so as to show few appreciable effects. A second explanation, supported by the correlations in Table 4.1, is that the relationship between school SES and student learning diminishes with greater time in school; as students progress through the early elementary grades, learning may become more a function of what happens in school rather than of the ascriptive characteristics students bring with them. Finally, the TIERS conversions, having sacrificed no small amount of resolution, may have attenuated the relationship between school SES and math achievement in our sample. These latter two arguments can be applied as well to other demographic or teacher background variables, each of which in other studies relates to student achievement.

The interplay between teacher learning and student outcomes is a game of constant questioning and it is a challenging one, not only because teachers might be fighting the enemy of low student achievement, but also because they can never permit themselves to linger on the comfortable solid ground of absolute security where dwell those who have ceased to question and who fail to grow.

SUMMARY

In this chapter we first identified the social organizational conditions of schools that influence teachers' opportunities to learn. Our analysis of quantitative data indicated that 79% of the variance in teachers' learning opportunities were explained by four organizational arrangements: (1) goal-setting activities that accentuate specific instructional objectives (students' basic skills mastery) toward which to point one's improvement; (2) clear and frequent evaluation by principals, who identify specific improvement needs, and who monitor the progress teachers make in achieving them; (3) shared teaching goals that give legitimacy and support and create pressure to conform to norms of school renewal; and (4) collaboration that at once enables and compels teachers to offer and request advice in helping each other improve instructionally.

In our examination of qualitative data, teachers' beliefs about the time required to master their art, and precisely what that artistry entails, tended to conform largely to their schools' social organization. In learning-enriched schools, teachers tended to hold a sustained view of their learning so as to better meet the challenge of students' diverse learning needs. In learning-impoverished schools, teachers tended to hold a terminal view of their learning, entailing mastery of routine practices and procedures, that, like an endless conveyor belt, process students uniformly. In impoverished schools, teacher learning seemed to result at the end of a brief voyage. In enriched schools, any voyage of teacher learning seemed ongoing.

Schools' social organization also tended to influence teachers' selection and assessment of their strongest professional skills and the manner in which they acquired them. In learning-enriched settings the predominant accomplishment of teachers was basic skills instruction, which they learned primarily in concert with colleagues. In learning-impoverished settings, teaching achievements included motivating students and designing creative activities, which, because they resided in personal traits, were explained more as innate properties or gifts than acquired talents and knowledge. Where teachers' essential nourishment brewed in utter isolation, they appeared to use neither colleagues nor outside resources to further their professional growth.

In examining how teaching deficiencies were dealt with under contextual conditions of varied circumstance, we found that principals and teachers in learning-enriched schools tended to respond with consistent feedback about the need to improve, with helpful advice, support, and assistance to buttress that need, and to optimize the odds of teacher improvement. In learning-impoverished schools, principals and teachers seemed to believe that little could be done to improve ineffective teaching, and thus responded to troubled teachers with little or no intervention, but rather with covert, unbridled ridicule.

When we asked teachers to identify sources of their professional renewal, those in learning-enriched settings primarily cited colleagues in conjunction with their own problem-solving and creative capacities, actions requiring substantial effort. But in learning-impoverished settings, teachers used primarily those material resources that were immediately accessible to them and that required only minimal effort.

Finally, returning to the quantitative data, we examined the relationship between teachers' and students' learning. The extent of teachers' learning opportunities increased the performance gains of one cohort of youngsters in both reading and math over a two-year period, regardless of pupil–teacher ratio or the extent of teachers' professional training. We also found that school SES and teachers' mean experience, albeit far more modestly, related negatively to students' reading gains.

All of this means that it is far easier to learn to teach, and to learn to teach better, in some schools than in others. It means that students in learning-enriched schools profit more in their mastery of basic skills. Finally, it means that the opportunities provided and constraints imposed on teacher learning may carry profound implications for teachers' professional certainty and their willingness and commitment to meet new situations and challenges. In the next two chapters we examine these latter implications.

5

Teacher Certainty

In this chapter we explore possible social organizational influences and outcomes of teachers' certainty about a technical culture and their own instructional practice. As part of that task, we must again be mindful of the differences between teachers' task conceptions as routine or nonroutine. Where teachers conceive of their work as routine, they perform standardized tasks over and over, despite variations in the students that they serve. But when teachers' view their work as nonroutine, they place more emphasis on feeling their way, on experimenting and collaborating with colleagues and principals, on developing more unique than standardized solutions to students' varied problems.

Indeed, our knowledge of the ways in which teachers' certainty (or efficacy) affect student learning gains is in its infancy, but results indicate a robust, positive relationship (Ashton & Webb 1986; Berman & McLaughlin 1977; Gibson & Dembo 1979). We will examine this relationship later in the chapter. Presently, however, we are interested in the ways teachers derive a degree of uncertainty from their environment; how uncertainty is influenced by, and in turn influences, their social organizational lives.

We frame the effects of school context on teacher uncertainty with the theoretical scaffolding of prior chapters, arguing that the attributions teachers cast for their performance are reasonable responses to their organizational constraints and opportunities. The parent community impinging on the school is also examined here—teachers' sentiments toward parents and the subsequent effects on their uncertainty. We will back into the parent community gently, by first looking at the problem that most clearly has its roots within the school.

The Technical Culture of Teaching

In Chapter 4 we saw that teachers from learning-impoverished settings (that is, routine technical cultures) held little awareness that their standardized instructional practice was in large part the reason they performed none too well. There seemed little to learn and little to guide their teaching efforts. Teachers from learning-enriched schools (that is, nonroutine technical cultures), by contrast, continuously acquired knowledge, techniques, and skills, and were better prepared to grapple with the diversified needs of their students.

Equally relevant to the contextual basis of technical knowledge is Ashton and Webb's (1986) interviews with and observations of teachers from two middle schools and two junior high schools, each serving low SES students. Middle school teachers worked with colleagues to broaden their knowledge of pupils' problems and needs, made technical decisions, set teaching goals, and emphasized the importance of adapting instructional methods to meet individual student requirements. They implemented a variety of teaching strategies, stressed comprehension of material over coverage, and frequently grouped and regrouped students to meet individual needs—a nonroutine technical culture. Professionally isolated and uninvolved junior high school teachers, on the other hand, relied instructionally on whole-class lecture and recitation, rarely taught to individual needs, and stressed coverage of material over comprehension—a routine technical culture. Not surprisingly, middle school teachers felt far more efficacious (that is, certain) than their junior high counterparts.

These findings lead logically to assertions we will test in this chapter. If uncertainty exists in the absence of a technical culture, and if organizational members define the state of their technical culture by their social organizational circumstances, it follows that their uncertainty should be minimized where workplace conditions make performance success more attainable. That is, to the extent that social organizational arrangements enable teachers to believe in a technical culture, and from that knowledge to pursue alternative and more successful courses of action, they should experience themselves as causal agents in their performance, more certain about a technical culture and their own instructional practice. Next we specify two conditions thought necessary for this to occur.

The Social Organization of Teacher Certainty

Positive Feedback. First, to perceive themselves as knowledgable and to believe in a technical culture, organizational members need their efforts to be noticed. Without some sense of how well one performs, there is little reason for self-congratulatory sentiments. Acknowledgment of workplace efforts is directly related to the amount of performance feedback people receive. Feedback can result directly from the task itself, as when a dishwasher repairperson turns on the machine and discovers that it does in fact work; or from approval that may be offered by others in the organizational setting, as when a supervisor commends a subordinate for a job well done.

In a like manner, most teachers derive such positive feedback from being instrumental to student growth and development (Lortie 1975) or from recognition they may receive from colleagues, parents, and principal (Kasten 1984; Rosenholtz 1985). Positive feedback may also be viewed as *psychic rewards*, where teachers gain some on-the-job estimate of their particular competence and worth. Yet as we glimpsed in Chapter 3, most teachers and principals become so professionally estranged in their workplace isolation that they neglect each other. They do not often compliment, support, and acknowledge each other's positive efforts. Indeed, strong norms of self-reliance may even evoke adversive reactions to a teacher's successful performance.

Learning Opportunities. Organizational resources should also attenuate teacher uncertainty by actually providing greater technical assistance. One obvious resource is teachers' opportunities to learn. The proposition that learning opportunities expand teachers' pedagogical options and so enhance student learning follows directly from Chapter 4. Teaching dilemmas calling for reasoned intentions, informed choices, and responsible actions are better resolved where the social organization of schools facilitates those processes, and teachers having the capacity to transform less into more successful practices should therefore experience less uncertainty about their work.

Learning opportunities, as revealed in the previous chapter, involve two elemental factors that by themselves may develop better instructional practice. The first is frequent and clear evaluation. Helpful suggestions and assistance by principals arm teachers with greater technical knowledge and greater certainty that their target of student learning is within sight (see Azumi & Madhere 1983; Natriello 1983). Beyond that is faculty collaboration. Collegial requests for, and offers of, advice and assistance increase the number of knowledge exchangers within schools, augmenting teachers' pedagogical options in the face of classroom decisions and, in turn, their belief in a technical culture and instructional certainty as well (Glidewell et al. 1983). Moreover, teachers' uncertainty may be diminished indirectly by any positive feedback colleagues and principal may render in the course of frequent evaluation and collaboration.

Managing Student Behavior. A second resource for teachers, and preemptive action against disorderly classroom conduct, is schoolwide management of student behavior. Collectively enforced standards for student conduct seem to operate synergistically within a school by raising the general level of classroom control above the average for any one teacher working alone (Denscombe 1985). The economy of such collective action is enormous. It frees teachers and students to engage in the matters of learning. Consequently, teachers need not resort to custodial control tactics that so patently undermine their sense of instructional possibilities.

Alternatively, disruptive students interfere with the process of teaching and, in the broader view, upset the running of the school, producing greater uncertainty about a technical culture and the prospects for instructional success. And where teachers perceive that student misbehavior is insurmountable, it may seem (and may well be) beyond their capacity to succeed instructionally. To buffer themselves from feelings of personal inadequacy, teachers tend to follow two common paths: they abdicate responsibility for teaching by reining in too tight or too loose, and/or they attribute the source of their uncertainty to intransigent students themselves (e.g., Ashton & Webb 1986; Blase 1986; Metz 1978). The transfer of blame from teachers onto students, recall from Chapter 3, proceeds most successfully and relieves most responsibility through experience-swapping with colleagues concerning hopelessly incorrigible students. And the more frequent their complaints, it seems likely, the greater their conviction that no teacher can reasonably expect to succeed.

School SES. A third resource in their quest for greater certainty is the raw materials of teaching: Students and their socioeconomic backgrounds. In low SES urban schools, the long-standing primacy of student control over learning becomes apparent even cursorily to those who spend time engaged there. It comes as no surprise, therefore, that those who work in low SES urban schools, when compared to teachers in other settings, tend to blame students more than themselves for any lackluster classroom performance (Peterson & Barger 1985) and to rely more heavily on punitive control tactics (Metz 1978; Denscombe 1985). Strategically, these actions put teachers into something of a dilemma. Students react derisively, seeing teachers' claim to complex professional knowledge weakened as a basis of status and control (Metz 1978). For their part, students believe that a teacher should try whenever possible to discover the reason for students' misbehavior and respond to that cause instead of simply punishing them (Metz 1978). They therefore show even less respect for the school's moral authority, which seems likely to attenuate positive feedback to teachers and increase their uncertainty.

Parent Involvement. Still another resource that may reduce teacher uncertainty is the cooperation and involvement of parents. Elementary teachers use several strategies that increase the willingness and capability of parents to help their children do better academically, irrespective of parents' SES, race, and working or marital status. These include "home-based reinforcement programs," where teachers call or send a note to parents who then institute some prearranged contingency depending on the behavior the teacher seeks to change; greater parent voluntarism in the classroom; and parent home tutoring, where teachers ask parents to read aloud to their children, to listen to their children's reading, to help with homework, to give spelling or math drills, and so forth (Epstein 1986; 1987).

Most schools ignore this potentially powerful resource, however. Epstein (1986, 1987), in surveying a Maryland sample of parents, students, and teachers from 600 elementary schools, found that 58% of the parents seldom or never received requests from teachers to become involved in their children's learning. Over 70% were never involved in any activity assisting teachers. Fewer than 30% reported that teachers gave them ideas on how to help their child in reading and math. Yet 85% of the parents spent 15 minutes or more per day helping their children at home when asked to do so. Matters were even worse in school–home communications: Over 35% of the parents never had a parent–teacher conference during the year, while 60% never spoke to their child's teacher on the phone. Not surprisingly, greater parent involvement and communications between home and school resulted where principals actively supported and encouraged these efforts.

Apart from the obvious provision of additional learning resources, teachers' involvement and communication with parents may decrease their uncertainty in several ways. First, teachers working with parents may come to better understand their students, enabling unique rather than routine solutions to classroom difficulties (e.g., Ashton, Webb & Doda 1983). Second, parent involvement may reduce distrust and distance between the home and school by forging shared understandings and efforts (Epstein 1986, 1987). Where teachers work with parents toward achievable ends and realize some benefit from their efforts, they may experience greater certainty about their technical culture and their own instructional practice. Third, involved and informed parents focus their children's attention on the importance of schooling, reducing the likelihood of their disengagement or misbehavior (e.g., Epstein 1986) and instructional uncertainty as well. Finally, parents who are involved and informed hold greater respect for teachers (Epstein 1986; Metz 1978), which may augment positive feedback thereby bolstering teachers' sense that they can in fact succeed.

At the same time, the more parents believe the school has failed to do what it is supposed to do for want of frequent communication about or active participation in their children's learning, the more teachers may suffer low approval and support, greater conflict with parents and students, and therefore greater prospects of instructional failure. And if teachers perceive that parents do not support or respect their efforts, the nature of work may appear (and again may be) less controllable and even beyond their ability. To minimize threats to their own self-worth, teachers may attribute the source of their uncertainty to parents themselves (e.g., Becker & Epstein 1982). And the more teachers complain about uncooperative parents, the more they tend to believe there is little they can do. There is something of a self-fulfilling prophecy in all this: Teachers who view parents adversatively often reduce or altogether cease communicating with them (Ashton, Webb & Doda 1983), substantially diminishing their opportunities for successful instruction.

To briefly review our argument, underlying teacher certainty are at least two primary factors. The first is the amount of positive feedback teachers receive. The greater the recognition flowing to teachers, the more certain they will feel about a technical culture and their own instructional practice. Second, the greater the organizational resources available to teachers, the greater their opportunity to make work-enhancing decisions, and the more they will experience themselves as causal agents in their own performance, less uncertain about their technical culture and teaching practice.

QUANTITATIVE MEASUREMENT AND FINDINGS

Operational Definitions

Quantitative testing of our hypotheses requires the specification of three new variables—positive feedback (or psychic rewards), complaints about students and parents, and parent involvement in children's learning. Box 5.1 introduces the operational definitions of these new variables.

Although the case might be made that the latter three indicators of parent involvement measure efforts made more by parents than teachers, we assumed that individual teacher responses aggregated to the school level would reflect schoolwide practice.

Results

With the exception of teacher experience and pupil–teacher ratio, which show only weak correlations with teacher certainty, all other variables, as presented in Table 5.1, show at least moderate relationships. From this data we again turn to LISREL to construct a path model. Significant path estimates from the final LISREL results appear in Figure 5.1.

The goodness of fit index showed an acceptable fit—.973. Its chi-square with 9 degrees of freedom equals 8.55, a .48 level of probability. The average residual size equals .03.

Direct Effects. Turning first to direct effects, we see as anticipated that the amount of positive feedback flowing to teachers has the strongest influence; the greater the feedback, the greater teachers' certainty in a technical culture and their own instructional practice. However, there is no indication from the LISREL analysis of a reciprocal effect; that is, teacher certainty appears *not* to influence positive feedback—it is instead a unidirectional relationship.

But contrary to expectations, learning opportunities, when measured

---

BOX 5.1   Construction of Scales

Positive Feedback (or Psychic Rewards)

1. I take pride in the things my students accomplish.
2. My students show that they appreciate me.
3. My principal recognizes the good teaching I do.
4. Other teachers in my school recognize my teaching competence.
5. There aren't many rewards for being a teacher anymore.*
6. I feel a sense of pride in my work at this school.
7. Most of my students' parents support the things I do.

Alpha = .68; item-to-scale correlations = .26 to .45.

*Teacher Complaints about Students or Parents***

Teachers complain about difficult students or parents at this school when they get together (e.g., in the lunch room).

Parent Involvement in Children's Learning

We calculated this scale by dividing answers to the following questions by the number of students in each respondent's class:

1. Sometimes teachers are able to work with students' parents to develop home-study programs for parents to work with their children at home. Have you been able to do this with any of your students? If so, how many?
2. What is your estimate of the total number of students in your class (or the average number of students in your classes, if you teach in a departmentalized school) whose parents attend scheduled parent–teacher conferences?
3. How many of your students' parents do volunteer work in your classroom?
4. What is your estimate of the number of students in your class (or the average number of students in your classes if you teach in a departmentalized school) whose parents regularly spend time with them on academic instruction at home (e.g., helping with homework, reading to them, etc.)?

Alpha = .53; item-to-scale correlations = .19 to .29

*We recorded this item in calculating scale scores.
**Scale reliabilities can be computed only with three or more items.

---

alongside one of its components, shows no significant effect. Instead, the degree of teacher collaboration strongly and independently predicts teacher certainty. Teachers who share their ideas, who unabashedly offer and solicit advice and assistance, and who interact substantively with a greater number of colleagues, expand their pedagogical options and minimize their uncertainty. These findings suggest that in schools where uncertainty is reduced, there *is* a technical culture of teaching, a codified base of professional

TABLE 5.1. Correlation Coefficients, Means (M), and Standard Deviations (SD) for Variables Examined with the Dependent Variable Teacher Certainty

	2	3	4	5	6	7	8	9	10	11	M	SD
1. Learning opportunities	.60	.74	.66	.07	-.30	-.30	-.07	-.01	.69	.43	17.38	2.67
2. Collaboration		.38	.42	-.01	.18	-.31	-.09	-.30	.54	.59	20.49	1.56
3. Evaluation			.45	-.01	.44	-.24	-.06	-.00	.60	.46	20.21	2.80
4. Managing student behavior				.08	.13	-.48	-.14	-.07	.52	.50	13.40	2.19
5. School SES					-.45	.09	-.29	-.18	-.24	-.20	.41	.22
6. Parent involvement						.09	-.02	.15	.45	.52	.33	.09
7. Complaints about parents and students							-.08	.12	.35	.32	1.80	.31
8. Pupil–teacher ratio								-.25	-.04	-.13	24.47	2.69
9. Teaching experience									.09	.15	12.73	3.00
10. Positive feedback (psychic rewards)										.69	20.81	1.30
11. Teacher certainty											27.94	1.98

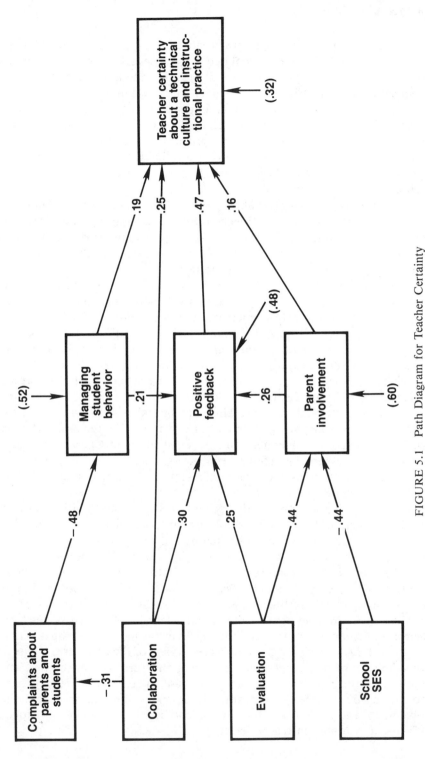

FIGURE 5.1 Path Diagram for Teacher Certainty

113

knowledge which is ever-expanding because of new problems, fresh goals, and either serendipitous or calculated discoveries of alternative teaching practices. Indeed, the path model indicates that the absence of faith in a technical culture, in situated knowledge, tends to diminish teachers' sense of what they are able to do. Of equal importance, when the full structural model of collaboration and its antecedents is elaborated with the model in Figure 5.1, the data indicate a reciprocal relationship between teacher collaboration and their certainty. This means that the greater the collaboration, the stronger teachers' certainty, which then circles back to strengthen their collaborative efforts.

Surprisingly, teacher evaluation makes no independent contribution to teacher certainty. Its direct influence on positive feedback and parent involvement, however, may indicate that good principals encourage teachers and provide them resources, but teacher evaluation may not be the primary source from which their certainty is derived.

Parent involvement in their children's learning is yet another direct, independent contributor to teacher certainty. Schools that enable parents to help their child at home, to participate in teachers' instructional programs, and to become better informed about their childrens' progress increase teachers' certainty about a technical culture and their own instructional practice. We shall see explicit examples of this in the qualitative data below.

Finally, student behavior coordinated at the school level also directly and independently augments teacher certainty about a technical culture and their own instructional practice. This finding makes sense in light of the body of technical knowledge that currently exists in the realm of effective schools and classroom management. As we shall see in Chapter 8, in successful districts, superintendents keep both principals and teachers well-informed about findings in educational research to improve their classroom and over-all school performance.

It is somewhat unexpected that school SES shows no significant, direct effect. Teachers in lower SES schools are no more likely than others elsewhere to perceive themselves as limited by the background of the students that they serve. Nor do teachers working in lower SES schools complain more frequently about students or parents. Both of these findings, anomalous to extant research conducted between low SES urban schools and those in more middle-class settings, suggest that low SES rural schools—which constitute the large majority of our sample—may qualitatively differ from their urban counterparts in either the degree or the nature of student behavior. Indeed, DeYoung (1987), in his recent review of the literature, points to a multiplicity of differences between urban and rural school settings, and emphasizes the paucity of research of these differences. In the present model, the direct effects of positive feedback, collaboration, parent involvement, and school-coordinated student behavior combine to explain 60% of the variance in teacher certainty.

Indirect Effects. Turning next to indirect or mediating effects, we find that teachers' complaints about students and parents are reduced by teacher collaboration and school management of student behavior, as indicated by their negative path coefficients. This is as it should be. As the exchange of collegial advice and assistance may solve more and cause fewer problems, and as teachers tend to deal with fewer instances of student misconduct, their reasons for experience-swapping should diminish. In the absence of these social organizational conditions, everyday experience-swapping about the pathology of parents and their children tends to make teachers feel that school life itself is pathological. Teachers from routine school cultures express vivid exemplars of this in the qualitative data below.

A second mediating variable, the extent of positive feedback, is predicted with comparable strength by several factors in the model: parent involvement, school-managed student behavior, teacher collaboration, and teacher evaluation. Together these variables account for 52% of the variance in positive feedback. Their relationships are not difficult to explain: (1) parents who are involved and informed apparently show their appreciation to teachers; (2) students who are orderly allow teachers to teach and students to learn, increasing teachers' psychic rewards; (3) teachers who collaborate may acknowledge colleagues' unique talents and skills; and (4) principals, in evaluating teachers, appear to express a valued measure of their work or improvement.

Finally, two variables independently influence parent involvement in their children's learning: teacher evaluation and school SES. The lower the SES of the school, the less teachers keep parents involved and informed. Combined, these variables explain 40% of the variance in parent involvement. The reason for the negative influence of school SES is not hard to locate. Greater communicative distance and misunderstandings between home and school develop here (e.g., Epstein 1986). The substantial effect of teacher evaluation on parent involvement raises two compatible interpretations: In their dealing with parents over children's classroom problems, teachers may directly involve principals, or alternatively, principals may suggest different parent involvement strategies to increase the possibility of instructional success and to reduce the bases for home–school conflict. We see examples supporting both these explanations in the qualitative analyses that follow.

THE SOCIAL CONSTRUCT
OF TEACHER CERTAINTY

Teachers usually find in their students what they look for. Consequently, their opinions often reveal more about themselves than their students. Our qualitative analysis thus begins by melding teachers' task conceptions with threats to their self-esteem, and the manner in which these ingredients may stir teacher sentiments about a technical culture, their own instructional practice, and the learning potential of their students. We then explore how teachers deal with classroom difficulties. Finally, we return to the quantitative data to test the relationship between teacher certainty and student learning.

By now our methodological procedures for assigning school values should be familiar to the reader. Averaging z-scores from those quantitative variables directly implicated in teacher certainty about a technical culture and their own instructional practice (that is, school-coordinated discipline policies, parent involvement, teacher collaboration, positive feedback, and teacher certainty), from the total sample we identified 13 schools with high teacher certainty, referred to here as *nonroutine technical cultures*, 15 schools with low teacher certainty, which we call *routine technical cultures*, and 50 schools where teacher certainty falls close to the mean, labelled here as *moderately routine technical cultures*. We conducted interviews with 25 teachers from 7 nonroutine technical cultures, 20 teachers from 6 routine technical cultures, and 29 teachers from 10 moderately routine technical cultures.

We asked three interview questions to explore teachers' certainty. The first two—"Tell me about a time you felt good about your work," and "Tell me about a time you felt bad about your work"—were especially revealing of teacher perceptions of their capacity to teach and that of students to learn. Overwhelmingly, and regardless of contextual circumstance, teachers referred to some aspect of student progress in answering both queries. (For the first question, 100% in nonroutine technical cultures, 61% in moderately routine technical cultures, and 58% in routine technical cultures. For the second question, 73% in nonroutine technical cultures, 70% in moderately routine technical cultures, and 87% in routine technical cultures.) As with other qualitative data, however, the nature of teachers' triumphs or failures was imputed to altogether different causes in accord with their particular contextual circumstance. In this section of the chapter, then, using this qualitative data, we explore the meaning teachers assign to their own and their students' performance.

Students' Learning Potential

Routine Technical Cultures. Whenever teachers from routine technical cultures make mention of low-achieving students' progress, the single shared experience is a sense of overwhelming fatalism, a feeling that students circumscribe their own learning potential, and that the burden of instructional frustration is persistent. Roughly half the teachers (52%) from moderately routine technical cultures express these same views. Teachers assail students for two reasons. The first is that students had poor attitudes—they are unwilling to put forth any academic effort:

> I think the caliber of [the third grade] students has generally been the same [over the years]. Of course, there have been some students who didn't progress. Some students didn't progress because they didn't want to improve. That's their own decision. You can't do much about them; you can't really help them.

> I have one [fourth grade] reading group that is especially bad. The children have no interest in learning. They have no concern with helping themselves. I tried to get them interested in their grades but they just don't care. I talked to the principal and the other homeroom teacher. It seems to be a schoolwide problem. All the teachers say they are having problems with these students. We discuss it a lot.

> We have some particularly unmotivated students. They're always up to something. For example one of them was climbing the flagpole last week. I don't know what to do with these children. It's the same thing with other teachers. The principal can't motivate them either. He agrees that these children are real behavior problems. Now it's to the point where we just ignore them the best we can. That's not right, I know, but we just have to do the best we can, just to get by.

The second reason teachers offer for their limited academic progress is students' natural depravity and their fixed levels of ability:

> Students with low ability are the most difficult. No matter what you do, they have trouble learning. I really think we should have special classes that handle these students.

> Children who have the ability are learning. You can't expect those children with low IQs to learn as much as those [with IQs] over 100. There are definite limitations in what low ability students can do.

> It seems that somewhere along the line we have lost the concept that most children are average, which is somewhere in the "C" range.

Threatened self-esteem, applied here from the vantage point of both students and teachers, helps explain these remarks. There is substantial evidence that to protect their own self-worth, students respond to chronic academic failure by withholding classroom effort (e.g., Metz 1978; Rosenholtz & Simpson 1984). That is, for students to exert maximum effort and fail anyway would establish beyond all doubt that they lack ability, and bring about feelings of inadequacy. One logical way for them to stave off acceptance of some fixed low level of academic ability, then, is to exert only minimal effort.

The same may hold true for teachers. Attributing poor performance either to students' unwillingness to work or to their outright lack of ability to do so takes teachers off the hook instructionally—they need not accept professional responsibility for students' inconsiderable performance academically. But external attributions tell us something more. Because teachers feel uncertain about how best to proceed in teaching these students, because they have limited faith in students' ability to succeed and their technical knowledge, they may not persist instructionally with them (e.g., Ashton &

Webb 1986; Good & Brophy 1987). That is, teachers may indulge normally unacceptable work, oblivious of any clangorous students about them, rather than engage in possibly self-defeating efforts to help them learn. And by perceiving students as ineducable—by putting on filtered lenses that let only the bright events shine through—they keep threatened self-esteem from making its dangerous presence known. But what promises to be a way out of these ego-endangering circumstances, as we shall see in Chapter 6, may actually conceal the greater danger of being trapped by them.

Nonroutine Technical Cultures. Whenever they referred to low-achieving students' progress, almost all teachers (92%) from nonroutine technical cultures and approximately half of the teachers (48%) from moderately routine cultures emphasized that there were few limitations to students' growth given appropriate classroom instruction:

> If there's one thing I've learned it is that they [kindergartners] can learn anything and you can teach them anything if it is put on their level. Children will make an effort to learn if they trust you. Children can learn if they know you care about them and are putting things on their level.

> If you love teaching, that motivates children to learn and for teachers to take on their [students'] learning problems. You have to motivate children and give them work they can be successful at. If you can get the students motivated you can do anything. I love math and my [fourth grade] students all know that. If they don't love it at the beginning of the year, they know I will teach them to love it by the end.

> I guess I pressure my [first grade] children a lot at the beginning. They find out that this is what she wants. She wants me to read. She wants me to like reading. She wants me to think school is fun. I hope I do a good job. I think I do. I've had students say, "I can read all through the years." "I can go to the library now." It's important for me to do this for *all* my students. Some first-graders are not ready for it yet. I try to keep the environment hopeful, give them special help, and they will come around. If they have a specific learning problem, I always try to help.

We immediately recognize from these comments that student motivation, rather than being used to justify poor student performance, is consciously cultivated by teachers as the sod of greater instructional success. Their intent, it appears, is to literally awaken and capture students' interest in learning, and, to the extent they are successful, arouse those who might otherwise find their attention diverted to less constructive pursuits. Indeed, the last teacher we heard from held uncanny patience and willingness, waiting for the appropriate, teachable moment. Students' academic success depends to no small extent on a classroom atmosphere of encouragement, optimism, and promise. Each is necessary for the other but neither can be pushed to extremes without unwittingly negating its companion (Good & Brophy 1987; Metz 1978).

And while teachers from routine technical cultures suffer recurrent bouts of doom—all the miseries teachers come to accept as others do chronic asthma or rheumatic pains—teachers in nonroutine cultures concordantly voiced optimism and promise about *all* students' academic growth. Directly related to their optimism is the emphasis teachers place on pitching learning tasks at the appropriate level of difficulty, on properly paced instruction, and on rendering individual assistance to needy students ("In order to be effective, you have to remember that you cannot teach every child in the same way"). This nonroutine technology is basic to classroom learning (Good & Brophy 1987) and thus explains a part of teachers' certainty.

Contrasting Technical Cultures. No less critical in interpreting teachers' remarks is the reminder that 84% of the teachers in our sample teach classes with mixed levels of achievement, information that takes on greater significance with the knowledge that, as the academic heterogeneity of the classroom increases, student learning gains decline (Beckerman & Good 1979; Peterson, Janicki & Swing 1981). This results in part from standardized classroom tasks that exacerbate the chance of students' off-task behavior (for want of work that is neither too difficult nor too easy), threatening to disrupt the teacher's classroom control (Denscombe 1985). That is, boredom and frustration are hardly the recipe for student motivation, academic growth, and proper classroom conduct, and so they become the very ingredients that maximize teacher uncertainty.

All of this means that teacher consciousness of children's potential may be shaped, at least in part, by the classroom structure in which they and their students perform. Indeed, where teachers feel uncertain, the presence of routine instructional practice protects them from unexpected situations in which they may not be able to maintain control (Metz 1978). Then essentially victimized by their own classroom structure, teachers using routine instructional practices are far more likely to reify ability as a stable trait on which students are highly stratified (Rosenholtz & Simpson 1984). Because children at the lower end of the spectrum consistently perform poorly, teachers seldom expect them to adequately complete their work. With nonroutine instructional practices, practices better suited to students' diversified needs, teachers tend to see children as far more malleable and far less stratified academically, and they expect almost all to perform reasonably well (Rosenholtz & Simpson 1984).

Against this lengthy backdrop we come to some final observations about teachers' perceptions of the capabilities of low-achieving students, culled from their comments above. Those embedded in nonroutine technical cultures are more likely to define students' learning potential as alterable and indeterminate, whereas those situated in routine technical cultures tend to define students' learning potential as widely dispersed and intractable.

What is especially remarkable here is that undernourished teachers appear to view their *own* learning in precisely the same way.

Ashton and Webb (1986) tie these contrasting task conceptions more explicitly to the classroom practices of teachers with high or low efficacy. To teachers with high efficacy, most low-achieving students can be reached and are therefore worthy of instructional time and effort. Observations in these classrooms revealed less routine instruction and atmospheres of greater warmth and friendliness. Teachers kept both students and themselves more on task academically, and handled student misconduct discretely and propitiously, without punitive tactics. Low efficacy teachers, who used only routine instructional practice, believe that low-achieving students were simply not smart enough to learn, and far worse, posed ever-present threats of classroom disruption. Accordingly, teachers define success with these students by their ability to exert control. They waste little instructional effort, but rather dwell on punitive control—screaming, scolding, and demeaning students publicly. In addition, low efficacy teachers experience far more instances of student misbehavior overall.

The latter finding makes sense in terms of ego-defensive maneuvers: The more teachers publicly demean students, the greater the threat to students' self-esteem, and the less willing they are to work. That is, student dignity, as with those who govern them, is particularly vulnerable when called into question, and they too recast their definitions of classroom success in ways that place themselves in the most favorable light. Especially in the later elementary grades and beyond, deviant peer cultures based on resistance to classroom control take precedence over learning, and instances of pupil misbehavior increase in attempts to limit the extent of teacher control. In this way, students derive alternative sources of self-esteem and status from their peers (e.g., Denscombe 1985; Metz 1978). Therein, however, lies a fundamental paradox: Where student aspirations and teacher expectations complement each other in mutually held views of limited academic progress, control orientations tend to become highly salient features of their classroom lives. Each battles the other to protect their respective dignity— teachers by controlling, students by refusing to be controlled—and each contributes willfully to the other's instructional demise.

Taken together, these data reveal fundamental differences between teachers from routine and nonroutine technical cultures. Utterly entrapped by their uncertainty, teachers cast aside their now threadbare idealism about tending to students' individual needs and wrap themselves in a custodial and punitive wardrobe, signifying their arrival to a less lofty place. And very few of their experiences there cause teachers to think seriously about changing their tailors. Nonroutinely situated teachers, on the other hand, profess a good deal more faith in student learning potential and grant greater supremacy to properly paced instruction than to the unsuccessful lurchings of standardized practice. And very few of their experiences cause these teachers to renounce their steadfast beliefs.

Still, it is no easy undertaking for teachers to recant their initially optimistic sentiments; to be defeated honorably by the underpredictable; to lose control of the instructional process and live within the limits of what is known technically in their schools. Teachers' succession from idealism to cynicism, from hope to despair, transpires through a series of noteworthy reinterpretations. And the continuum between nonroutine and routine technical cultures in our data offers an entry point from which to observe their passage from that of internal control of student learning, to that of external, unalterable fact. To explore teacher certainty and the way it, on the one hand, may be shaped by the social organization of schools and, on the other, may influence their interactions with parents, students, principals, and colleagues, we asked teachers, "When you have a particularly difficult problem with a student, what do you do?" Teachers' answers, summed by the level of their school's technical culture, appear in Table 5.2.

Handling Problems Alone

Less than a quarter of the nonroutinely situated teachers mentioned dealing with student problems by themselves, whereas the majority of teachers from both moderately routine and routine schools did so. In fact, the more routine the technical culture, the more teachers reported handling student problems alone. Far more pertinent to the question of how cognitions are organized and defined by school context, however, is the fact that teachers attach different meanings to this solution. In nonroutine technical cultures, teachers tend to emphasize two things: that trying to resolve problems on their own was only the initial step in a series of possibilities, and that talking to children was one way to better understand their classroom difficulties. Roughly a third of the teachers in moderately routine settings concur with this view:

> Immediately after the problem situation occurs I talk with the student. My action depends on the type of problem. First I want to see if it is a problem with me, if it is a problem with the school, or if it might be some kind of problem at home. If I need to, I'll call in the parents and talk and sometimes I will call in other teachers. Last, I will go to the principal if I want some advice.

> First I try to talk with the student privately, like while the rest of the class is in P.E. I try to find out what the problem is. Is it something I've done? Is it a problem at home? Is their best friend moving? Was their dog killed? When students are 10 years old they carry the world on their shoulders. They want to be little and big at the same time. They have a lot of trouble dealing with their emotions.

> I talk to the student first. There's always a source for the problem. It could be something that happened at school or at home. It might even be something that happened with me. Then, if that doesn't work, I'll call the parents. They're usually very helpful and we can work out some kind of strategy that will help

TABLE 5.2. Dealing With Problem Students

WHEN YOU HAVE A PARTICULARLY DIFFICULT PROBLEM WITH A STUDENT, WHAT DO YOU DO?*

Level of school's technical culture	Handle it by myself	Contact parents	Contact principal	Contact colleagues
Nonroutine (*n* = 65)	23%	31%	26%	20%
Moderately routine(*n* = 53)	49%	13%	28%	9%
Routine (*n* = 27)	67%	4%	18%	11%

*Teachers frequently offered multiple responses to this question. Percentages therefore reflect the number of times each category was mentioned.

the child. And if that doesn't work, I'll consult the principal or other teachers. They're always helpful in bouncing around ideas. The problem usually does get solved through one of these ways.

Teachers in nonroutine technical cultures, then, tend to cast external attributions for the source of children's problems. They examine specific factors that impinge on student performance—including shouldering some of the responsibility themselves. In more routine settings, however, the large majority of teachers attribute the source of their classroom problems to students themselves. Consequently, dealing with student difficulties on one's own most often meant conducting an interrogation and then executing the appropriate and frequently punitive response:

> I take the child into the hall or keep him in the room. I sit him down and point out the reason what he did was wrong, what happened because he misbehaved, why he shouldn't have that happen, and what are the consequences of his actions. Sometimes I'll keep the student after school or take away his play period. [Do you go to the principal for help?] I haven't had to have any outside help. And I haven't had to use any corporal punishment this year. I've had a really good year with a really good group of kids. I think that's the secret to it.

> I usually try to talk with students. I have enough control to handle the students without going to the principal. I keep them in from recess or take away their play privileges for a couple of days. I haven't had to paddle anyone so far this year. I set as a goal for myself that I would try not to do it this year. I don't like to do it. I used to like to paddle; there was a time when I used it quite a bit.

It is instructive that the first teacher attributes her successful year—not using corporal punishment—to having a "good" class, rather than to something *she* had done. This reminds us that external attributions need not be negative; at the same time, they still beg the question of teachers' professional responsibility.

Quite apart from blaming students for their inadequacies, there is an equally fundamental way in which handling problems alone helps teachers who will not stand up to scrutiny. It is far safer to confine teaching problems to the most solitary place, to distance themselves from others, to stay put in their own classrooms. In this way teachers keep problems under wraps, away from the ubiquitous and ego-endangering aspersions of colleagues and principals. For routinely situated teachers, what others did not know, did not, for all practical purposes, exist:

> The way I see it, you have to work things out for yourself.

> Teachers here see it as their job to do what they're doing and yours to do what you're doing.

> Discipline-wise it should be handled in the classroom.

Not untinged by these same sentiments, one teacher also unknowingly stressed the standardized treatment of students underlying the routine technical culture in which she works. Even for serious offenses, teachers had a prepared script:

> I think teachers should handle their own problems unless it's a major offense. [What constitutes a major offense?] Drugs. Fights. Of course, even with these things there are district rules and regulations. There are district policies and teachers should follow them.

Here lies the direct consequences of threatened self-esteem. Believing that the cause of the problem inheres in students, routinely situated teachers most often punish them. Believing that the cause of the problem is external to students, nonroutinely situated teachers tend to search for the problem's origin to find an acceptable solution. What is at issue here is not just the problem but the extent to which it can be known, and by whom.

Contacting Parents

Contacting parents was a second alternative to deal with problem students. As Table 5.2 reveals, over twice the percentage of teachers from nonroutine as compared to moderately routine cultures pursued this option, and in routine settings, teachers seldom made mention of parent contacts at all. As with student contacts, parent contacts varied by school culture and were made by teachers for altogether different reasons.

Routine Technical Cultures. One straightforward explanation for the lack of parent contacts on the part of more routinely situated teachers is the transfer of blame for children's attitudes and unruly behavior squarely onto parents themselves. In this way, students' problems become nothing more than manifestations of parents' problems. And if parents are part and parcel of the problem, it serves no constructive purpose to consult them when difficulties with their children arise:

> I keep kids after school all the time to punish them. You're not supposed to do that without parents' approval. But I do it anyway because I think that problem children have problem parents. And if the parents don't support me, how am I ever going to be able to control their kids? There's got to be some punishment for bad behavior.

> If you don't have parent support and backing, when you have discipline problems, they don't discuss it at home and they don't go along with some of the things you have done. When the child knows that whatever he does at school, when he goes home his parents are going to say, "They shouldn't have done that," they know how their parents feel and they know the parents don't care, so they're not really too concerned about it either.

Discontent breeds resentment. And in routine technical cultures, teachers foster their righteous indignation about the wrongs of parents through experience-swapping. A group interest shaping a group attitude will much more convincingly prove that parents are largely culpable for student problems. Possibilities for student learning, after all, make themselves felt as more or less fixed where complaints about students and parents tend to become commonplace occurrences. And the more concrete the complaint, the more rational the belief that instructional failure inheres in parents and students more than in teachers:

> Students have an attitude problem. They really don't seem to care. It seems like each year it becomes more and more difficult. [Why do you think that is?] Well, we've [teachers] discussed this and we think probably it's the home situation. We think they have less discipline at home, less parental involvement.

> Parents cause me the most problems. There seems to be more apathy than in previous years. [What have you done to deal with this situation?] We [the first grade teachers] have sat down as a group in order to try to figure out what to do about it. So far all we have decided is that the parents' apathy is reflected in the students' attitudes. It shows there isn't much direction at home.

> Right now I'm having a problem where the student just won't accept the facts. I have a student who says I'm constantly picking on him, but I know that he says that just because he doesn't want to behave. I know that he goes home and stretches the truth. The parents and the student have to be ready to accept the facts. [Do you discuss this problem with other teachers?] Yes, I talked with other teachers and found out that the parent was not ready to accept the problem. I was not the only teacher who had problems with this particular kid. So it felt good to know I was not alone.

A story is constitutive; it makes for collective identification. It bonds less accomplished teachers, giving them something to live by, if they can only keep telling their stories. In stories that finesse the burden of responsibility for classroom problems from teachers onto students and parents, teachers seldom falter in their own esteem or that of their colleagues. They complain, after all, to spawn new selves, to be uplifted in self-esteem, more persuasive and resolute, until internal blame loses itself in darkness and silence. They can therefore see any self they wish; yet ironically, they tend to see a good deal less than the teachers they once envisioned themselves becoming. Their once blazing vitality becomes a mere flicker now, low and blue.

Beginning teachers often tell the most revealing tales in this regard. Veterans, needing to keep their stories alive, offer preparatory comfort and forewarning to new teaching recruits. Thus, when novices contact parents, they often channel the maelstrom of their own experiences along the same hopeless reality that breaks over them, with blinding force, as a storm at sea:

> [From a second year teacher] I made a home visit early last year because the mother couldn't come in for a conference. I wanted her to understand the problems I was having with her son, and try to find a way to solve them. I found the mother unwilling to talk about her child—she seemed so defensive! When I didn't get any backup from anyone [at home], eventually I just gave up trying. [Have you made any home visits since then?] No. It probably wouldn't do any good.

Although beginners may initially find colleagues' helpless lamentations stupefying, in inheriting their legacy they seem to eventually learn that these comments are nothing more than condensed stories waiting to be brought to life by their own dealings with parents:

> When I first started teaching here [two years ago] I wanted to get parents more involved. I thought about making home visits, but I was advised not to do that. [Who advised you against home visits?] Teachers who lived in certain areas and have grown up and gone to school there. They thought that the parents would think I was judging them—that parents would resent that. It was really depressing, but now I know what they meant.

Initially then, beginners may stand up to the collective winds of despair, but gradually tend to droop under the constant burden of parent and student offenses, the sense of fit between their own observations and their colleagues' complaints withering them bit by bit, until their teaching passion and zeal one day seem to disappear altogether. In growing more and more detached, novices abandon some of the gentle nurturing of students that was once their greatest vision. Ultimately, in mastering their environment, they seem to have come to let their environment master them.

Nonroutine Technical Cultures. In nonroutine technical cultures, teachers often contact parents to help them better understand their child's problem and solve it. Approximately half of the teachers from moderately routine technical cultures use this same strategy:

> The only problem I've had, and just with a few children, is with raising their grades. They're not careful. They don't proofread. If you want improvement, you have to understand the nature of the problem. I talk with the child and the parents. I try to keep the parents informed about what I've done so far. I ask parents to help at home. I try to praise the child a lot to keep him working, and ask his parents to do the same.

> I talk with the parents first. I try to check and see if they are having some problem with the child. Is there something unusual going on? I also try to involve the parents in solving the problem.

Seldom do teachers in nonroutine technical cultures attribute classroom problems to parents or students. Instead they assume personal responsibility, a view that reflects belief in a technical culture which compels teachers to investigate the source of student problems. A necessary sign in that process, as the next teachers make patently clear, is greater parent involvement:

> Transfer students sometimes come with negative attitudes. Who wouldn't if they were just uprooted? The children and I work together to make new students feel welcome. One child is assigned to be a buddy in the classroom and on the playground. It makes their adjustment easy, and they learn about what we expect of them. I also call the parents to introduce myself, and sometimes I'll suggest ways they can help their child adjust.

> When we have students with attitude problems, we deal with them by getting parents involved in helping us solve them. [How do you do this?] By calling them all the time, by sending notes home, and by asking them to praise their child when he's had a good day. We ask them to ask their child what kind of day it's been, too. That way we don't get our signals crossed and students get the same message from their parents as from teachers.

Notice the sense that positive things can happen, that teachers can make positive things happen, by eliciting parent involvement. To elaborate this point more fully, we hear several strategies nonroutinely situated teachers use to keep parents informed and involved:

> We have a club for our students. They read a certain number of books that we assign or they choose. Parents have to sign a paper saying that they read the book with them. [Then we have] the Memorial Banquet. At the banquet we pass out medals and a story teller comes. It's for parents and students both. I think it's a real nice thing to do for the little people.

> [From a second year teacher:] We've worked out a system to have parents drill their kids on multiplication and division facts at home so that we can work earlier [in the year] on higher order skills. [How did you learn to do this?] I think mostly because there was a need and that other teachers had worked out these things and shared them with me.

> One thing we do in kindergarten is a newsletter and we call it "Kinder News." We cover each subject area and we tell the parents what we're working on, what they can expect to hear from their child. We give them little activity ideas and games that they can do at home with their children. Sometimes we'll hide a little clue that says, "Mother, if you read this, cut out this happy face, sign your name to it, and send it to school with your child, and your child gets a reward." That has worked out real well and it helps to keep parents informed. [Do you find that most parents will follow the clues?] Yes. Especially after the first couple of news letters, the other children catch on. They start nagging their parents.

Hear the resounding "We" in these teachers' remarks. Collegial support and assistance in nonroutine cultures does not seem to build a helpless reality to explain classroom failure, but rather tends to galvanize parents' support and participation to better ensure classroom success. Here we are reminded again that teachers who collaborate invent a dazzling array of possibilities and in this way may diminish their instructional uncertainty and build a technical culture.

Contacting Principals

Teachers proposed a third strategy to deal with student problems—contacting principals. While over a quarter of the nonroutinely situated teachers pursued this option, as Table 5.2 indicates, it was far less popular with teachers from routine technical cultures. These findings make sense when we recall from Chapter 3 that principals offered more helpful advice in collaborative than isolated settings and that they posed fewer threats to teachers' self-esteem. Although there were no numerable differences between nonroutine and moderately routine technical cultures, as with other strategies, teachers from varied social organizations attached different meanings to principal contacts.

Nonroutine Technical Cultures. Teachers from nonroutine technical cultures, as the reader might surmise, contacted principals to seek help:

> [From a second year teacher:] There was an incident that happened last year. I really blew up at one of my kids because he repeatedly refused to finish his work. Well, he got fairly abusive. The principal and his teacher from the year before and I had a meeting and they went over the progress he had made last year, and then I understood why he wasn't working for me. I didn't supervise his work too closely and the work I was giving him was too hard. They gave me some ideas about how to help him. Like having another boy in the class work alongside him, and not giving him assignments unless he really understood what he was supposed to do. It was rocky at first, but things did get better. I had to consult the principal a whole lot less this year.

> Probably, if the problem continued I would contact the parents. If the problem is not resolved I would go to the principal. There was one instance recently. It was a combination of an academic and behavior problem which was getting progressively worse. I didn't know exactly what to do, so I went to the principal. He suggested things to help remediate the problem.

> I often go to the principal. He will talk to the students if he thinks that talking with them will solve the problem. Sometimes he will go to a class: he will speak to an entire group of students if he thinks that will help. He's not shy about calling in parents either. He works with parents a lot.

As the last comment suggests, principals from nonroutine schools often marshall parent involvement and support, ostensibly reducing some of the endemic uncertainties of teaching:

The principal gets parents involved with their child's education. He sets up parent committees to organize parent volunteers in classrooms. He encourages us to keep parents informed, and to work with them when problems with their children come up.

He gives us ideas about how to approach parents, how to have them help their child, and when he finds someone doing something special with parents, he shares the idea with everybody else.

Further, in their interactions with parents about students' classroom problems, principals in nonroutine technical cultures appeared to uphold teachers' instructional decisions and enforcement of school rules, largely because they were also their own:

He makes sure that all parents understand our school rules.

He will explain school policies to parents who aren't familiar with them.

If parents are upset he will remain calm and explain our rules.

There appeared to be a dual emphasis in principals' contact with parents: to keep them abreast of matters and to enlist their help in improving children's performance:

When I have a problem, I'll call a conference with the parents and the principal. He gives parents reasons why their child is not succeeding, and encourages them to remind their child about obeying our school rules. That way, parents come away feeling that they can help their child become more successful.

He can figure out the best way to approach parents, particularly when you're thinking about retaining their child. He can reason with them and help them see how their child needs extra work. And he follows through with the child the next year to make sure he's getting the extra help we promised. We don't retain children here unless we can give them that extra help next year.

Principals' swift acts of decisiveness in students' favor seemed to dispel in a single stroke any turmoil unsettling the parents. Perhaps the best weapon principals can wield against parents' anger is such straightforward, helpful communication.

More Routine Technical Cultures. Teachers in routine technical cultures frequently voiced complaints about principals' lack of involvement with parents, as the almost palpable frustrations of this transferred veteran illustrate:

[In this school] I see good parents willing to help. The potential is there, but the management is so loose that things are not as good as they could be. This could really be a super school if it had a tighter ship. It all goes back to the question of leadership.

This teacher, new to the school, apparently experienced a different and better reality somewhere else. Retrospective comparisons of this sort enable teachers to identify the most salient school problems. Such is also the case for two other routinely situated veterans, who interpret their principals' unwillingness to entertain parent involvement consistent with our theoretical underpinnings:

> My last school merged with this one. I admit that the last school I was in was not perfect in all ways, but we built a reputation that we were proud of. But my present principal couldn't accept the idea that there might be a school that is better than his. He couldn't handle it. I think he was intimidated. When the two schools merged, they weren't formed into an *idea*; rather, they were combined in his way. Parents used to help a lot in my other school. They would volunteer their time. Now that the schools have merged, most of these parents have stopped their volunteer work because of our principal. I think the problem is he interpreted their efforts in the wrong way. He has been very defensive.

> At our school parents are sometimes a real problem. The principal can't handle it if he thinks parents are overstepping their bounds. He gets angry. At my other school parents did a lot in classrooms. They helped teachers. Here the principal gets angry if he thinks they're in his territory.

Through their divergent school experiences, these teachers see that school possibilities for parent participation were larger than the confined reality currently confronting them—larger, more hopeful, and far more compelling. There is a kind of danger in too much comparative knowledge, however—a kind of powerlessness and sadness that is born of such knowledge. These teachers see their principals' turf-mindedness with parents as an emblem of fear; fear about losing control and with it principals' own sense of worth. With the exception of two teachers from routine technical cultures, parents' classroom involvement was never mentioned.

In more routine technical cultures, teachers identified one of three paths their principals pursued in dealing with parents. One path, clearly more prevalent in moderately routine than routine settings, led principals to "back their teachers" by confronting parents with their child's intransigent behavior:

> He will stand behind you. He may come back to you and let you have it. He'll tell you you were wrong, and not to do it that way again.

> The principal will back you up with parents, even if he thinks you're wrong. He lets you know afterward, though.

There is a striking paradox in this course of action. Principals who staunchly defend teachers in the face of questionable if not wholly unjustified circumstances may leave parents hostile and alienated, enlarging more than diminishing the communicative distance between home and school. Children exposed to parents' repudiation of the school may feel psychically and morally upheld, perhaps even victimized by their teachers, and in this way continue the very classroom misbehavior the conference convened to improve.

It is at this point that we come full circle in understanding more routinely situated teachers' complaints about parents and students and the external attributions they cast. When deprived of a fair and open airing of grievances, parents may repudiate the school's authority and their children may respond in kind. In other words, the cynical reality that teachers come to construct may rest, at least in part, on the school's disenfranchisement of parents.

The second path principals pursued led again not to conflict resolution but rather to gestures of appeasement. In their dealings with parents, teachers explained, principals simply "smoothed things over," just as road gangs fill in potholes, hopeful that the temporary fix will suffice. The consequence of this patchwork requires no additional elaboration, as teachers from three moderately routine settings make it plain enough:

> He generally tries to smooth things over with parents. Sometimes it helps and sometimes it doesn't. Principals I guess should back up their teachers but when they don't it's because they'll catch it from the superintendent if parents complain. So they smooth things over a lot.

> He is very diplomatic. I don't know if he really *solves* problems, mostly he just *handles* them. He soothes parents' feelings well. He cools people down.

> If there's a problem with a teacher, sometimes he'll use achievement test scores to put parents' minds at ease. It doesn't really solve the problem, though.

Notice in the last comment that although school goals may be internally incoherent, unstated, or merely professed, this principal defined them here *post hoc* in order to justify teachers' actions.

Finally, and more typical of routine than moderately routine technical cultures, some principals chose the path of least resistance. They simply abdicated responsibility for solving problems with parents, and, in the midst of the pandemonium of dissent, escaped to a comforting, numbing sensation of utter irresponsibility. Three teachers explain woefully:

> She can't handle parents. She makes teachers deal with parent problems—she never gets involved herself. We have very little interaction because she stays in her office all the time. I think that she may not know how to deal with all the problems—maybe that's why she's so standoffish.

> My old principal was wonderful. She always supported teachers. If a parent complained, they always have to go to her first. They just couldn't come up to the school and jump on the teacher. She wouldn't always say you were right, but she would try and support you in front of the kids and parents. My present principal makes teachers stand up to the parents by themselves, even if they are accused unjustly.

> The principal doesn't back teachers with parents. He makes teachers solve their

own problems with parents—he won't deal with them. He takes the attitude that we've created the problem, so we have to solve it.

Principals choosing the path of least resistance seem to put down roots in a place where they may cultivate their own self-esteem rather than their school's technical culture. What grows in its stead, however, is greater instructional uncertainty. For one thing, teachers left to fend entirely for themselves come to resent principals, problematic parents, and their students. For another, in warding parents off, teachers divert needless psychic energy and attention away from classroom instruction before the act of teaching has even begun. Finally, principals' noninvolvement not only exposes their schools to public criticism; it clearly invites it.

How principals deal with parents in regard to student problems, then, has all the ingredients of a self-fulfilling prophecy. If principals encourage and help teachers to keep parents informed, to involve parents in solving problems and give them constructive measures to follow, reasonable solutions to classroom problems can be found. These actions strengthen teacher's beliefs in a technical culture and their certainty about instructional success. But if principals merely placate, altogether ignore, or unintentionally alienate parents, teachers discover that bothersome students continue to give them the same disconcerting trouble, and all too soon they abandon their hopes for classroom and pupils' success.

Provided little constructive support, routinely situated teachers rarely consult principals about student problems. Their assistance, most of them ruefully agreed, is altogether inadequate:

Well, I don't talk to my principal. I don't think he understands children's problems. [Do you think that other teachers at your school feel the same way?] I'm sure that 100% of them feel that he doesn't understand discipline and that he doesn't understand children's problems and what to do about them.

Actually, I can't say that I have any real support from the administration. I have a couple of extremely difficult kids this year. For example, one of them flushed a library book down the toilet. I was in a big hurry at that time; I didn't have time to take out and deal with that particular child. So I sent him directly to the principal's office. He was totally ineffective in the situation. That's why I think teachers in general don't consult our principal very often. They find he's very ineffective when they do consult him. Since we have no counselor and the principal doesn't help, most teachers try to solve their problems on their own.

The possibility of only limited, if any, administrative support, as implied in the last comment, is exactly how teachers and students become casualties in the skirmish for classroom control. One teacher from a routine technical culture recounts:

The principal goes so far as to publicly recommend that teachers handle their own discipline problems. Also, the principal commends those teachers who don't bring their discipline problems to her. I don't think that is the best way to handle those situations. I think there is a lot of abuse of children just because teachers get so frustrated. I know teachers who swat kids, put their jobs on the line, but I do think that they feel as if it's their only recourse, because they can't consult with the principal. Oftentimes we beg for other ways to deal with problems. We really wanted to have an in-school detention room. We had a lot of meetings where we asked the principal for that kind of room. But our proposal never got anywhere. No one in the administration wants to take responsibility. No one is willing to pull the bull by the horns.

That principals overlook parent and student difficulties, then, carries dramatic implications for teachers' dealings with problem students: nothing can be done except punishment. In this way, principal uncertainty defines school character and the actors engaged in its drama no matter how disingenuous or wounded they become. For teachers who survive this ordeal, the only apparent recourse may be coercive control and punitive punishment. Indeed, the indifferent, unapologetic sarcasm of a routinely situated veteran testifies to the abuse children sometimes suffer at the hands of teachers who receive no administrative support:

> I usually try to dismiss the student from the room. I continue with whatever I was doing so that when I confront them I don't slug them. One time I didn't do that and I immediately paddled the child. The mother called and said that the kid had bruises. I didn't believe it but I *was* mad. If there was ever a time that I was mad enough to hurt a child, it was that time. Usually, though, I try to shame kids rather than using physical punishment. Most kids just act up for attention anyhow. They don't give a darn about what kind of punishment is used with them. [Do you ever consult the principal about these problems?] If I can't solve the problem, my principal certainly can't either. Proceed to the next question.

The pathology here could be missed only by those too ensconced to look. These comments exemplify the hard-boiled, cynical teachers who talk destructively, distrust students, punish them harshly, and take no problems on themselves without complaint. Here it becomes apparent that the reduction of students to a singular negative profile serves a reflexive attempt at relief, an unburdening function, that spares teachers the need to deal individually with pupils' problems.

There is an especially wrenching irony to all of this: Principals' self-defensive tactics that result in classroom and parent noninvolvement produce the most harrowing costs for teachers and their students—costs that go almost beyond calculation—a handicap to éclat which speaks almost entirely for itself.

Routinely situated teachers who did bring problem students to their principals invariably saw this not as a solution but simply as their last resort. Students were yielded up to the kind of sentence only a frustrated teacher could hand down:

I usually isolate the student and if he needs to be spanked I send him to the principal. We have this thing about spanking kids in class. So if worse comes to worse, I send the kid to the principal.

Sometimes I send a note home to parents. If there is no response, then I go to the principal as the last resort. I rarely paddle students. That's more the principal's job.

I try to resolve it myself. Then I will go to the principal if I need to. But that's usually only as a last resort. I usually let him question the children. He decides if they are in the wrong and he punishes them—usually it's a paddling they get.

Cooling these teachers' once altruistic intent is their chilled, implacable indifference to any student consideration; they underwent for an interval a mental somersault, during which they were upside down, their perspective topsy-turvy, until a steady and sometimes deep-seated contempt for students put their classroom affairs tightly in hand. We need not dwell further on this heavy-handedness, except to be mindful that punitive treatment does little to nourish student learning and offers few deterrents against future infractions, given its cyclical nature (e.g., Ashton & Webb 1986; Metz 1978).

Contacting Colleagues

Finally, when student problems arose, some teachers consulted colleagues. Teachers from nonroutine technical cultures exercised this option, Table 5.2 reveals, twice as often as those more routinely situated. A straightforward explanation for this finding, and one that underscores the contextual nature of teacher beliefs in a technical culture, is that, in more routine schools, teachers invariably defined "a particularly difficult problem" as student misbehavior, whereas in nonroutine settings "a particularly difficult problem" often encompassed instructional difficulties, too.

In more routine technical cultures, teachers' threatened self-esteem accounts at least in part for the absence of collegial consultation. In the two comments that follow, notice particularly that teaching competence in these settings creates its own resentment:

You have to be careful about talking to other teachers about being successful, so that you don't come across as bragging. Sometimes you can make another teacher feel bad, like, "You didn't do as good a job as you could have with a particular student." You can make another teacher not want to talk to you about *anything*. You have to be careful about that.

[Do other teachers help you with teaching problems?] I guess they would if I asked. [Do you ask for help?] Once. But some teachers here brag about their classrooms. People won't listen to teachers who brag—like they're just trying to earn brownie points by making other teachers feel bad.

Nonroutine technical cultures were of an entirely different nature. Here we find the perfect antidote for norms of self-reliance and threatened self-esteem, and teachers who mentioned this problem-solving strategy tended often to undauntingly counsel each other in times of trouble, frustration, or uncertainty:

> I always go to other teachers if it's a teaching problem that I can't handle. Of course, you have your favorite people that you go to for special problems. [How do you know who has special expertise?] Oh, you find out walking down the halls. You grab snatches of what's going on in different teachers' rooms and just know through talking with them who's doing a good job. [Do you think most teachers find out about each others' special skills?] Yes. You can't always get around to all the grade levels—there are still some 5th grade classrooms downstairs that I don't get a chance to visit and I'm dying to see what they do. But you do find out a lot by talking with different people. After you talk to someone about a problem and their suggestions help you to figure out where you're going wrong, you sort of find out who knows what.

> Actually, I check with other teachers. I see what they have done with similar problems, and I try to get their input. Dealing with a problem child is a process of elimination. You have to try out different processes to see which will work. The more ideas you have the better.

In technically routine stories, teachers spoke in the diction of fear and defeat. Beneath the civility that accompanied their experience–swapping, there were strident messages: Messages that it was all right to talk about students and parents as long as these conversations strengthened rather than challenged their collectively constructed reality; that thoughtful and successful guesswork in the classroom should stay hidden lest teachers incur strong moral censure for "besting behavior" that made others feel somewhat inept; that teaching, after all, was about the confidential interactions that transpire between students and their teacher.

In technically nonroutine stories, teachers spoke in the eloquence of hope, illumination, and progress. There were always organizational signals beckoning for greater collegial involvement, more inventive possibilities, and higher professional responsibility to better meet the challenge of students whose learning needs still exceeded their grasp. Because the challenges of teaching were great even under the best of circumstances, it was necessary to turn to others for help.

TEACHER CERTAINTY
AND STUDENT ACHIEVEMENT

If our argument is correct, that nonroutine schools better accommodate students' individual needs than routine schools, it seems reasonable to predict that the more uncertainty suffered by teachers, the less students will learn. We return now to the quantitative data to test this proposition directly.

The correlation coefficients show moderate relationships between teacher certainty and fourth-grade reading (.31) and math (.38); but nonsig-

nificant relationships between teacher certainty and second-grade reading
(.13) and math (.09). The reader is again referred to Chapter 4, Table 4.4,
for discussion of the correlations between achievement test scores, school
demographic variables, and teacher background variables.

Table 5.3 presents the results of separate hierarchical regression equations for reading and math on teacher certainty for significant coefficients
only. Again we controlled first for school demographic and teacher background variables.

Turning first to fourth-grade reading achievement, students' second-
grade reading shows a robust effect. The better students read in second
grade, the more likely they will excel in fourth grade. Teaching experience
is inversely related to student learning gains in reading, a finding that repli-
cates other studies. The more experienced the teachers within a school, the
lower the probability of students' basic skills mastery. Of greater statistical
significance than teacher experience, and of equal strength to second grade
reading, is teacher certainty. The more certain teachers feel about their technical knowledge, the greater students' progress in reading. These three independent predictors combine to explain 49% of the variance in students'
fourth-grade reading results.

For students' math achievement, school size and teachers' undergraduate status, despite their significant correlation, again yield no independent
effects. Instead, teacher certainty and students' second-grade scores each
make unique contributions, combining to account for 58% of the variance
in fourth-grade math scores. Comparing standardized beta weights, we find
that second-grade reading performance is substantially more powerful than
teacher certainty in explaining fourth-grade math results. Thus, when we
compare students' second-grade achievement and when we examine the total amount of variance that each regression equation explains, teacher certainty moderately influences students' basic skills mastery.

Teachers' success in the enterprise of teaching seems to fortify them in
their careers, giving them confidence in their right to pursue it, and in the
rightness of their pursuit. It is this scintillating glory of their mission that
brings teachers their conviction of strength, their sense of technical knowl-

TABLE 5.3. Multiple Regression Analysis of Teacher Certainty on Reading
and Math Gains

A. Reading, Grade 4	Variable	Beta	F	R^2
	Reading, grade 2	.57	43.37***	.38
	Teaching experience	−.16	3.39*	.40
	Teacher certainty	.56	8.55**	.49
B. Math, Grade 4	Math, grade 2	.63	69.42***	.46
	Teacher certainty	.34	20.32***	.58
	Multiple $R = .76$			

*$p < 08$.
**$p < .01$.
***$p < .001$.

edge, of certainty, of power; this possibility that invests them with the shimmering inspiration and patient care of a master artist bent over canvas.

Perhaps it is the numbing sameness lurking in the work of routinely situated teachers—their lack of opportunity for new vision—that is responsible for the negatively inspired questions ("Why aren't students learning?") and the same answers ("Because they can't; because they don't care"). Each is a measure of teachers' failure to nourish and be nourished, to encourage and be encouraged. The worst sameness is that of teachers' failure in the face of everyday demands; for many, a professional promise broken long ago.

SUMMARY

In this chapter we have argued that teacher uncertainty about a technical culture and their instructional practice could be diminished in at least two ways. The first is by providing teachers positive feedback, encouragement, nurturing inspiration to persist in their instructional efforts. The second is by mobilizing the organizational resources of schools: resources that help teachers acquire greater technical knowledge to solve the ubiquitous and nonroutine problems of their students; resources that involve parents in their children's learning; and resources that optimize students' on-task behavior through consistently enforced policies for appropriate student conduct. To the extent these conditions absent themselves in the school culture, we predicted, teachers would complain more about parents and students, believe less in a technical culture of teaching, and convince each other that teaching itself was futile business. Our quantitative data, with structural modeling, supported this argument. Specifically, we learned that where teachers request from and offer technical assistance to each other, and where school staff enforces consistent standards for student behavior, teachers tend to complain less about students and parents. Further, where teachers collaborate, where they keep parents involved and informed about their children's progress, where teachers and principal work together to consistently enforce standards for student behavior, and where teachers celebrate their achievements through positive feedback from students, parents, principal, colleagues, and their own sense, they collectively tend to believe in a technical culture and their instructional practice. We also learned that involvement of parents in their children's learning tends to occur less in low SES schools but is more likely to occur where principals work hard to see this happen as part of their evaluative efforts—their continual measure of school needs.

Our qualitative data, like our quantitative data, revealed dramatic contextual differences. In routine as compared to nonroutine technical cultures, we encountered far less use of colleagues' expertise, more punitive and standardized treatment of students, less parent involvement, collective faculty complaints about poor student attitudes that pinned their origins to the home, beliefs about students' fixed learning potential, and with all of this, external attributions that tended to relieve teachers of the need to shoulder personal responsibility for solving student problems. Principals appear to influence these patterns by either unequivocal noninvolvement or by unwitting exacerbation of the relationship between the home and school. In fact, many of the negative attributions teachers impute both to parents and students may rest, at least in part, on the intransigent treatment of parents by the school. In nonroutine settings blame of students or of parents neither invites nor jeers. Teachers instead proclaim their sense of confidence. They appear to know just where they stand and seem sure of the foundations below them—their already existing technical culture and their knowledge of how to expand it.

Returning to the quantitative data, we next examined the relationship between teacher certainty and student achievement. Statistics testify just as eloquently as the qualitative data that teacher certainty makes a difference in students' mastery of basic skills. Controlling for prior student learning and other teacher background characteristics, teacher certainty contributes significantly to student learning gains in reading and math over a two-year period.

All of this means that what teachers perceive as real in their workplace circumstances tends to become real in their consequences. Where teachers collectively perceive students as capable learners, and themselves as capable teachers vested with a technical culture to help them learn and grow, they seem more likely to persevere, to define problem students as a challenge, to seek outside resources to conquer that challenge, and, in this way, to actually foster students' academic gains. But when teachers collectively perceive that students' potential is circumscribed by either their background or manner, they are less apt to respond to student difficulties with increased effort, to view such adverse circumstances as surmountable, to avail themselves of outside resources for help, and, in the end, to help students learn basic skills. Perhaps our most important lesson is that teachers' optimism and enthusiasm are tractable virtues by which students grow, and schools can either strengthen or weaken them through the contextual design of teachers' work. We delve deeper into the consequences of teachers' enthusiasm or despair in the chapter that follows.

6

Teacher Commitment

In this chapter we explore the social organization of teachers' workplace commitment. The first section begins by defining school commitment, a definition that has much to do with teachers' loss of visionary promise, or alternatively, their still high-spirited determination; their hard-won conclusions about students that were better understood once we looked (in Chapter 5) at the social organization in which they worked. Next we specify the social organizational circumstances that affect teacher commitment and, as with previous chapters, test the model empirically.

THEORETICAL FRAMEWORK

The Definition of Workplace Commitment

The basic sentiment that compels a high level of commitment to work has been described by some organizational social psychologists as *internal motivation*. Where people are highly motivated, their feelings are closely tied to how well they perform; good performance is self-rewarding and provides the incentive for continuing to perform well. Alternatively, poor performance is an occasion for distress that causes internally motivated people to search for ways to avoid such feelings in the future and to regain those pleasurable feelings that accompany good performance (Hackman & Old-

139

ham 1980). However, when people experience low internal motivation, they suffer feelings of alienation and disaffection from work and engage in a variety of behaviors that produce self-fulfilling prophecies affecting their ability to acquire performance-based rewards. These behaviors include absenteeism, low effort expenditure, and outright defection, a definition of low commitment we will pursue in this chapter.

There are, in fact, sound theoretical and empirical grounds for the clustering of these variables. On the theoretical level, dissatisfaction with the conditions of work may manifest itself most dramatically in a decision to defect from the workplace. The link between dissatisfaction and actual defection, however, may be mediated by the alternatives individuals perceive to be available (March & Simon 1958). A lack of alternative employment or declining enrollments that limit opportunities for teachers to transfer to more favorably perceived schools, for example, may cause dissatisfied teachers to stay where they are, withhold service, and "settle for less." As the ultimate manifestation of withheld service, teachers may resort to chronic absenteeism.

On the empirical level, a growing body of evidence from industrial social psychology reveals that the same elements predicting turnover can be used successfully to predict disaffection and absenteeism (Marcus & Smith 1985; Johns & Nicholson 1982). For teachers, too, disaffection, absenteeism, and attrition are highly intercorrelated (Litt & Turk 1985; Rosenholtz 1985).

The Social Organization of Workplace Commitment

Of the many resources required by schools, the most vital are the contributions—of effort, involvement, and commitment—from teachers. Not only are the quality of these contributions related integrally to school goals; they are ultimately the means by which other resources are acquired. Successful schools, as we have seen, are better able to marshall parent involvement and support and to attract more academically talented teachers than unsuccessful schools. Thus, central to a school's quality is its ability to motivate teachers to make continuing contributions to it rather than to some competing organization.

Psychic Rewards. Organizational members are motivated to remain within a setting and to contribute productively only so long as the inducements offered are as great or greater than the contributions they are asked to make (March & Simon 1958). That is, the psychic rewards of teaching must outweigh the frustrations. As we saw from quantitative analysis in the previous chapter, most teachers' psychic rewards derive from helping students grow and develop—from estimates of their own performance as well as external recognition of their work received from parents, colleagues, principals, and students themselves. Where their work is perceived as unsuccessful, or where their efforts go unnoticed, teachers' disaffection, their absenteeism, and their desire to leave the workforce loom large (e.g., Kasten 1984; Litt & Turk 1985).

Managing Student Behavior. We also saw in Chapter 5 that just as student progress is the primary source of psychic rewards for teachers, difficult relations with pupils is a primary source of psychic debilitation. Thus teachers are far more apt to obtain psychic rewards, to take greater pleasure in their work, to the extent that schools succeed in maintaining orderly student conduct. Indeed, failure to deal successfully with student behavior problems is strongly related to teachers' loss of workplace commitment (e.g., Blase 1986; Rosenholtz 1985).

Task Autonomy and Discretion. Workplace commitment also results where people experience personal responsibility for the outcomes of work—the sense that they can make things happen with their own intentional striving. If the outcomes of work can be explained more by external factors than by people's own contributions, there is little reason for performance-based fulfillment, even when particularly positive job outcomes result. This organizational dimension involves the extent to which work provides substantial freedom, independence, and individual discretion in carrying out tasks (Hackman & Oldham 1980; Gecas & Schwalbe 1983). Jobs that give people more autonomy and discretion require that they exercise judgment and choice; in doing so, they become the main causal agents in their own performance. Losing the capacity to control the terms of work, to determine what is to be done, how it is to be done or what its aim is to be, on the contrary, widens the gap between the knowledge of one's unique contributions to the work and any performance-based fulfillment that can be derived from it. The products of work no longer reflect one's personal intentions, and one becomes estranged and alienated from them, unwilling to accept personal responsibility for, or ownership of, job outcomes (Gecas & Schwalbe 1983).

For the teacher workforce as well, there is substantial evidence that professional autonomy and discretion increases motivation, responsibility, and commitment, and that a lack of workplace discretion is often cited as a reason for their disaffection, absenteeism, and defection (Ashton & Webb 1986; Blase 1986), particularly for the most academically talented teachers (Chapman 1983).

Teachers' Learning Opportunities. Workplace commitment also results when people experience work as meaningful—something that is important to their personal values and beliefs. If work is perceived as trivial or unimportant, no matter how many psychic rewards people receive, and no matter how much task autonomy they possess, there is precious little basis for internal motivation (Hackman & Oldham 1980).

Work can elicit feelings of personal meaningfulness in a variety of ways. One way is through opportunities for learning, for mastering skills that are then used in a variety of different and increasingly challenging activities. Once jobs have been mastered, they become routine, tedious, and monotonous unless there is still further challenge that stretches people's talents and skills. Work that allows people to grow and develop, to perfect current skills and learn new ones, gives them a sense of challenge and personal progress that compels greater workplace commitment (Hackman & Oldham 1980).

For their part, teachers sometimes complain of monotony, boredom, professional stagnation, and lack of direction where they have continued to use the same instructional techniques and practices year after year; quite often they become unenthusiastic and unable to motivate students (Ashton & Webb 1986; Blase 1986). Indeed, the opportunity to confront new challenges, to test and expand their professional repertoires, is the primary reason teachers involve themselves in innovative instructional programs (Huberman & Miles 1984). People confront new task challenges not just because they are interesting and exciting, but because their goal is to learn, to become better skilled and more knowledgeable. This explains more fully why teachers include the absence of professional stimulation and growth in their reasons for disaffection, absenteeism, and attrition from work (Kasten 1984; Rosenholtz 1985).

But for new tasks to have high motivating potential, people must feel that they possess sufficient knowledge and adequate skills that can stretch with increased work challenges. That is, people move initially toward confronting new challenges only where there is a reasonable chance of success—some assurance that their efforts will produce the positive outcomes sought.

Teacher Certainty. In the case of teachers, commitment to meet classroom challenges may pivot on their certainty about a technical culture and their instructional practice. That is, when teachers feel certain about their professional practices and know how to expand them, they devote themselves to greater instructional effort and involvement particularly with low-achieving students, which in turn strengthens their expectations that these children can learn. The opposite side of the coin is that challenges perceived as too great or costly may cause uncertain teachers to anticipate frustration and failure; not wanting to run that risk, they therefore become less demanding of low-achieving students, less apt to praise their performance, and less likely to provide feedback about their work (see Good & Brophy 1987). These and other such negative classroom practices in turn heighten teachers' uncertainty (Ashton & Webb 1986; Dembo & Gibson 1979).

As we saw in Chapter 5, much of teachers' certainty and willingness to confront new challenges hinges on the meaning they impute to their own teaching failure or success. Those who are confident about instructional practices are more likely to attribute successful or unsuccessful performance to something *they* have done, rather than to luck, chance, or an easy undertaking. They quite willingly take credit for their successes and are inclined to believe that their failures are simply a matter of not trying hard enough. We would expect them to confront new challenges, therefore, with greater optimism and promise. We also saw that uncertain teachers are most apt to attribute teaching success and failure to external causes, such as having a "good" class in the former case and a "bad" class in the latter. Believing that external causes put instructional success beyond their collective grasp, uncertain teachers may shy away from new job challenges that seem likely to rekindle the same sense of frustration and persistent workplace problems.

The point worth emphasizing here is that external attributions construct the belief that teachers can exert little influence or control over conditions of work. And because teachers attribute their uncertainty to external causes over which they have no control, those who feel they can make little contribution to student growth and development tend to lower their professional aspirations, become less involved with students, absent themselves more frequently, and defect more often from the workforce. This is especially true for teachers who work in low SES urban settings (Litt & Turk 1985; Rosenholtz 1985).

Negative Consequences of Low Commitment

The absence of conditions for high internal motivation has profound and deleterious consequences for people's workplace commitment. They fully recognize the constraints and deprivations inflicted on their performance and have an immediate sense of their low work-based self-fulfillment. But because of their need to make self-enhancing judgments, the definition of success in these settings is often recast among the working community in terms of behaviors and values that still allow them opportunity to derive status, esteem, and control (Gecas & Schwalbe 1983).

Instead of rewards earned through performance-based action, people redefine their mission as simply to "make do." "Making do" behaviors provide temporary relief from boredom, pass the time, invent ways to leave the job, focus more on social than work relationships with colleagues. Such behaviors—and the sense of esteem derived from them—are, of course, contrary to productive work. Stated differently, tasks no longer become a source from which self-fulfillment is derived; work becomes devalued and at the same time oriented toward satisfactions other than those that come from successful job performance (Gecas & Schwalbe 1983).

Within each chapter thus far we can identify several dysfunctional redefinitions of work by teachers in less nurturing schools. They may control their students rather than teach them, they may focus more on social than

on substantive relations with colleagues, they may become professional isolates in the school, and they may complain about and belittle students, parents, and principals. Each behavior, as we have seen, unwittingly undermines their chances for professional fulfillment.

Summary. To review, we have argued that several conditions are necessary
to sustain teachers' commitment to the workplace. These factors include
psychic rewards, where teachers are acknowledged for their special competencies and worth; task autonomy and discretion, where teachers control
the terms of work and are therefore able to assess their unique contributions
to it; learning opportunities that provide an ongoing challenge and a sense
of personal accomplishment; and teacher certainty, which lends the confidence needed to approach new work challenges. In addition, low school
SES may negatively affect teacher perceptions about their ability to succeed
professionally, diminishing their commitment.

QUANTITATIVE MEASUREMENT AND FINDINGS

Operational Definitions

To test this model, in Box 6.1 we provide the operational definitions of two
new variables: teacher commitment and task autonomy and discretion.

Results and Interpretation

In Table 6.1 we find the correlation coefficients between social organizational and school demographic variables. Included here as well is a measure
of teacher absenteeism that surfaces later in this chapter as an objective
rather than perceptual definition of commitment. Each of the social organizational variables shows moderate to strong correlations with teacher commitment and absenteeism, as does school SES. We therefore proceeded with
multiple regression analysis. The significant beta weights in the final regression equation appear in Table 6.2. Three social organizational factors significantly affect teacher commitment and combine to explain 76% of its
variance.

   Comparing standardized beta weights, we find that one of the most
powerful explanatory factors is task autonomy and discretion. When principals relinquish their need to control, trusting faculty with discretionary decisions, decisions that may result in greater performance fulfillment, teachers tend to become more unstinting contributors to the workplace.
Teachers' psychic rewards also contribute in an equally meaningful way to
their workplace commitment. Indeed, as we shall see in the qualitative data
that follows, their sense of pride in success not only enhances their commitment but also the amount of effort they are willing to put forth in future

BOX 6.1   Construction of Scales

Teacher Commitment

1. I enjoy teaching.
2. I feel the need to take R and R days.*
3. I think that the stress and disappointments involved in teaching at this school aren't really worth it.*
4. The teachers at this school like being here; I would describe us as a satisfied group.
5. I like the way things are run at this school.
6. If I could get a higher paying job, I'd leave teaching in a minute.*
7. In general, I really enjoy my students.
8. I don't seem to have as much enthusiasm now as I did when I began teaching.*
9. I think about transferring to another school.*
10. By the middle of the day, I can't wait for my students to go home.*
11. I think about staying home for school because I'm just too tired to go.*
12. What percentage of teachers do you think would like to leave this school?*
    a. none or few
    b. 25%
    c. 50%
    d. 75%
    e. almost everyone, or close to 100%

Alpha = .82; item-to-scale correlations = .36 to .67.

Task Autonomy and Discretion

1. I have to follow rules at this school that conflict with my best professional judgment.*
2. I can take little action at this school until a superior approves it.*
3. I have "freedom within limits" at this school; I know what is expected of me but I also have freedom to be creative.
4. The rules and regulations at this school don't make my job any easier.*
5. The principal of this school is a trustworthy, approachable person.
6. The rules and regulations at this school are rigid and inflexible.*
7. I have to buck school rules in order to do what I think needs to be done for my students.*
8. At my school, I am allowed to teach in my own style.

Alpha = .61; item-to-scale correlations = .25 to .48.

*We recorded these items in calculating scale scores.

TABLE 6.1. Correlations, Means (M), and Standard Deviations (SD) for Variables Examined with the Dependent Variable Teacher Commitment

	2	3	4	5	6	7	8	M	SD
1. Commitment	.75	.71	.73	.45	−.25	−.65	.58	34.35	3.10
2. Psychic rewards (positive feedback)		.49	.69	.69	−.24	−.60	.52	20.81	1.30
3. Autonomy and discretion			.64	.07	−.45	−.49	.41	23.06	2.95
4. Learning opportunities				.48	.07	−.69	.66	17.38	2.67
5. Teacher certainty					−.20	−.46	.45	27.94	1.98
6. School SES						−.06	.09	.41	.22
7. Teacher absenteeism							−.61	.07	.01
8. Managing student behavior								13.40	2.19

TABLE 6.2. Multiple Regression Analysis of Teacher Commitment

Variable	Beta	R^2	F
Learning opportunities	.18	.54	3.88*
Task autonomy and discretion	.40	.65	28.32**
Psychic rewards	.44	.76	30.85**
Multiple R	.87		

*$p < .05$.
**$p < .001$.

planning. Finally, although to a somewhat lesser extent, teachers' learning opportunities show a significant independent effect on teacher commitment, underscoring the likely importance of new work challenges in combating workplace alienation and boredom and in increasing their sense of control over their professional environment.

Neither teacher certainty nor managing student behavior, despite their moderate correlation with commitment, enter as independent variables in the equation. These findings may result from two factors: (1) the limited sample size that permits but a few independent variables to be considered (e.g., Rosenholtz & Simpson in press) and (2) the shared variance between each of the independent variables, as we saw in Chapter 5, which renders both teacher certainty and managing student behavior less unique predictors in the regression equation.

Teacher Absenteeism

Next we examine the quantitative relationship between teacher perceptions of their commitment and their actual school-level absenteeism, a tacit acknowledgment of their utter workplace despair. Teacher defection could not be examined for several reasons. For one thing, restrictive labor market conditions during the time of our study caused extremely low turnover samplewide. For another, district personnel indicated that the scarcity of positions prompted teachers to take leaves of absence rather than resigning. But leaves of absence due to disaffection could not be distinguished in our data from leaves for personal reasons. But recall that the same elements that predict turnover can be used successfully to predict absenteeism. Under conditions of low attrition, absenteeism is an alternative behavioral response that measures workplace commitment.

To distinguish between voluntary and involuntary absenteeism, as the industrial literature recommends, we calculated the total number of teachers' one-day absences within each school and divided this sum by the total number of teaching days per school year. This proportion was then regressed on the same school-level variables identified above. Results of this analysis appear in Table 6.3.

Among the variables, three are significant, together accounting for 54% of the variance in teacher absenteeism: managing student behavior,

TABLE 6.3 Multiple Regression Analysis of Teacher Absenteeism

Variable	Beta	R^2	F
Learning opportunities	−.38	.47	8.94*
Managing student behavior	−.44	.51	5.24**
Psychic rewards	−.21	.54	3.84**
Multiple R	−.73		

*$p < .01$.
**$p = .05$.

teachers' learning opportunities, and their psychic rewards. Schools' management of student behavior shows the strongest influence; the better the relations between students and teachers, the less stress teachers accrue, and the less they tend to absent themselves from the workplace. Teachers' learning opportunities follows next in the size of its effect. Where teachers feel challenged to learn new skills, especially if their efforts are successful, their absenteeism appears to lessen considerably. Finally, among the significant variables, psychic rewards shows somewhat less influence, albeit still substantial. To the extent that teachers receive positive feedback about their performance and see their work-related efforts as self-fulfilling, reasons for their absenteeism tend to diminish. Neither task autonomy nor teacher certainty significantly affected their one-day absenteeism. Nor, contrary to the literature, did school SES. Nonetheless, we locate in these data, then, two fundamentally important findings: objective, external validation for teachers' perceptions of their workplace commitment, and partial explanation for a critical and costly program plaguing many school districts.

To review, our quantitative data indicate that three social organizational conditions of schools strongly relate to teachers' commitment to the workplace: the extent of their opportunities for learning, their psychic rewards, and their task autonomy and discretion. Validating teacher perceptions, the degree to which they absent themselves from work appears also to be determined in part by teachers' psychic rewards, school efforts toward orderly student conduct, and teachers' learning opportunities. Thus work commitment seems to have less to do with the personal qualities people bring with them to the workplace than how tasks are designed and managed within it.

In the qualitative analysis that follows, we consider the meaning of school commitment for teachers' professional investment, and how their task autonomy and discretion tends to affect their commitment to work. In the final section, we again return to the quantitative data to test the relationships between teacher commitment and absenteeism, on the one hand, and student learning gains on the other.

THE SOCIAL CONSTRUCT OF WORKPLACE COMMITMENT

Low investment in work is one of the consequences of lost commitment. Particularly in service professions, if workplace conditions deny the very inducements that make people unstinting contributors to the clients they serve, people find that they cannot sustain the kind of initial commitment they once had. They lose positive feelings, sympathy, and respect for the clients they serve and, as we have seen, develop cynical perspectives that encourage them to label and treat clients in demeaning ways (Maslach 1982).

Throughout our analysis we have noted these same attitudes in teachers' frustration with principals, students, and parents, which left them only a residue of collective resentment and despair; in their lack of nourishment from colleagues, which consumed the inner resources that in their entry to the profession had once inspired high aspirations and promise; and in the absence of professional growth, which stunted their anticipation of new teaching challenges and possibilities.

From her organizational analysis of corporate life, Kanter's (1968) distinction between the "stuck" and the "moving" is useful here. The stuck feel no sense of progress, growth, or development and so tend to lower their aspirations and appear less motivated to achieve. They shy away from risks in the workplace and proceed in cautious, conservative ways. The moving, by contrast, tend to recognize and use more of their skills and aim still higher. Their sense of progress and future gain encourages them to look forward, to take risks, and to grow.

Two of our interview questions sought to capture the ways in which teachers' workplace circumstances pinned them somewhere between hope and despair—between being stuck or moving. Computations of z-scores on the variables directly related to, and including, teacher commitment (i.e., learning opportunities, psychic rewards, task autonomy and control) produced 17 "moving" schools with highly committed faculties. From 8 of these, 28 teachers were interviewed. Our analysis also pinpointed 15 "stuck" schools whose faculties reported low commitment. We sampled 24 teachers from 8 of these schools. Finally, we identified 46 "moderately stuck" schools with teachers situated between the "stuck" and the "moving." From 7 of these, we interviewed 22 teachers.

Teachers' Future Plans

We know that individuals who are provided opportunities for independent and successful action in challenging work increase not only their motivation to excel but also their willingness to attempt new tasks. Thus, in one question we asked, "Do you have any specific future plans for your classroom?" We expected that teachers from moving schools would tend to welcome new challenges with greater certainty and promise, look for better ways of doing things, and respond to our question with specific ideas and goals for instruction. Believing that instructional success is beyond their collective grasp, we reasoned, teachers from stuck schools would tend to shy away from new job challenges that might only confirm their absence of psychic rewards and would plan few new instructional ventures. Teachers from moderately stuck schools, we anticipated, would locate the extent of their future planning somewhere between these extremes. Teachers' answers, presented in Table 6.4, categorize the substance of their future plans within each school typology.

Strikingly consistent with predictions, whether or not teachers held future plans co-varied with the level of their school commitment. Ambitions lie fallow for the clear majority of teachers from moderately stuck and stuck schools, whereas only a handful of teachers from moving schools envisioned no future plans or aspirations. Typical of the responses by those who specified no plans:

No, just to continue on as I have.

I'm not doing what I didn't do before.

Right now I'm waiting to see what class I'm going to have.

I usually don't think about those things 'til summer.

I haven't really thought about it.

Teachers suffered a loss of ambition and drive in stuck schools, just as overgrown elms and sycamores poach sunlight from the lawn and cause it to wither and brown. In place of their once high ideals and aspirations, inertia and boredom now grew. Indeed, boredom is a kind of pain born of unused powers, the pain of wasted talents and possibilities. Now teachers tended to live only for the moment; brooking the next obstacle, crossing the next tributary, getting past the next whirlpool of countercurrents. Following the stream of the day-to-day appeared to become an end in itself, not because it would take them anywhere, but because it was among the few things that gave them any direction, any purpose, any course of action. It was likely better than doing nothing at all.

Academic Plans. As to the content of teachers' future plans, we find a pattern that recalls earlier analyses of the nature of teacher talk in Chapter 2, the type of teacher sharing and leadership in Chapter 3, and teachers' greatest pedagogical talents in Chapter 4. The extent to which teachers specified academic content as the stuff of their future plans tended to relate directly to the level of their school commitment. Overwhelmingly, teachers from moving schools more often than the rest envisioned plans that expanded their professional talents and repertoires in subject-specific areas:

[From a second-year teacher:] There's so much I want to try next year. My reading program needs work—you can't do everything at once, and this year I concentrated on math. But next year I'm going to work out a way to teach specific skills in reading. I'm already gathering materials for it.

[From a veteran ending her 17th year:] Oh my yes! I try to do something new

TABLE 6.4. Teachers' Future Plans

	DO YOU HAVE ANY SPECIFIC PLANS FOR YOUR CLASSROOM?*				
Level of school commitment	No plans	Academic plans	Parental involvement plans	Non-academic/ affective plans	Classroom management plans
Moving (n = 25)	4%	73%	16%	0%	4%
Moderately stuck (n = 23)	48%	13%	4%	4%	13%
Stuck (n = 23)	65%	4%	0%	13%	14%

*Teachers offered multiple responses to this question. Percentages therefore reflect the number of times each category was mentioned.

every year. Next year I'm going to work on thinking skills. I asked a professor at [a nearby college] for some materials. She's going to help me. And I want to emphasize writing more. I always work on it, but I want to do it more. It is really important that children be able to express themselves.

[From a fourth-year kindergarten teacher:] This summer we are starting to work on a new math curriculum. We're developing special materials to use in a new skills program. We're hoping to develop the math program as thoroughly as we did the language arts program. We'll start testing it in the Fall. [What happens if it doesn't work?] We are always modifying the language arts program to make it better. We'll do the same thing with the math program.

We note with particular emphasis that the academic plans of teachers from moving schools did not relate to their years of classroom experience. Experienced teachers, when compared to their younger counterparts, were equally likely to seek out better ways of doing things, to take risks, to avoid sameness and routine, and to move on from what they had been doing to something more challenging and new. These were the pedagogical tightrope walkers, the river rafters, the mountain climbers. They appear to bring a sense of adventure and thrill to each new lesson they perform, no matter how many variations of it they had played in the past. Teachers' responses rang with enthusiasm and hope about new instructional ventures. Doing something different implied doing something *better* than before. In this way, faulty experiments would be overtaken by the headlong possibilities of tomorrow, the adrenal rush of high expectations.

Plans for Parent Involvement. Consistent with findings from Chapter 5, stuck teachers held no goals for parent participation, perhaps because parents' negative attitudes protected their self-esteem. In other words, teachers did nothing about parents' obvious disregard for the learning welfare of their children for there was nothing to be done. At the same time, this course became the perfect vindication for their own instructional uncertainty.

Although the plans of teachers from both moving and moderately stuck schools centered around eliciting greater parent interest and involvement in their children's school lives, fundamental differences between them existed. There was little apparent about the intent of parent involvement plans from most moderately stuck teachers, save their consciousness that a gap between home and school existed. Teachers from moving schools narrowly focused their efforts on involving parents with academic content, thereby bridging the learning chasm between home and school. Perhaps exemplifying these contextual differences best are the plans of an 11-year veteran from a moving school, juxtaposed against a fourth-year novice from a stuck school. Both teachers serve comparable low SES, rural populations:

I want to get children's literature more into the classroom. I'd like to get parents more involved with the children's reading. This year in my class most of the children were reading. Toward the end of the year we had a "Parents as Partners" class [that kindergarten teachers taught in the evening] and the parents would read stories to the children for about 15 minutes. [Did all of the parents do that?] No. I would like to make it more accepted and used by parents, by getting them started earlier [in the school year]. I found some literature I want to send them, showing them the importance of reading to their children.

Not right off hand, I can't think of any. I do want to get more parent involvement in the classroom. That is my goal next year, to have them come in and be more aware of what's going on. I haven't planned any particular program. I have thought about having a big party at my house and inviting them to an open-house type thing. Just let them come in and see where I live and that I am just plain as day. And that I am willing to listen to anything they have to say, or discuss any problems that they want to discuss. I don't know how this will work in this particular school area, whether they would come or not. I had first thought about home visits, but I have been advised not to do that. [Who advised you against home visits?] Teachers. They thought that the parents would think I was judging them.

There are several intriguing points here. The moving teacher, aided by colleagues, tried to involve parents directly in their children's learning by giving them specific activities to do at home. And her dogged persistence in this strategy, despite its limited initial success, seemed to come from her own initiative in seeking out better strategies, and the hope of rising to new heights. This typifies the optimism of the moving: teachers seem inspired by their failures, not defeated. By contrast, the moderately stuck teacher sought not to improve the academic efforts of students through parent involvement, but rather to establish greater social connectedness between home and classroom. This is a laudable goal; nonetheless the means she chose will acquaint parents neither with her specific classroom practice nor her teaching competence. Of equal if not greater importance is the fact that colleagues seem to shape this teacher's consciousness of the acceptable way in which to accomplish her goal, with the ultimate idea—hosting an open house—actually far less effective than the original one—home visitations. The raw power of colleagues to mediate school reality is here again patently clear.

Affective Plans. Teachers from moving schools reported no affective plans for their classroom. This comes as no surprise. As the reader will recall from Chapter 5, teachers saw children's affective development as not inseparable from their learning; that is, they treated student problems individually rather than routinely; they perceived student motivation as essential to their learning; and they encouraged and celebrated student enthusiasm for learning. In sum, children's affective sentiments were essential means for greater instructional success.

It *is* perplexing, however, that teachers from moderately stuck and stuck schools reported few affective plans for their teaching. These were the teachers who, in Chapter 4, reported affective skills as their major strength in teaching. In stuck schools, the preponderance of means over ends seems almost predictable. Their future plans, rather than revealing some means to make their classroom climate more conducive to student learning, emphasized affective activities as ends in themselves. In their comments below, note how stuck teachers unwittingly sponsor only cosmetic alterations of the status quo:

> I have a large empty photo album, and I'll start taking pictures of my classroom before the children get there. Then I'll take pictures of my class all during the year. The children can look at them and say something if they flip back to something we did in September and it's January. I'm hoping they can say, "Oh, I remember when we did that. It was fun."

> Well, I have specific goals. I like my children to be happy. I want them to feel good about themselves. One of my goals is to present the image that we are all part of one big family. If anyone ever needs anything, or anything comes up, we can all talk together.

> I've written a little song to give them [students] more of a sense of unity and pride, like, "This is the greatest fourth grade and we'll do our best and we want to feel good about ourselves."

These activities, exasperatingly, suggest no obvious outcomes for children's affective growth. This clear disjuncture between means and ends again can be understood with references to the social organization in which stuck teachers function. Without substantive dialogue between colleagues and principals about teaching goals and purposive means to attain them, these teachers may lack clear direction in how to define, operationalize, and evaluate future plans. With goals evolved from the curricular anarchy that surrounds their every day, they appear left with activities that serve little purpose. These activities may ultimately falter in bringing about the affective outcomes teachers seek, and, when this occurs, they carry precious few implications for greater professional growth, psychic rewards, and workplace commitment.

Plans for Student Discipline. Teachers working under different contextual arrangements also varied in the content of their plans for dealing with student discipline. The minority of teachers from moving schools who expressed such plans stressed the articulation of goals for student behavior at the school level through active involvement of teachers and principals. Their stuck counterparts instead emphasized norms of self-reliance in confronting student misbehavior by resisting any outside interference. These perspectives are highlighted nowhere more clearly than in responses from two teachers in the same district whose superintendent had directed all principals to institute consistent disciplinary practices in their schools. First we hear from a teacher with 25 years' experience in a stuck school, followed by a 14-year veteran in a moving school:

> Well, I'm going to have to try a new type of discipline. I believe in having my own way of doing it, but I guess everyone is going to do the same thing, and I really haven't heard what they're going to do. I have used a reward system and I have found it works beautifully. So I don't see why I have to change.

> I'm going to work up a behavior management system based on Assertive Discipline. We're going to submit our plans to the principal. He plans to work with different grade levels to develop similar plans and implement them uniformly.

We hear in the first teacher's comments the defeat of the future and the defense of the past. She seems to feel no sense of communal responsibility for behavior problems in her school and instead chafes against every attempt to alter her current system, a system that already conforms to her conception of good classroom management. She is reluctant (if not altogether unwilling) to consider alternative possibilities and challenges, or to sacrifice her own management strategy for the school's common good. This is the paradox of uninvolved teachers. With announced change, they tend to withdraw in ambivalence or anger without mounting any counteraction. Their noninvolvement in turn leaves an open door for principals to actively define the nature of school reality, a reality that teachers may come later to resent. By contrast, the moving teacher views the assignment with clear understanding of her school's need and the importance of her involvement in it, and she welcomes her principal's invitation to participate. Although there is little reason for optimism about greater professional growth, psychic rewards, and commitment in the former instance, in the latter they abound.

That the majority of teachers in moderately stuck and stuck schools formulated fewer future plans than teachers from moving schools can be explained in two mutually compatible ways: by looking at the implications of planning vis-à-vis threatened self-esteem, and by articulating these qualitative data with our earlier quantitative findings.

We have argued throughout that possible threats to uncertain teachers engage them in a variety of tactical maneuvers that deflect attention from measures of their professional worth. The moderately stuck and stuck reported far less future planning than the moving, which is precisely the sort of defensive strategy that deflects such self-attention. To avoid any inferences about performance inadequacies that the moderately stuck or stuck might draw, they can choose to devote less effort to teaching, to think less about it, especially where it is headed. In this way teachers maintain some degree of control over their contextual circumstances. Any given instructional failure may simply result from their lack of classroom planning.

Alternatively, the contextual nature of teacher planning may be better explained with reference to our quantitative findings. For one thing, the relatively low task autonomy and discretion exercised by teachers in moderately stuck and stuck schools may actually thwart their attempts to control future actions. If teachers find themselves powerless to shape the nature and conditions of their work, if every plan they envision must first be approved by administrators who appear to know little about conditions of their work, teachers' forward thinking, their anticipation and drive, cannot possibly be sustained. Powerlessness, first and foremost, is the enemy of teacher planning.

Second, in that teachers from moderately stuck and stuck schools lack opportunities for professional growth, little *substance* is provided for future plans. With limited access to principals' or colleagues' ideas, feedback, and encouragement, they may be sentenced to repeat the same instructional strategies without pardon, forfeiting any sense of professional progress and accomplishment as they serve. Without the challenge and inspiration that would carry them out of the tedium that crowds every day, they may find no new frontiers beckoning, and no promising new hopes, and so they shun reinvestment in the same instructional enterprise that proved so unrewarding in the past.

Finally, in stuck and moderately stuck settings, teachers' instructional uncertainty and their belief that students possess only limited potential promises them little hope of improving their performance, so the task of future planning carries little, if any, meaningfulness. Uncertainty functions as a self-fulfilling prophecy that dampens teachers' enthusiasm and willingness to exert the undaunted effort necessary to bring them up to par with the moving. The most frightening deficit here is in boldness. New approaches and strategies for teaching lie dormant because the results of their efforts will, as before, carry few self-congratulatory sentiments. It is a chronic no-win situation—if teachers expend no effort they receive nothing, save hopelessness, in return. Hope seems not so much a virtue as an essential part of successful teaching. But in stuck settings, hope, like other essentials, appears long relegated to the school's dustier corridors.

The content of teachers' plans in varied contextual settings, then, suggests how the regularities of school life influence teachers' hopes and aspirations. As we saw in Chapter 4, the single-minded dedication of teachers to shared instructional ventures lends direction, substance, and support for academic planning in moving schools. As these conditions wane in moderately stuck and stuck schools, teachers presume greater pedagogical latitude to pursue future plans, or more patently, to seek refuge and solace in inertia. Indeed, the very act of instructional planning by teachers in moving schools seems to affirm a robust commitment to the future and their own professional growth, whereas the absence of planning in more stuck settings may portend the moribund prophecy that teacher growth may be neither expected nor likely. Instead, teachers tend only to have stayed the course through all the arduous dramas. With no fresh ideas from old colleagues there may be nothing left to say. All the topics have been tried; they have come up against the incorrigible in each other. They are left with time itself, sitting in silence, reeling it in together.

Teacher Conformity

Given the primacy of teachers' task autonomy and discretion in regard to their workplace commitment, we asked a second question: "Do you ever have to do things that are against the rules in order to do what's best for your students?" Our purpose here was twofold: To explore the extent to which professional empowerment affects teachers' conformity to state, district, or school mandates, and second, to examine whether the policies found most objectionable reflected different teachers' task conceptions of their work.

One historical caveat in Tennessee schools warrants mention here. In contrast to the previous year when we administered questionnaires, early in the course of the second school year, when we conducted interviews, the Tennessee Department of Education instituted two major education reforms: a career ladder plan and minimum competency testing for all elementary grade students. The Basic Skills Program and the voluntary career ladder plan carried with them the burden of new and voluminous record-keeping demands. Partly for this reason, both reforms were regarded as anathema to over 75% of our sample (Rosenholtz 1987). The influence of this confounding factor is clearly evident in the next segment of interview data we consider.

Despite these state reforms, we nonetheless expected that moving teachers, confident of their instructional skills and empowered by their schools, would ignore perniciously perceived policies that stood in the way of children's learning welfare and their own professional fulfillment. Stuck teachers, we expected, would confront restrictive rules or policies as yet another instance of their powerlessness and would collectively bemoan their fate rather than mobilize to combat it. Moderately stuck teachers, we again anticipated, would locate themselves somewhere between these extremes.

Moving Teachers. Consistent with predictions about moving teachers, 79% responded that they would break rules that stood in the way of what they regarded as a higher cause:

> [From a 12-year veteran:] Yes, I probably do. [Could you give me an example?] Sometimes I give the Basic Skills Tests at a different time than I'm supposed to. I'll teach the skills first, and then give the test, regardless of when they [the state] say I'm supposed to give the test. It doesn't make much sense to test kids on stuff they haven't studied.

> [From a fourth-year novice:] Yes, I always have and I always will. In this district we aren't supposed to go beyond the fourth grade skills. I never have gone

along with this policy. It is not that many students are affected. But it kills me to see these students stuck behind. So I don't submit complete plans for these children. I do other things like that if it is for the good of the students. For example, with the Basic Skills Program, all kids are supposed to be exposed to all skills. I don't think that does any good. If you progress too fast, the kids will lose out. The kids have to learn the basics first, or it won't do any good to expose them to other skills.

[From a 14-year veteran:] Definitely. I can think of one instance immediately: the central office policy that reading books are not to leave school grounds. I don't see how they're supposed to learn how to read without taking the readers home with them. I mean, you'd think someone would've thought about that one! I think that happens a lot. We have a class for advanced children, and a teacher who has free time to work with these children. This teacher can't tell anyone outside of the school that she's working with them. We put these kids through the first-grade readers already. That was illegal. We're not supposed to let students go beyond their grade level. But we're still going ahead with our program. I don't see what's wrong with doing that. I think most teachers would be willing to do that if it was for the betterment of the child.

In each instance, the fists of the moving seemed to swing from the arms of a confident future; teachers undauntingly violated district or state mandates that ran contrary to their conception of appropriate classroom practice. Although they now perceived teaching as more a bureaucratic obstacle course, perhaps even as a treacherous interval between success and failure, little seemed to dim their determination and their transparent, energetic locomotion. Policies that dictated that they could not infringe territorily on the content of succeeding grade levels, that wasted precious instructional time, or that prevented them from rendering individual academic assistance were deemed ill-conceived obstacles that warranted total disregard whenever the issue of student learning was at stake. Moving teachers apparently knew no complacent servitude. While they taught, the bureaucracy around them could not claim their attention against the strong and pressing needs within their classrooms.

That moving teachers exercised professional discretion in these matters emphasizes the extent to which they are empowered by their contextual surroundings. Here they stood in all the vigor of their profession, accomplished, acknowledged, and inspired. This is no more potently underscored than in the last teacher's observation: "I think most teachers would be willing to do that if it was for the betterment of the child." The regularities of her everyday life forged a reality that most teachers would not falter; that they, too, would undauntingly dismantle restrictive regulations in the best interests of their students. Yet, far to the contrary, the majority of teachers working under less empowering circumstances were not willing to break or bend rules, even under the most dire circumstances.

But we are getting ahead of the story. We must first consider one alternative response of the moving. Of the 21% of moving teachers who replied they would not break rules, one third explained that because school policies were set by teachers themselves, professional compromises were seldom if ever called for:

> I can't think of any now. I don't think we have rules that are rigid and most of the rules generate around the welfare of the children here. I can't think of any that I would really want to break. The philosophy of the school was prepared by the principal and the teachers together. We set our own rules.

> Teachers here make the rules. We're all pretty focused on helping children learn, and all our rules revolve around that. If we don't find a rule useful, we change it.

Moderately Stuck and Stuck Teachers. Foreshadowed above, 61% of the moderately stuck and 75% of the stuck teachers responded that they would *not* break rules that interfered with the interests of their students:

> Wouldn't do it. There was a time, maybe, when I was younger, that I might have. But now if it meant going against the rules, I wouldn't do it.

> No. I have basically taught myself to accept them and go on. I know there's not much I can do to change things; there's nothing much you can do about them.

> I just sort of accept everything. You get used to accepting things after a while.

> At an earlier time in my career I would have fought for what I thought was right for students, but not any longer.

Consistent with our thinking, those whose professional discretion is subjugated by a muscle-flexing bureaucracy seem to view their powerlessness as though it were a verdict without appeal. Teachers continue on, but without enthusiasm, automatically, in forced complicity with ideas that have become, by their own admission, agents of professional destruction. Equally noteworthy is teachers' gradual acceptance of their low professional empowerment over time. Unlike the moving who even at more advanced career stages continue to press their professional judgment, authority, and wisdom against ill-conceived state or district mandates, the clear majority of moderately stuck and stuck teachers were again overcome by inertia, as though their talents had been ground down to a blunt instrument for fighting the doldrums of teaching itself. Conscious of their powerlessness, they appear now to accede to overly restrictive policies because "there's not much you can do about them." The deepening detachment, the resigned pessimism, the paralysis of the spirit, and the stagnation of vision, are all present and accounted for in the utterly tragic reality of stuck schools.

Then, too, obstacles loom much larger where teachers suffer lost commitment. They appear less willing to forge ahead and more willing to cave in; "Why bother? The rules are here to stay." The spark of enthusiasm seems difficult to kindle in the everyday monotony of teaching. Teachers' lack of determination and drive may become self-perpetuating: If they succumb in the face of bureaucratic obstacles, their powerlessness is only confirmed, which in turn provides further reason not to resist in the future.

Keeping faith with the enterprise of survival, most teachers from moderately stuck and stuck schools, unlike the moving, appeared to bemoan their oppression without mobilizing to defeat it. The exasperating, open despair of the stuck teacher we hear from next fully captures these pent-up frustrations:

> Probably not. A lot of teachers would rather let it slide, than go through the hassle. I think this is what's happening. They don't resist, they just give in. Sometimes I think that we take things that we shouldn't. You feel sometimes like you're beating your head against the wall. You try and you're pushing and you get criticized for it. You just don't have the enthusiasm you once had. You think, "I'm taking all this abuse." There are times when maybe I have not been as patient as I should have been [with students]. I realize this. It's like a cycle. You seem to get wound tighter and tighter. Between you and me, I started working on my Masters and I quit because I thought, "There's no future in it." I have made the comment time and time again, if I thought I could get out of teaching and into something else, I would. I've heard that from a lot of teachers. Sometimes you can put up with certain things, but when things begin to overwhelm you, everything seems just to drag you down. You feel like you're swamped to start with. I've discouraged any child that's ever come to talk to me from going into teaching. I tell them there's no future in it and there isn't.

The professional death rattle in this teacher's remarks is almost audible. The possibilities of mastering the environment, of deriving a sense of professional self-worth, and the deleterious consequences that result when such needs go unfulfilled here seem patently clear. This teacher has grown frustrated, angry, and intolerant, no longer able to give herself time to reflect or gain perspective on the problems she confronts—her idealism and hope long since relegated to a pedagogical graveyard.

But it is perhaps more to the point to observe that emotions like indignation or despair will not generate constructive action. Teachers themselves appear transformed into bureaucratic functionaries, no longer able to instruct flexibly and responsively. Not only does teaching become more routine (as we saw in Chapter 4), but teachers become less sensitive to children's feelings or needs, and say or do punitive or callous things (as we saw in Chapter 5). In a last ditch effort to stave off feelings of powerlessness, teachers may take actions that risk their own professional status, by abusing children through physical or psychic means (as we saw in Chapter 5).

Where moderately stuck and stuck teachers *did* report violating policies, they reflected altogether different concerns from those expressed by the moving. Specifically, 86% of the moving teachers reportedly violated policies that impinged on and interfered with academic instruction, whereas 71% of the moderately stuck and 83% of the stuck identified non-academic policies as those most apt to be ignored:

> Yes. We are required by the state to have thirty minutes of P.E. everyday. But I feel that kids need time to be loose and to have free play. So since the P.E. class is structured [and taught by another teacher], I go way beyond that— fifteen to thirty minutes more. Those children are just cooped up too much as it is. I disagree with that rule. I'm not the only one either. I know several teachers who do it. [Does anyone feel you shouldn't?] No, because no one keeps up with the next person here. If the principal actually came and checked, the situation would be different. But he hasn't said anything to me yet.

> Yes. I don't do anything that is that bad. You know there is a law that you can not have any prayer or religious things in school. You are not even supposed to talk about religious things. However, if a child brings a book to school like at Christmas time that refers to the birth of the Child, or at Easter, I can't refuse to read his book. That would really hurt the child. I think that refusing to read the religious book would be refusing that child his rights as much as reading it would infringe on the rights of others.

> I had a student who I have talked to nicely and who still didn't get the idea. Finally, I had to take him out in the hall and sit him down and speak to him in language he could understand. I'm sure what I said was against the rules, but it worked. I made my point.

> I can't think of any off hand. Oh yeah. There was this one kid who would strangle other kids and took their lunch money all the time. In order to avoid him [in monitoring the playground during recess duty], I would take rest breaks at a time when I knew he would be around. The principal didn't want me to do that and made a big stink. Then later he admitted he would have done things the same way.

It is precisely at this point that schools face a major dilemma. If they allow too great freedom for their faculty, they are apt to confront erratic and sometimes organizationally irrelevant or destructive behaviors. If they allow too little freedom for their faculty, they are likely to produce oppressed, alienated, and uncaring teachers who are equally unproductive. Indeed, stuck schools seemed the perfect breeding ground for organizational anarchy: teachers extended P.E. periods, introduced irrelevant content into the classroom, punitively violated policies for dealing with student misbehavior, or enforced them only selectively, all with seeming impunity. The ill-conceived bureaucratic control exercised over teachers, as we shall see next, weakened their effectiveness and fouled their commitment— effects precisely the opposite of those intended.

TEACHER COMMITMENT AND STUDENT ACHIEVEMENT

As we have seen, teachers who are powerless to shape the substance of their classroom plans or the policies of their school not only profess no ownership of them, but tend to become alienated from the essence of their work. Given the attitudinal and behavioral manifestations of alienation, it follows logically that student achievement should suffer at the hands of teachers not committed to the programs they must teach or the policies they must follow. The other side of the argument is that teachers who deliberately balk at formal rules and prescriptions for practice because such policies require them to treat pupils routinely should better meet students' learning needs.

Furthermore, teachers who seem hopeful about and responsive to students' learning, who take time to reflect on their pedagogical practices, and who then plan different approaches and try different things tend to put forth greater effort than their unacknowledged, undernourished counterparts. With greater effort teachers should experience more instructional success, and their students should demonstrate greater mastery of basic skills. Next we test these propositions using both our perceptual measure of teacher commitment and our objective measure of teacher absenteeism.

In examining the correlation coefficients between student achievement, teacher commitment, and teacher absenteeism, we find moderate correlations between teacher commitment and fourth-grade reading (.41) and math (.39) and, likewise, between teacher absenteeism and students' fourth-grade reading (-.38) and math (-.39). Teacher commitment is unrelated to second-grade reading (-.04) and math (-.07) test scores. Nor is teacher absenteeism significantly related to second-grade reading (.11) or math (.11). The reader is again referred to Chapter 4, Table 4.4, for a full discussion of the correlations between school demographic and teacher background variables.

Next we regressed students' fourth-grade achievement in reading and math on each indicator of commitment, controlling, of course, for students' second-grade test scores, school SES, teachers' mean undergraduate status, their mean educational attainment, and their mean years of experience. The results of these four equations, for significant variables only, appear in Table 6.5.

First we consider the effects of commitment on students' reading achievement. As seen in the first equation, prior achievement again shows the strongest independent relationship to students' fourth-grade reading test scores. The reading skills students bring with them to the classroom determine in no small way how successfully they will read in the future. Teachers' undergraduate status makes a more modest contribution. The greater the prestige of teachers' undergraduate institutions, the more likely it is that students will progress in reading. Sandwiched between these two variables in terms of its relative strength is teacher commitment. The less teachers' workplace alienation, the more students achieve in reading. These three variables combine to explain 59% of the variance in fourth-grade reading achievement.

Turning next to math, and holding constant students' second-grade test scores, teacher commitment is the only significant predictor. Together these

TABLE 6.5. Multiple Regression Analysis of Teacher Commitment and Teacher Absenteeism on Reading and Math Gains

	TEACHER COMMITMENT			
A. Reading, Grade 4	*Variable*	*Beta*	*F*	R^2
	Reading, grade 2	.59	52.88**	.38
	Undergraduate status	.14	2.85*	.42
	Commitment	.42	30.17**	.59
	Multiple $R = .77$			
B. Math, Grade 4	Math, grade 2	.71	105.91**	.46
	Commitment	.44	40.48**	.65
	Multiple $R = .80$			
	TEACHER ABSENTEEISM			
A. Reading, Grade 4	*Variable*	*Beta*	*F*	R^2
	Reading, grade 2	.67	78.44**	.38
	Teacher absenteeism	−.45	35.30*	.58
	Multiple $R = .76$			
B. Math, Grade 4	Math, grade 2	.71	81.02*	.46
	Teacher absenteeism	−.29	13.34*	.54
	Multiple $R = .76$			

*$p < .09$.
**$p < .001$.

two variables account for 65% of the variance in students' fourth-grade math achievement.

In a parallel manner, teachers' actual absence from work, ostensibly a direct measure of alienated labor, is independently and negatively related to students' reading and math gains, even after controlling for second-grade test scores. In reading, 58% of the variance is accounted for by prior achievement and teacher absenteeism. Similarly, in math, 54% of the variance is explained. That student learning is negatively affected by teacher absenteeism seems reasonable and intuitively sound. In most schools, especially in the upper elementary grades, students spend considerable energy plotting strategies and weaving traps into which an unwary substitute might easily fall. There is little continuity of instruction. Indeed, this is the stuff that prompts alternative definitions of classroom success for those students who do not derive their self-esteem from routine classroom work.

SUMMARY

This chapter examined the social organization of schools that induced teachers to remain in the workplace and contribute productively to schools. Productive contributions, we argued, were a direct function of the professional fulfillment teachers derived from their work. Our conceptual argument and later quantitative analysis identified three conditions necessary for such fulfillment. The first is teachers' task autonomy and discretion—the sense that achieving work goals results directly from purposive actions, or teachers' feeling that their own intentional efforts cause positive changes to occur. The second condition deals with teachers' psychic rewards. If teachers' rewards do not outweigh their frustrations, particularly in their relationships with students, work tends to lose its meaning and alienation increases dramatically. The final condition is learning opportunities, opportunities to increase one's talents and instructional strategies to better master one's environment, to repel professional stagnation, and to experience a sense of continuous progress and growth. These three workplace arrangements combine to explain 76% in teachers' commitment. When we examined the effect of these variables on teachers' one-day absenteeism, 54% of the variance was explained by their learning opportunities, their psychic rewards, and school management of student behavior.

Two questions in our qualitative data allowed us to explore the effects of teacher commitment with greater sensitivity. When asked if they had any specific future plans for their classroom, most moving teachers specified academic plans as the stuff of their forward thinking. There seemed to be goals in their journey and there were arrivals. Inquisitive explorers who brought back more than a memory or a story, moving teachers tend to bring back new visions, fresh starts, and blazing hopes. Indeed, it appears to be only by their strength to push forward that teachers might live at the peak of their potential.

Moderately stuck and stuck teachers far more frequently hold no future plans and tend to aspire to no new heights in their professional goals. Most are unable to conceive a future different from the past, unable to devise alternatives for tomorrow to correct any deficiencies of today. Almost everything they do seems to be a repetition of something that had been done before. For those few who did specify future plans, the context tended to be considerably remote from student learning.

We also asked teachers if they would alter bureaucratic rules that interfered with the best interests of their students. Moving teachers tend to quickly exclaim that they *do* break rules wherever district or state policies contradicted their best professional judgment. In the main, moderately stuck and stuck teachers deny any power by their contextual entrapment, appear to have little fortitude to break rules. Their lack of passion for teaching ostensibly makes them passively suffer until the current storm, whatever its point of departure, has passed. Neither self-effacing nor self-confident, teachers seem like victims of a disease who are given only a placebo—affirming their powerlessness through complaints to colleagues. It may well have been a delusion through these complaints to avoid fundamental issues about classroom failings, but it proved also a relief. When stuck teachers did break rules they were entirely of a nonacademic nature, whereas the rules that moving teachers broke had almost exclusively to do with those impeding the academic progress of their students.

Finally, with quantitative data we examined the relationship between teacher commitment, their absenteeism, and student learning gains. Controlling for second-grade achievement, we found that both perceptual and objective measures of commitment showed significant independent effects on students' fourth-grade achievement in both reading and math.

In sum, teachers' regard for their work—their sense of optimism, hope, and commitment—tends to reside in workplace conditions that enable them to feel professionally empowered and self-fulfilled, that keep them reaching for new teaching challenges, fresh opportunities, and ever-expanding technical knowledge. On the other hand, teachers' terminal boredom, the loss of their original meaning, their overwhelming sense of unappreciation, and their lack of professional empowerment costs stuck schools dearly: they usurp teachers' capacity to dream. Thus the expectation that bureaucratic control will quickly lead to the promised land of better teaching and student learning cannot be sustained, even by those who most sincerely believe it. We will affirm this point even more dramatically as we examine district-level differences next.

7

Teacher Commitment: District-Level Influences

As researchers have paid progressively greater attention to school effects, as they have flagged and codified things we should look for, it was inevitable and appropriate that they should also examine interorganizational relations—the district conditions that drive schools to more or less efficient ends. Interorganizational analysis is the study of two or more interacting organizations, with emphasis on how the "focal" organization affects others in the environment (Perrow 1979). Imagine the environment as a set of concentric circles; inside each circle is a smaller one whose dimensions are constrained by the larger circle. Each circle is independent to some extent of the larger one and can be analyzed accordingly, as we have done thus far. But one cannot fully grasp the nature of schools without analyzing the still larger environment in which they are embedded. Recent investigations suggest that those smaller circles are also quite dependent on the shape of the larger ones on the outside (Gersten et al. 1986; LaRocque & Coleman 1987; McLaughlin & Pfeifer 1988; Murphy & Hallinger 1987).

As we move from organizational to interorganizational analysis in the present chapter, we again note the contrasts between routine and nonroutine settings. When organizational tasks are routine, people can perform them over and over with exactly the same result. A bureaucratic structure is most efficient under these conditions. But when tasks are not well understood, people require more discretion in their performance; more interaction among them is needed and more emphasis is placed on collaborative consultation. Because teaching is nonroutine, because there are more art, craft, and finely honed skills involved, traditional bureaucratic structures are operationally dysfunctional to the work of successful schools.

The interorganizational analysis presented here serves as a capstone to previous chapters. In it we will address those district-level practices that bear directly or indirectly on some of the most critical dimensions of school success as we broadly define it. As with prior chapters, we look first to quantitative data aggregated to the district level. We find substantial variance between districts on factors related to and including teacher commitment. We then analyze qualitative data from interviews conducted with key personnel from the most "stuck" and "moving" districts to better understand and expand on those quantitative differences. Here schools seem to be a microcosm for what happens in their districts. How districts select principals and teachers, whether districts offer them continuous opportunities for learning, and whether task autonomy is delegated to schools and thereafter monitored are the keys to unlocking sustained teacher commitment and the capacity for schools' continuous renewal.

DISTRICT-LEVEL DIFFERENCES: A QUANTITATIVE ANALYSIS

Our analysis of quantitative data is straightforward. To maximize variability, we aggregated individual-level data ($n = 1,213$) to the district level and performed one-way analysis of variance on each scale related to, and including, teacher commitment. These results appear in Table 7.1.

The analysis produced two important findings. First, with each scale, statistically significant differences between districts exist. Second, district differences are fairly consistent across scales—two districts, Sunnyview and Richland, consistently score highest, and three districts, Jefferson, Eastside, and Hillcrest, tend to score lowest. In examining specific differences, multiple range tests reveal on each scale that the two moving districts differ significantly from the three stuck ones ($p < .05$).

These same findings are sustained at the school level. When samplewide z-scores on teacher commitment are compared between schools aggregated to the district level, moving districts share a disproportionately high percentage of moving schools (Sunnyview = 67%; Richland = 60%) and a disproportionately low percentage of stuck (Sunnyview = 17%; Richland = 0%). Conversely, stuck districts contain a disproportionately low share of moving schools (Jefferson = 9%; Eastside = 9%; Hillcrest = 0%) and a disproportionately high share of stuck schools (Jefferson = 45%; Eastside = 63%; Hillcrest = 57%).

Several background characteristics of districts, however, may indirectly mediate the effects of workplace conditions on teacher commitment and thus deserve considerable scrutiny here. These include the socioeconomic level of the student population served, per-pupil expenditures, district size, pupil–teacher ratio, the educational attainment of teachers within each district, their mean years of teaching experience, the mean status of their un-

TABLE 7.1. Analysis of Variance between Districts on Five Organizational Variables

		DISTRICT MEANS		
District*	Teacher commitment	Learning opportunities	Task autonomy	Psychic rewards
Sunnyview	36.46	24.03	23.94	20.81
Richland	35.64	23.01	23.73	20.48
Westend	34.55	22.89	23.46	19.33
Warner	34.52	21.67	22.35	19.47
Percy	34.53	21.81	22.39	19.15
Jefferson	34.98	20.17	23.68	18.90
Eastside	32.77	19.46	22.08	18.25
Hillcrest	32.08	19.11	22.02	17.75
F	4.70	7.63	10.26	10.56
Sig	.001	.001	.001	.001

*To ensure anonymity these names are fictitious.

dergraduate degree, the tenure and appointment terms of the superintendent, and the type of community the districts serve (LaRocque & Coleman 1987; Walberg & Fowler 1987). Although the small sample size precludes detailed multivariate analysis, Table 7.2 presents district means for each of these possibly confounding background variables.

Table 7.2 shows several fundamental differences between districts on several background variables. First, moving districts—Sunnyview and Richland—have the largest per-pupil expenditure, whereas the three stuck districts—Jefferson, Eastside, and Hillcrest—have the lowest. Second, moving districts tend to employ teachers with the highest educational attainment from the highest status universities, while superintendents of stuck districts employ those with the lowest educational attainment from the lowest status colleges. Also, school boards appoint superintendents in moving districts, while the public elects them in stuck districts. Third, Sunnyview and Richland are also the smallest districts in the sample—a consistent district correlate of student achievement (Walberg & Fowler 1987).

Finally, district SES, while varying considerably, shows no linear trend; moving districts were equally likely to serve low SES students as their stuck counterparts. Nor did teacher–pupil ratio, the status of teachers' undergraduate degree, or the type of community served show consistent linear patterns, although the three stuck districts are invariably rural.

DISTRICT-LEVEL DIFFERENCES:
A QUALITATIVE ANALYSIS

To examine district-level practices that might relate to analysis of variance results, in the second year of the study we interviewed each of the eight superintendents and at least one high-ranking member of each central office staff, most commonly, the assistant superintendent of elementary education. Responses were recorded by two research staff members, independent of the interviewer. Reliability checks between observers' notes revealed high consistency. To clarify responses and to forge greater understanding of quantitative results, follow-up phone interviews were also conducted with selected superintendents or their assistants at the end of the school year. Those were tape-recorded and transcribed for analysis.

We conducted the initial interviews immediately prior to our inservice for principals—the inducement originally offered superintendents to entice their participation in the study. Following these interviews, we shared and discussed with each superintendent (or in one case the assistant superintendent) graphed profiles for each of their elementary schools. Profiles encompassed those variables related to, and including, teachers' learning opportunities, their certainty, their psychic rewards, and their commitment. Each variable was standardized by z-scores computed on the basis of *district* means. With the exception of only one school, superintendents or their as-

TABLE 7.2. Mean District Demographic Characteristics, Superintendent and Teacher Qualities

District	Student SES*	Per-pupil expenditure	District size**	Pupil–teacher ratio	Teachers' educational attainment***	Years teaching experience	Superintendent tenure and appointment terms	Type of community
Sunnyview	.43	$2,800	5,200	20.31	1.51	17.27	16 years; Appointed	Rural/suburban
Richland	.28	1,900	3,200	25.79	1.71	13.16	3 years; Appointed	Urban/suburban
Westend	.25	1,800	29,600	24.42	1.31	13.05	9 years; Elected	Rural/suburban
Percy	.46	2,300	5,800	23.61	1.37	12.48	2 years; Appointed	Urban/suburban
Warner	.45	1,900	6,000	25.80	1.56	11.72	1 year; Appointed	Rural/suburban
Jefferson	.41	1,500	9,800	23.91	1.32	12.35	2 years; Elected	Rural
Eastside	.74	1,600	7,200	23.77	1.12	11.27	7 years; Elected	Rural
Hillcrest	.24	1,600	7,200	27.43	1.30	12.79	7 years; Elected	Rural

*Percentage of students receiving Aid to Families with Dependent Children.
**Includes all elementary, junior, and senior high school students.
***Measured by teachers' highest degree (1 = B.A., 2 = M.A., 3 = Ed.M., 4 = Ed.D.).

sistants whole-heartedly agreed that the profiles accurately reflected the status of outlier schools—both strong and weak—within their district.

Our search for parsimony in the qualitative analysis will be guided by two considerations: (1) those districts with distinctly different patterns of social organizational activity, and (2) those differences that yield the most bountiful harvest of policy implications. Hence we will concentrate upon interview data collected from the two moving districts—Sunnyview and Richland—and the three stuck ones—Hillcrest, Eastside, and Jefferson.

District Goals

In examining superintendents' cognitions and behaviors, we find it appropriate to ask whether those who administer districts are themselves models for how principals should treat their teachers, and teachers their students. We begin by asking whether superintendents clarify the locus for improvement—that is, what they want to see accomplished in each school—and convey this sense of direction and purpose to those involved. The literature on organizational change reminds us that in utilizing their resources, the most successful districts designate someone as the local facilitator—a member of the district staff who both organizes and advocates improvement and arranges technical assistance for schools. That is, change facilitators mobilize the commitment of teachers and principals, help schools set programmatic goals, monitor goal attainment, acquire necessary resources, arrange learning opportunities, and plan for ongoing change. Each of these functions will be discussed in this chapter. Presently, however, we focus on the linchpin driving organizational improvement—district goal-setting. Where superintendents articulate abstract and operational goals, change facilitators have clear rationales for action—what to monitor, evaluate, improve. To explore district goal-setting in stuck and moving districts, we asked superintendents and staff, "What are your current improvement goals for the district?" We expected that moving more than stuck superintendents would have their sights set on clear-minded goals.

Goal-setting in Moving Districts. Sunnyview's superintendent not only identified district goals, but also outlined the district's means for continuous organizational improvement:

> We have an ongoing goal of improving basic skills. We were into it long before the state ever got into it. We had devised a checklist of 700–800 items. We constantly update and monitor this checklist. We have been very successful in reading and math. I think our success has come because we have monitored ourselves so carefully. We try to do that kind of research, monitoring as we go along, trying to correct any weak areas. Every first and third Tuesday we hold regular staff meetings [with principals and district personnel]. First on the agenda is instructional matters. We do a great deal of brainstorming in those meetings, trying to solve instructional problems, trying to help mediocre princi-

pals, just generally trying to make things run smoother from this office. [Do principals suggest ways to improve the district?] They give suggestions about how we can better help them or their teachers. We decide a lot of district policies that way—always trying to get better at what we do.

Richland's superintendent literally illustrated many district goals even before our inquiry began. Taking control at the onset, he proudly presented a thickly bound survey of teacher attitudes toward several aspects of school and district functioning, including the instructional helpfulness of the principal, the physical maintenance of school, available teaching resources in both the school and district, teachers' learning opportunities, parental involvement in schools, school discipline, and so forth. This particular survey had been conducted the previous year, a practice begun in 1977 and repeated every three years. The superintendent leafed through the report, stopping periodically to show us graphs of teacher responses and discussing at some length what district actions were taken to solve the most immediate and meaningful problems to teachers. Data were plotted both by school and district, showing nearly identical results. It was evident that he *knew* the results of the survey like the back of his hand. When asked directly about district goals, Richland's superintendent replied: "To get better every year in helping teachers teach."

> Every year we [the district staff and building principal] do a needs and a wants assessment. Last time we did it, we took as many statements as we could find about the research on effective schools and effective teaching and said, "On a scale of one to five, What's our implementation of this?" We used the information to guide our inservice topics for principals. [During the school year] we meet every other week. We talk about needs assessment. Sometimes principals set the agenda. The problem-solving sessions are the best ones; sometimes they'll last two or three sessions. If we ask what principals think about something, we want to know. But when we make a decision, then we all need to go with that.

In both moving districts, superintendents involve principals in setting district goals or policy, in determining their school's technical needs, and in specific problem-solving, forging a shared reality about district and school-level practice. More than that, ties between schools and districts indicated strong mutual influence; it went both ways. Renewing, revising, and reconstituting goals over time required frequent task-focused interaction. And if it is true that reality is socially constructed through recurrent patterns of interaction, superintendents' reiterative calls for wholeness, harmony, and solidarity should have resulted in greater consensus among principals about district goals.

Of equal if not greater importance, moving superintendents establish through their goals that district policy relates integrally to teachers' practice and that there are also corresponding linkages between the behaviors of principals and teachers and student learning outcomes. There seems to be a certain rationality about each district. From here it is but a short leap to identify those negotiated beliefs as fundamental reality-definers for principals' certainty about instructional practice and goals within their schools.

Goal-setting in Stuck Districts. In stuck districts, by contrast, uncertainty about the technology of teaching and its capacity to bring about changes in student performance appear to be the adversary of rational planning and action. In this regard, Jefferson's and Hillcrest's superintendents revealed with remarkable candor that their abstract and operational goals of school improvement had little to do with any academic substance:

> [Jefferson:] My expertise is in physical plant, food services, some in curriculum. I inherited a lot of problems when I started as superintendent. It's been rough. Let me give you an example. We have 180 acres of grass, and we had 2 lawn mowers when I started. Today we have four mowers. We had the same number of mechanics and tire changers for the buses when I started as we did 30 years ago. Now we have four full-time mechanics and one body repair person and two tire changers. I've been in seven schools with maintenance crews. We painted gyms that hadn't been painted since 1953. When I came, our cafeteria served chicken with the blood running out of it. One day during lunch I went into the cafeteria and tasted the lima beans. They were so bad, I threw the plate on the floor in the middle of the cafeteria and all food service stopped. And it stayed stopped until the food was fit to eat. Now I require all school personnel to eat in the cafeteria. [Next the superintendent pulled out a photo, pointing to it with pride. The picture showed a long table of first-graders, eating off plates on trays and smiling at the camera.] Last year we had most children eating in classrooms with cockroaches and everything. Now *that's* one of the things I've been able to accomplish.

> [Hillcrest:] The key thing is the community. We're interested in keeping the schools up in appearance. What's important in getting confidence from the community is a good-looking facility. If you have a clean building, if the grass is cut, and if the halls are shiny, you're going to have a greater degree of tolerance from parents. If you want them to have confidence in you, you have to do those sort of things.

Hillcrest's and Jefferson's assistant superintendents confirmed their district leaders' lack of instructional emphasis:

> [Hillcrest:] If the superintendent has goals, he hasn't told me about them. He sits in his office. When he comes out, it's usually to do some kind of politicking—he's in an elected office, you know. He meets the same group of businessmen everyday for breakfast. *Nothing* happens in this district unless it is done by one of us in the central office. We do things on our own instincts. You know, you see a problem and you try to patch it up. There are so many problems in our school system that we seem to spend all our time struggling day-to-day with them. But the superintendent doesn't get involved. [Have you asked for his help?] Yes, but it's better just to do things ourselves and maybe tell him about it afterwards.

[Jefferson:] Before, we didn't need a central office. The principals had total control of everything. The maintenance department met every morning and said, "What y'all want to do today?" For example, at Central School there was a light bulb that was out. Seven men and three trucks went to see what size it was, came back here, had lunch, and the same 7 men and 3 trucks went to change the lightbulb that afternoon. It took the whole day. We have a new maintenance supervisor now. He is accountable. There is a strong sense of order now. Our food service is also on the way up.

Noticeable at once are distinct differences in the goals of moving and stuck districts. Moving superintendents apparently know that norms of continuous academic improvement across all levels of the district are essential preconditions for strengthening teachers' commitment and school quality. Stuck superintendents seem to understand instead that cosmetic improvements are necessary to counter unfavorable political trends that might threaten their survival in the district. That is, moving superintendents tend to direct their districts toward student learning, whereas the direction for stuck districts tends to emerge as random and disorderly, the product of political interests. In the ebb and flow of opportunities for short-term gains, stuck superintendents put their own interests in preserving leadership of the district ahead of the interests of any of its members (e.g., Perrow 1979). There was little in the elected superintendency itself to guarantee accountability or responsibility for schools' academic performance.

But to continue to maintain the value of their currency, elected superintendents cannot stray too far, lest popular support collapse and confidence evaporate. So it was that Eastside's superintendent boasted a five-year plan for the improvement of proficiency test scores in basic skills. Declining our invitation to outline specific steps or procedures taken, he nonetheless proudly proclaimed its success—in the past year alone, a 4% increase in math and a 2% increase in reading district-wide. We questioned his assistant superintendent about these results:

Teachers are teaching to the test now, rather than using their texts or other materials. We are asking principals to get all their teachers to do this. Our test scores were very low. The superintendent ran his campaign for election on the theme of raising students' test scores.

Covert practices such as these recommend themselves to superintendents of uncertain status, ever-wary of their precarious political position. They tend to harbor low regard for principals' and teachers' capabilities. Hence we find one possible source for the maladroit if not pernicious behavior of stuck principals, as they search for some solid ground from which to protect their self-esteem. Political pressure from the superintendent forced them to abandon their innocuous live-and-let-live etiquette as their schools became subject to more formal review and evaluation. The conspiracy of silence, as well as the conspiracy of tolerance, had been seriously breached by coercive accountability to the superintendent, and his in turn to his constituents.

Districtwide demands of "teaching to the test" also in part address stuck teachers' routine technical culture. Increasingly told what to teach, when to teach it, and how to evaluate, teachers may come to abandon their own pedagogical judgments about tending to the varied learning needs of students. That is, caught in the dilemma between *coverage* of basic skills and rudimentary *mastery* of them, most teachers will standardize instruction, assuring that only the most average students will grow academically (Darling-Hammond & Wise 1985; Rosenholtz 1987; Shannon 1986). And where students' opportunities to master a broader base of knowledge are undermined because teachers must divert their instructional emphasis to material that is tested, to material too difficult for some and too easy for others, and to material that they have had no hand in shaping, students' learning success and teachers' workplace commitment suffer dramatically (Rosenholtz 1987; Shannon 1986).

SCHOOL GOAL-SETTING
AND DISTRICT MONITORING

Recent case studies of school improvement as well as those of highly effective districts consistently recognize the centrality of district diagnosis, evaluation, and feedback to schools to achieve their goals (e.g., LaRocque & Coleman 1987; McLaughlin & Pfeifer 1988; Murphy & Hallinger 1986). We therefore asked superintendents and their assistants a series of questions to gauge district monitoring practices. The first few concerned the assessment of principals' performance: "How do you evaluate principals? How often do you evaluate them? What do you do with the evaluation?"

Performance Monitoring in Moving Districts

Richland's superintendent began his answer by outlining the practice of school goal-setting, a policy demanded ("Sometimes it takes a little pushing") and carefully monitored by the central office staff. The superintendent requires principals and teachers to collectively set school learning goals relevant to the students that they serve. Principals and their faculties also make policy decisions for their schools on wide-ranging issues, as explained by the assistant superintendent:

> He [the superintendent] gives people freedom, but all the responsibility that goes with it, too. When schools are given the freedom to determine their curriculum, their budgetary allocations, the kinds of [teacher] inservices they want and so forth, they have to follow through by showing improvement with students. [So principals are evaluated by the progress their schools make in meeting learning goals?] Yes. We do that through conferences and written evaluations. [How frequently do principals receive feedback about their progress?] Informally, it's on a regular basis, depending, of course, on the school. Weak

principals get more time and attention from our office than strong ones. Formally, they are all evaluated every year.

In both moving districts, superintendents demand accountability in the policies of schools and from those who make such policies. Although each seemed to have a finely tuned sense about how far to push, sometimes he or she had extracted accountability from unwilling and uncomfortable principals, as Sunnyview's superintendent hinted:

> Each principal must develop school goals for the year. We approve them on the basis of their needs and our district priorities. [Do you reject some principals' goals?] Only rarely. By now they're very good at identifying their needs. We have one principal ready for retirement who is resistant. We work with him, trying to steer him in the right direction. We evaluate principals on their ability to reach their goals. That way principals are realistic; they *have to* involve teachers because it's the only way that they're going to be able to reach their goals. I give them a lot of authority but I have very high expectations. Some can't manage it—setting their own goals and living by them. I tell them, "I can deal with some failure, but you have to succeed overall." The principals have authority to decide which books they want, how many books, inservice topics and speakers, things like that. Principals have total control of their budget. The principal can put all the money, if he chooses, into reading, for example, if he can justify it. It's decided between the faculty and the principal.

These proactive measures did not escape the attention of teachers. In their interviews they invoked, as if by incantation, their district's commitment to moving their schools in new directions. They seemed proud of their traditions, but they apparently do not rest on them. Their greatest tradition seems their commitment to shaping a better school:

> [From Richland:] We emphasize excellence a lot in this district. I think it's good. We've gotten a lot of parents involved; teachers expect more from all students and I think it's made a difference across the board here.

> [From Richland:] The state has minimum standards. We do *more* than the minimum in this system. They [students] learn more than the minimum in our classes. We're proud we promote excellence. We work hard, but we don't feel that anything is held over our heads. By striving toward excellence we can hopefully raise the public's point of view. We have always tried to be the best.

> [From Sunnyview:] In our school system, we have a very good monitoring program. We are all on top of what our children know. We do sequential ordering as to the things that are taught. It is passed on from grade to grade exactly what they [students] have been taught, what they have mastered and what they haven't mastered.

> [From Sunnyview:] I'm proud to be in this school system and I want to know what goes on in it. I think it's an excellent system. Our system expects teachers to be at the top. I don't know this for sure, but that seems to create very different attitudes among us towards our work. We take things very seriously.

I think your degree of [job] satisfaction depends on how hard you're willing to work at it.

Three points arise from this. First and foremost, we find joint goal-setting and decision-making between principals and teachers, and schools' task autonomy and control contextually embedded within a larger sphere of district-level practice. Second, just as superintendents interact with principals to define a collective reality, they typify their desire for principals to offer similar opportunities to teachers. Third, when progress is not forthcoming, rather than abandon poorly performing principals, district staff help them, tenacious in their call for betterment, tacitly acknowledging the possibility of positive change even for those most resistant. With district norms of continuous renewal explicitly manifested all about, principals may be mindful to persist in their own attempts to help less effective teachers improve.

Performance Monitoring in Stuck Districts

In monitoring school progress, stuck districts are the quintessence of loose-coupling. Holding few operational goals for student learning, superintendents seem to undervalue, or let go unappreciated, the direct linkage between principals' activities, teachers' efforts, and students' learning outcomes. School goals, academic or otherwise, are therefore commodities in short supply. Never had there been a performance evaluation of Jefferson principals as confirmed by both superintendent and assistant superintendent. The two remaining stuck districts evaluated principals helter-skelter, adding no particular luster to individual or collective school improvement:

> [Eastside:] At the end of the year I ask principals to tell me what they've accomplished and I ask them to write down their strong points and their weak points. Of course, it's hard to do the weak points. But I ask them to do it, and then we look at it and see what they can do better next year. [Do you then use the weak points to evaluate the principal the following year?] I don't do yearly evaluations. The evaluation process for principals is not as extensive as I'd like it to be.

> [Hillcrest:] I let teachers evaluate the principal anonymously. They give the principal a copy and I get a copy. We have questions like, "Is your principal fair in making decisions?" You know, things like that. In evaluating the principals based on these forms, I look for major areas of weakness. For example, if 3 teachers in school say that a principal is unfair, I'll ignore it. But if 30 teachers say the principal is unfair, then I say, "Hey! We've got a problem," If something like that happens, I will use that information to remove a principal.

Observe that stuck superintendents' apparently anesthetized stock-taking is typified in principals' problem-solving as seen in Chapter 3. Hillcrest's superintendent neglects to monitor school progress and makes no intervention attempts in schools with weak principals at the helm, but to the contrary makes transfer decisions before remedial attempts are even contemplated. Notice further that no goals for student learning are embedded in either districts' evaluation procedures. Evaluation not tied to specific improvement criteria symbolically sanctions divergent school goals, so pronounced and professionally isolating for teachers, as we saw in Chapters 2 and 3. These districts have grown so underground, so wayward in tradition as to renounce easily the most fundamental axiom of a district: the delivery of educative services to schools and students. Under these conditions, overall needs for school improvement are neither likely to be sought nor easily found.

In stuck districts, at least as articulated by Hillcrest's assistant superintendent, the school only superficially ministers to the community around it, and topsy-turvy change holds primacy over deliberated action:

> We don't do formal evaluations of principals. [Do principals get any feedback from the district about how well they are dong?] No. [Do you use any achievement test data to evaluate the progress of schools?] Not really. The Superintendent assumes everything is going along okay unless he gets a lot of complaints from teachers or parents. If there are enough complaints, he moves the principal to another school.

School Visits

As we have stressed, a workaday reality is made infinitely more stable where leaders' actions typify organizational policy. Thus with focused school visits, superintendents can help institutionalize district norms by symbolically communicating their importance to principals and teachers, as they also monitor school progress. In some cases, looking at schools may reveal collective weaknesses within the system as a whole that may facilitate institutional change. Accordingly, we asked superintendents and staff another set of monitoring questions: "How many visits do you make to elementary schools per year?" "What do you look for?"

School Visits in Moving Districts. In moving districts, both superintendents and their assistants reported frequent visits to schools for the explicit purpose of global monitoring:

> [Sunnyview:] I'm in schools every week. I have close communications with the principals. When I go to a school I will go to the principal's office and we'll chat for a while and then I'll go through the building. I won't disturb the teachers unless that's the purpose of my going to school. I'm there to get a feel for what is going on. I'm looking for an overall feeling that there's learning going on. I'm very concerned if I see anything that I think will infringe on the students' time-on-task. When I see something I like, I give a lot of praise.

> [Richland:] Either I'm in the schools or [the assistant superintendent] is at least once a week. [What sorts of things do you look for?] Is the principal in his

office or in classrooms? What is he doing? Are children wandering about the corridors? Are teachers keeping students on task? Is there a warmth in each classroom, or do students appear ill at ease? We're there to look in general at how things are going.

Teachers' instructional time seems inviolable to these superintendents. In addition, both reportedly rely on the observation and advice of their assistant superintendents for shifts in district focus or for concentrated improvement in individual schools. Richland's assistant superintendent, for example, explained his designation as the local change facilitator:

> I'm in the schools daily. I spend more of my time there than here [at the district office]. I'm there to look for ways I can be helpful. I look for problems I can be useful in solving. It's my job to be available. I attend meetings held by specific groups of teachers. For example, last week I went to a problem-solving session held by the kindergarten teachers in one school. [What was the problem?] They were trying to drum up greater parent support for their program.

School Visits in Stuck Districts. Superintendents from stuck districts, clearly lacking any consensus with principals about what should occur in their schools, find nothing meaningful to monitor and nothing meaningful to observe. Without rationales for particular action, the frequency, duration, and substance of their visits vary widely. Whereas the assistant superintendents of both Eastside and Hillcrest reported that their superintendent made only occasional visits to schools, superintendents boasted otherwise. Regardless, none of them appear to monitor school progress, help teachers or principals solve problems, or communicate high expectations for school improvement:

> [Eastside:] I visit schools about once a week and I get into each classroom once a year. [What do you look for?] I look for the appearance of the room, like the bulletin boards, and how well the kids are behaving. Sometimes I'll talk with a teacher or principal. [What do you talk about?] Nothing specific I can recall. [What does the appearance of the room and the bulletin boards tell you?] That there is some order in the classroom. A bulletin board tells me whether or not teachers are making things interesting for students.

> [Hillcrest:] I visit each school about once a month. I just talk with teachers and gab about stuff. I tell them to blame their problems on the state. I don't take any responsibility for it. I don't sit in many classrooms. I usually just listen to teachers' problems; I don't do anything, you understand. I just listen.

Jefferson's superintendent, as confirmed by his assistant, did frequent the schools. Such a visit in fact was occurring during our prescheduled time to interview him at the district office. In the room where we waited, a prominently displayed blackboard clocked in district personnel by name, location, and ETA (estimated time of arrival). The blackboard even specified lunch time and location. For all this superintendent's efforts at exacting accountability, however, we found little constructive thrust to his school visitations:

> I get into schools every day. Yesterday I was in nine classrooms. I can read a classroom. [What sorts of things do you look for?] The first thing I notice is the floor. The condition of the floor can tell you a lot. [What does it tell you?] If it's clean, students have respect for their school. If it's dirty, the children and teacher obviously don't care. I also look at the chalk tray. [What does the chalk tray tell you?] If there's dust in the chalk tray, the teacher is teaching. If not, there's no teaching going on.

The political survival of all superintendents depends largely on their ability to respond effectively to constituent complaints. The constituency for appointed superintendents, of course, is schools within the district and all those associated with them. For elected superintendents there is a still broader constituency. Not only must they satisfy those associated with schools, but also the entire community in which those schools reside. In this way elected superintendents were at a decided disadvantage over appointed ones. Whoever succeeded a fallen superintendent invariably ended up with the legacy of some unwanted baggage. They were burdened, too, with all the impossible expectations they had awakened during their candidacy, and enjoyed no transitional period and no advanced planning or training. In light of this, it is not unexpected that district goals reflected these different constituencies. In fact, it can be reasonably if not decisively argued that elected superintendents' sense of community pressure led them to persist in their authoritarian, bureaucratic behavior. To still the demands of their respective communities, elected superintendents unabashedly described their feint and parry for positive political exposure, and their continual attempts at hard populist appeal:

> [Jefferson:] The superintendent has to have good public relations. I try to be on TV at least twicet [sic] a week. Once I had a newspaper call me an ogret [Some discussion among us here, arriving at the word ogre]. Now we don't let the press get ahold of negative things.

> [Hillcrest:] I'm seen all the time. I'm always going to baseball games and things like that. I eat breakfast with the same group everyday. There's a place where we all gather to eat and talk. Everyone from politicians to judges to people like me.

> [Eastside:] I get to understand the community's feelings just by talking to people. I visit businesses, ball games, athletic events, school functions, PTA meetings, and the Booster's Club. And they'll tell me what they think.

Instead of deploying their not inconsiderable resources to improve local schools, superintendents transform themselves into impresarios of contemporary political theater; temporarily crowned kings who disguise themselves in costumes of wisdom and strength. Theirs is the kind of world in which networking takes precedence over district problems and acquiring the right contacts overrules the insolence of school failures. And perhaps because they leave undisturbed the elemental myths surrounding their schools, they tend not to insist on too close a look.

If political patronage becomes a job in itself, it is no doubt troubling to districts' boards of education. Unlike the case in most school systems where the board appoints the superintendent and thereby exacts some measure of control, the elected superintendent, while perhaps responsive to certain pressure groups, is accountable to none. With all the political infighting that this suggests, stuck superintendents invariably curse their combative relations with school boards. Superintendents at odds with their school boards may encounter countless daily obstacles that diminish their work capabilities, increase their uncertainty, and pose threats to their self-esteem. Lest readers doubt the depths of such divisiveness, the school board in Eastside reportedly squabbled for five months with the superintendent before deciding to grant his request for an assistant. Moving superintendents' rapport with their school boards was, to them, beyond dispute (e.g., from Sunnyview's superintendent: "I always get what I want with a 7–0 vote"). With conflict of such magnitude alien to them, the attendant evils of uncertainty tend to vaporize too.

Goal-setting Practices and Superintendent Learning

What may in part explain the lack of academic rigor in stuck districts, and integral to superintendents' elected status, is the absence of technical knowledge about the substance of their work. Two of the stuck superintendents catapulted to their present position directly from the rank of classroom teacher, while the third had former experience as an elementary school principal. None held more than a B.A. from a local low-status college. By contrast, both moving superintendents held Ed.D. degrees from high status universities, and each benefited in his present position from successful previous experience as a superintendent.

There is another compelling explanation for superintendents' varied task conceptions of their work. Whereas stuck superintendents reported no efforts to advance their own technical knowledge, both moving superintendents availed themselves of opportunities to learn on an ongoing basis. Moving superintendents anticipated change because of their improvement efforts; otherwise, schools would tend to become brittle and frail—something other than vital educative places. Such anticipation and eagerness to learn led them to higher places, to a desire to advance and challenge the intellect, not only for themselves but for their schools—again typifying organizational norms through their action.

For example, a prominent Tennessee university offered bimonthly, two-day seminars for superintendents across the southern states. Although Tennessee superintendents received invitations, only those from moving districts attended. Having served as a presenter to Peabody's Leadership Conference on two occasions, the author was in a unique position to verify its synergistic effects. The seminar helped superintendents to interpret their experiences in more positive ways, saving them from responding to each problematic situation as a personal assault:

> [Richland:] I regularly attend the Superintendent Leadership Conference at Peabody College. Superintendents fly in from all over the South, not just Tennessee. There's usually about 15 to 20 of us. They bring in speakers to talk about the latest research in some area we want to know about. We talk that over for a long time—what it means for us; how it can be used to improve our schools. Some of the new research on superintendents has helped me analyze what I do, how I react, and what I can do to further our goals. We also share some of the programs we've introduced, how they are going, and what could be done to improve them. We share techniques and problems with each other, and try to brainstorm solutions. It's a real shot in the arm for me.

In Sunnyview, the assistant superintendent, also an Ed.D. and tenured in the district for over 20 years, shared equal power and authority with his immediate superior. He, too, served as the local change facilitator. Working with him as a team, Sunnyview's superintendent went further to emphasize his professional growth through research:

> We attend national and regional meetings to pick up new ideas, new research findings. [The assistant superintendent] is quite a researcher in his own right and keeps up with the latest research. He keeps us all abreast of ways to improve what we do. He keeps us up-to-date on things—like classroom computers, for example. He attends courses to learn about these things. He conducts his own research, and encourages research by doctoral students and professors at [a nearby research-oriented university]. The findings are taken seriously here. We try to implement a lot of new strategies or initiate change on that basis. We also try to encourage principals to do research. We stress that quite a bit.

In district efforts at continuous improvement, superintendents' own learning cannot be overestimated. They, too, need colleagues to encourage and inspire them to seek new vistas. Learning seems to fulfill a longing for adventure, discovery, challenge—a rebirth of the spirit from the weariness brought on by the routines, problems, and decision-making of everyday life. Without these experiences, superintendents—if they try at all—will likely elevate their schools far more slowly, less sure-footedly, making unanticipatable slippages and strenuous remountings alone. Under these conditions, some will inevitably surrender to the arduous uphill climb.

In fact, it may well be that moving superintendents' means and goals reflect their newly acquired knowledge. With infusions of better strategies and practices, or with help in solving persistent district problems, the expectation and possibility that things can improve becomes a far more certain reality. This vitality and hope may be passed along to principals as superintendents teach by example, believing that history can be reversed, constructing an alternative world and bringing that world to life.

Meanwhile, stuck superintendents, wholly analogous to the isolated teacher, appear to make no attempt to weave new technical knowledge into the old, faltering heartland of their small rural schools. Instead they tend to rely wholly on their own observational acumen and their own managerial and personal resources to solve difficult and sometimes politically pressing problems to the satisfaction of their constituents. The dither and dally of their amateur political tactics does not go unresented by teachers.

> [From Jefferson:] I'm all for an unelected superintendent to come and take over and get rid of the politics here. The morale is bad, as far as being treated like a professional and being respected. If I had my way I would get rid of those people who sit for the newspapers and get their pictures taken and make silly little quotes.

PRINCIPAL SELECTION AND LEARNING OPPORTUNITIES

Principle Selection

While relatively little empirical research has been conducted on interorganizational relations in general, and on school systems in particular, there has been much speculation by organizational theorists. Two widely accepted characterizations are that (a) districts serve as a source of information for schools, and (b) districts stock critical school resources (see Scott 1981). Certainly one key resource that districts "stock" is principals—their qualifications, background, and training. We have seen in previous chapters that principals' task conceptions are visited on teachers in ways that affect the quality of and the sentiments toward their work. How districts select and train principals, then, seems pivotal to teachers' learning, their certainty, and their commitment—in essence, to continuous school improvement.

As with individual schools, districts' selection criteria for principals serve dual functions. At the symbolic level they represent the values and norms of the district. At the practical level selection criteria help principals decide their professional identity, that is, what they ought to become. We explored this area by asking superintendents and their staff, "How are elementary school principals selected in this district?" If moving districts are tightly coupled with schools, they should select principals whose foremost concern is student learning. On the contrary, if loose-coupling characterizes stuck districts, principal selection criteria should bear little relationship to schools' academic progress.

Moving Districts. As expected, the selection of elementary principals in moving districts tightly couples with district goals; superintendents and staff rely thematically on instructional leadership and all that it entails:

> [Sunnyview:] The tradition we have moved away from is the stern, coach-oriented principal. Now there's more emphasis on academic preparation. There's more stress on this in the interview; also part of the general application

is written. It involves applicants applying their knowledge to a variety of hypothetical situations. Some of them have to do with solving problems of instruction. There are five of us on the [selection] committee: myself, the assistant superintendent, a principal and two teachers. [Do you generally choose your principals from within or outside the system?] Other things being equal, we prefer to hire from within the system; someone who has already demonstrated excellent teaching and school leadership. In making these decisions, of course, we have to make certain assumptions that certain qualities are already there in the applicant. For example, they have to have the ability to lead; they have to have the ability to get along with other people. We're always hoping to see, and we do look for, the ability to do research. We look for someone who is able to envision and implement new programs and evaluate them. We have one principal who is researching latch-key children with the aim of implementing some after school programs. So far, we have 196 students in that school interested in some type of after-school program. I think what he has found is very intriguing. Now we're trying to interest the Board of Education in our ideas.

[Richland:] We have had a leadership development program for the past 12 years. They [principal candidates] have to be recommended by other teachers and principals in order to get into the program. [On what basis?] For their instructional leadership with other teachers and their teaching abilities. [So principals are selected from within the district?] Yes, always. We begin with the competencies they need. There are some competencies they have to be trained in and there are some they just have to have. [What kind of principal competencies do you train and which competencies are those that principal candidates must have?] Evaluating teachers is something they are trained in. Honesty and good human relations skills are something they just have to have. They have to have had some very successful teaching experience, too. They also must be able to establish good working relations with almost all of the faculty. If they can't do that well, we make it clear that we'll replace them rather than replace the faculty. We place each candidate with a successful principal for an apprenticeship to develop their competencies. We like to have about three more in training than we can place.

In selecting principals, moving districts hold several common points. First, superintendents make clear through their actions that above all else, principals must be continuous learners, and through their leadership, entice teachers to be learners, too. Second, moving districts hire from within the system. This allows control over preservice training, the assurance of prior instructional leadership among colleagues, teaching excellence in their former schools, and a steady pool of tested candidates to fill any new opening.

Stuck Districts. Hillcrest's prescription for selecting principals as the superintendent enumerated it included a litany of qualities not dissimilar to those of Richland's: leadership ability, communications skills, and intellectual ability. His assistant superintendent, however, in direct contrast, stressed the superintendent's long-held tradition of invariably choosing candidates who appear most compliant, and at the same time, most autocratic:

He looks for principals who will be able to control teachers and what they do in their classrooms. He wants to be able to issue an order and have it carried out in every teacher's classroom in the school system. We see things differently because of our roles. He mostly has to deal with PR and stuff like that. [Could you elaborate on that?] Well, he is an elected superintendent; he is anxious to please the public. So whenever he gets a complaint, he wants his solution to be carried out down to every last classroom.

Autocratic and at once compliant behavior seemed to be the primary selection criterion for Jefferson's principals as well. Unruffled by trouble, undeterred by the legacy of former policies, this relatively new superintendent appeared to aim at instant, slapdash reform:

[Jefferson:] I haven't hired any principals yet. But I just got through moving all 27 principals and assistant principals. [Why?] Well, some were in the same slots for years. They went to school here, grew up here, taught in these schools, and are now principals there. They feel like they own the school. We can't have that. If they own the school they'll do what *they* want instead of what *I* want. Some have been in the schools so long they get to be friends with some of the teachers and *then they can't tell them what to do*. When you work with 35 females a day, some things go on. You don't see these things unless you go out after dark. I stay out after dark and I know what's going on. [Do you feel that all your principals perform poorly?] I have some good principals and good schools. But when you say, "This is *my* school," when a principal feels he *owns* a school, that's it.

After so many years of laissez-faire leadership, Jefferson's new superintendent felt free to write querulous memoranda, free to strut and bluster, free to meddle in everybody's business, free to indulge his apparent passion for rules, free to foreclose on any investment, continuity, and pride in one's school. That made decrements in teachers' workplace commitment something of an inevitability. Clearly those hardest hit by the coming metamorphosis were teachers from moving schools. But those from stuck schools also felt it too—that the end result would be only calamitous:

[From a moving school:] I guess you've heard that the superintendent intends to switch around all principals in our district next year. Our principal doesn't want to move to another school. He has pride in our school. Last year we got an award for being one of the top 100 schools in the nation. He [the principal] brought us up. But the district office will have their way. Our morale is very low.

[From a stuck school:] I think that the upheaval within the district of all these principals is a ridiculous thing. We [teachers] wonder what's going to happen next. We just don't get involved. The best thing you can do is just do your job and then go home.

This superintendent had just blown up with an earth-shattering blast the first teacher's once fervent commitment to the workplace; the second teacher seems simply to slide a little deeper into oblivion. This superintendent was the proverbial fighter, winning the battle of wills but overall losing the war.

Eastside's superintendent pursued additional and equally noxious criteria in his selection of principals:

> I look for their qualifications. Whether they're certified. I think experience as a teacher is very important. I check their standing in the community; I talk with people I know and they usually tell you what they think. I look for other things, too, like their appearance. It's my concern—how they look. You can tell a lot about their self-confidence by how they carry themselves. That small little guy that was in your presentation is an assistant principal. I'll be hiring two new principals for next year and he wants one of the jobs. I just can't give it to a whimpy-looking guy like that.

We asked the assistant superintendent why his superior placed primacy on personal appearance over other criteria:

> The superintendent only picks principals who he thinks will fit into the community's standards. He has to protect his job because he's elected. [He mentioned that the way a person looked was important in his selection of principals. Can you explain that?] If principals fit in with what the people think a principal should look like, there will be fewer problems for the superintendent. He wants strong principals that can keep a lid on things and have teachers do things he thinks should be done.

Here we find a superintendent anticipating ill-will among constituents and thus relying on mere cosmetic change that barely scratches the surface of the district's performance-based needs. Under these restraints it is easy to grasp the inadequacy of principals' technical and managerial preparation—preparation that may ultimately cost teachers' commitment to the workplace.

All three stuck superintendents punitively seek principals who will go quietly into the autocratic night but still deliver district policy to teachers with the tough-minded action of a John Wayne character. Such selection procedures give superintendents a greater span of control, and power to get things done. If they can control personnel, they may have the means to impose their own definition of schools, however ill-conceived, as they wish to see them shaped, to apply unilateral solutions to schools' nonroutine problems (Perrow 1979). Even if intending to restore school order, stuck superintendents, by expropriating schools' technical culture and their task autonomy, actually accelerate their demise. In brief, these superintendents have painted themselves—and their successors—into a corner from which there is no obvious escape. By contrast, it seems apparent to moving superintendents that the way local schools respond to district initiatives can be a source of new ideas rather than a threat to their technical knowledge, authority, and control.

Principals' Learning Opportunities

Teachers' learning opportunities, recall, grow with the hearty encouragement and substantive aid of their principals. The rendering of appropriate technical assistance, however, is not the result of serendipity; principals also need opportunities to refine and expand their pedagogical repertoires, opportunities for critical inquiry, rigorous discourse and analysis. And if superintendents keep themselves open to and abreast of new knowledge, there are implicit districtwide expectations that principals will do so, too. That is, just as principals of moving schools nourish teachers' learning opportunities in keeping with their operational goals, we anticipated that moving districts would also supply these same opportunities to principals, enabling them to render meaningful help. To explore this assumption we asked superintendents and staff, "How are principals made aware of new teaching practices?"

Principal Learning in Moving Districts. We found in fact that both moving districts rendered principals the chance to extend their instructional repertoires through extensive district inservice, with topics selected according to principals' own needs.

> [Richland:] Principals need to know a little more than the teachers, like the best techniques and trends. The principal needs to push a little, not be content with staying at the status quo. We have a principals' retreat for a week before school begins. We get away. We have a topic and we have a consultant. For example, each of our principals has gone through the Madeline Hunter Training Program. We set the agenda by some of the goals or concerns mentioned by principals.

> [Sunnyview:] We have two experts on our staff. One is on staff development, the other on evaluation. They're always in the schools. Principals learn that way. And on alternate Tuesdays, we will bring in someone to do an inservice for the principals. [How are the topics determined?] Mutually, by input from principals about what they'd like to know, and by our own assessment of where we should be headed, what our needs are.

Principal Learning in Stuck Districts. In answer to this question, and again typifying the absence of instructional goals and means, all three stuck superintendents made it perfectly clear that the responsibility for learning new instructional practice fell wholly on principals themselves:

> [Hillcrest:] Good principals go back [to school] to learn a lot of things for themselves. I have one, for instance, who's gone back to learn about computers and about basic skills programs. [What do you do if a principal is experiencing difficulty in his school?] I have one principal who is a very, very poor communicator. He is also well-educated. That turns teachers off, period. I told him months ago, "You are your own worst enemy. A lot of times you aggravate

people when you don't keep your mouth shut.'' I moved that principal from an elementary school to a high school five years ago. I'm not sure what difference this has made.

[Eastside:] Good principals learn new things on their own. They should be creative. They should take classes to keep up. I have one in particular who's always taking classes to learn the latest things. He introduces them to his teachers. [What do you do if a principal is experiencing difficulty in his school?] The worst principal I have has no rapport with the public. He makes decisions completely on his own and then he calls me. And then he calls parents and tells them that I made the decision. The parents lose respect for him. [Have you tried to correct these problems?] It wouldn't be worth the time. He's retiring in a few years, and I won't have to put up with him anymore. But I have about four or five more that are just like him.

[Jefferson:] You should stay on top of new things [to be a good principal]. My best principal does. But it's not a requirement for them if that's what you mean. [What do you do if a principal is experiencing difficulty in his school?] I move them or fire them.

The contrast between stuck and moving districts, nowhere more apparent than here, underscores how principals become helpful instructional advisors or maladroit managers of their schools. It is also clear that stuck superintendents attribute poor performance to principals themselves, rather than accepting any responsibility to help them learn and improve. This again may indicate their lack of technical knowledge and subsequent threats to their self-esteem. If districts take no responsibility for the inservice needs of principals, of course, principals become less able colleagues, less effective problem-solvers, more reluctant to refer school problems to the central office for outside assistance, more threatened by their lack of technical knowledge, and, most essential, of substantially less help to teachers. Of equal importance, with little helpful assistance, stuck superintendents symbolically communicate the norm of self-reliance and subsequently professional isolation—that improvement may not be possible, or worthy of their time and effort, or that principals should solve their school problems by themselves—lugubrious lessons principals may unwittingly hand down to poorly performing teachers, and thus teachers to students, as we saw in Chapters 4 and 5. In these data, then, we locate possible antecedents to principals' and teachers' uncertainty, their lack of learning opportunities and psychic rewards, and consequently uncover the reason for the defensive tactics they employ to protect their self-esteem.

TEACHER SELECTION AND LEARNING

Teacher Selection

At the heart of the educational system, and what may ultimately determine its success, is the quality of instruction by its teachers. The criteria used to select teachers, we have seen, holds dramatic consequences for the academic success of the school. To explore whether districts' selection of teachers corresponds in any way to school procedures and to their varying commitment, we asked superintendents and staff, "How are teachers selected in this district?"

Teacher Selection in Moving Districts. In Richland, where teachers possess a high degree of task autonomy and commitment, they also participate in selecting both faculty and principals. The superintendent explained the procedures, for instance, in selecting new teachers:

> They have a lot of freedom. We have a committee to do the screening. It's chaired by the Assistant Superintendent, and four others are on the committee; a principal, and three elementary teachers—both primary and middle. The applicants are screened by committee and lumped into categories. When a vacancy occurs, the Assistant Superintendent sits down with the principal and the list and the principal selects from that list. They [the principals] can get pretty much whom they want. I guess you could say we discriminate against teachers from the local state university. [How do you characterize your best teachers?] They are concerned with one thing: helping students learn in a positive, supportive way. That's what this district is all about. Excellence. We're good and getting better. We stand for those two mottoes.

Sunnyview follows parallel procedures:

> We have 300 to 400 applicants for seven or eight positions. For the most part, we give a few applicants teacher aide or teacher substitute positions. After principals have had a chance to observe those people for a year or two, we might end up offering them jobs. It's sort of an apprenticeship. Only rarely will we take someone on as a teacher from somewhere else where we have not had the opportunity to observe her in action. I want to point out that we do think it is good to bring in someone new, not local. We need people with new ideas, people who come from other places where they do things differently. [Are principals involved in the selection process?] Yes. I'll send the top three or so applicants to the principals to be interviewed. In most schools, principals have a committee of teachers to help. They select the one they want. [How do you characterize your best teachers?] If I can find a teacher who is actually concerned with achievement results, I know I've got a good teacher. You've *got* to think in terms of results. [Are a large percentage of your teachers results-oriented?] Yes. Because that's what we're talking about all the time!

Geographically, Richland and Sunnyview are each situated near small colleges of low academic status. They therefore deliberately recruit from higher status universities elsewhere for their applicant pool, like professional talent scouts scouring collegiate teams in anticipation of their draft. The quest for better qualified applicants, as we saw in Chapters 4, 5, and 6, has paid off handsomely in students' mastery of basic skills, urging districts to pursue this policy, perhaps even more so as the sun of success continues to shine on them.

Teacher Selection in Stuck Districts. Hillcrest's superintendent followed an altogether different procedure. Instead of involving principals and teachers, he himself hand-picked each new entrant. The applicant pool was entirely local:

> Principals don't have to accept them [new teachers], but they can't handpick the teachers that they want. I don't have a personnel director. I don't want one. *I* do all the employing here. I always hire teachers locally. I don't want to train someone and then send them on to someplace else.

When asked, Hillcrest's superintendent judged the quality of both principals and teachers by their ability to "carry out orders from this office." He, like Jefferson's superintendent, grows particularly petulant with teachers' ownership of school endeavors, and like Jefferson's, sees such possessiveness as grounds for their transfer. The picture conjured is that of an endless conveyor belt pouring teachers into schools, like dreary canning plants for California tomatoes. Yet stuck superintendents encounter no perceptible challenges by oppressed teachers struggling for greater freedom. As we saw in Chapter 6, there is reason for their reticence; stuck teachers have already capitulated to their powerlessness and the futility of any organized resistance.

In the culture of the stuck district, superintendents reject both the school that is unable to reform and the principal and teachers who were unwilling to conform:

> [Hillcrest:] As a principal, I moved my teachers every two years. I didn't like the way some of them started to get so possessive about things. They didn't follow my directives. I would go up to them and say, "What do you think you're doing? That's not *your* room. That's the *school system's* room." I don't believe that teachers should be so possessive about what they do. That's not the way it ought to be. And I tell principals to tell teachers that. If I had my way, teachers and principals would change schools every five years.

> [Jefferson:] When I select teachers, I interview every one. The number one thing I look for in a teacher is maturity. If I have a choice between a person 30 years and one younger, I'll go after the older. In case after case, it works better. Grades aren't that important. Someone with lots of "C's" can be a great teacher, and an "A" teacher can be not so good. [Where do your applicants come from?] Mostly from [the local college]. They know the students they'll be dealing with because they were students here too.

> [Eastside:] When we interview teachers, we [the assistant superintendent and superintendent] usually agree and the board goes along too. If they like a teacher and I don't, the board makes the decision. We actually have no hiring policy in the County. The board can put anyone in a school to teach that they want to. Most of our teachers come from [the local college]. Everyone here knows everyone, and everyone tries to play politics in getting teachers hired.

These examples of selection bias allow us to sort out a number of observations. First, in moving districts, teacher selection tends to follow directly from their goals of student learning, whereas stuck districts, apart from omnipresent nepotism, appear to have less coherent rationales or objective criteria from which to act. Second, stuck districts appeal to locals for their applicant pool, locals who, we might add, tend to graduate from nearby low status colleges, while moving districts look elsewhere for those with evidence of superior wisdom or training. This point corresponds particularly well with earlier school-level data and affords a district-level explanation for selecting and retaining the most academically talented teachers (e.g., Wise et al. 1987). Finally, we see further in districts' selection practices how teachers may come to acquire or be denied autonomy and discretion in their schools.

To summarize, in stuck districts, the most competent and skilled principals and teachers probably lack the social characteristics (e.g., docility) superintendents seek. And by covert discrimination against bright, independent, energetic personnel, the superintendent keeps control of the district, for ends principals and teachers eventually come to accept because they have few alternatives to consider. The problem here, of course, is that there is little if any relationship between the social criteria stuck districts employ and our broad measures of school success, a void that carries immense and probably insuperable difficulties for the practice of teaching.

Teachers' Learning Opportunities

Of all the information districts supply, perhaps the most essential is teachers' learning opportunities. We have already glimpsed into some of the ways moving districts select and prepare principals to offer sage advice and warm counsel to teachers. The task of helping inservice teachers learn devolves from districts through other means as well. We probed this area by asking superintendents and staff, "How are teachers made aware of new teaching practices?"

Teacher Learning in Moving Districts. In Sunnyview and Richland, individual schools determine their own inservice needs and how their fiscal resources should accordingly be spent. Selecting their own classroom resources gives teachers a forum in which to share their ideas, and opportunities to critically hone their craft as they scrutinize different techniques and materials. For example, in Richland, a committee of teacher representatives—popularly elected by school colleagues—study and recommend text selections for the district. Bringing together teachers from different schools invites broader views of instructional practice, and with them the possibility of infusing new knowledge into each school via teacher leaders. At the conclusion of their work, the committee recommends several texts within each subject area. With the adoption phase completed, each school then decides which texts to use—yet another opportunity for technical decision-making and collaborative consultation. Above all, empowering teachers in this way may ease the threat to their self-esteem during this fervent period of public unrest about their competence.

Both districts also house teacher resource centers of voluminous proportions, equipped not only with various materials, programs, and techniques, but also a full-time teacher who offers guidance in their use. District records revealed wide use of these resource centers, especially by teachers from moving schools. For those who put forth the effort, then, collegial advice and assistance sought through resource centers constitutes another opportunity for teacher learning.

Of greater importance to teacher learning, recall from Chapter 4, is the ongoing support, monitoring, and substantive help from principals. Accordingly, in Richland, teachers' individual improvement goals pivoted on principal evaluation following a clinical supervision model, as the assistant superintendent explained:

> As a principal does an evaluation on teachers, they agree on the needs for improvement and develop a plan for implementing the improvement. We tailor inservice options to meet those needs. For example, sometimes the principal or teacher requests additional assistance from specialists in the central office. They are always available to work with particular teachers in their classrooms.

To this Richland's superintendent added,

> First we have to have an evaluation. If a teacher has a weakness in an area, we accept responsibility for some kind of help for her. After the program is completed, we evaluate. If she doesn't come through, we continue with more help.

Sunnyview several years previously had trained all principals in Madeline Hunter's Model, which, when combined with clinical supervision, formed the basis for their teacher evaluation process in reading and math. Teachers' response, according to both superintendent and assistant superintendent, was overwhelmingly positive:

> [From the superintendent:] We have very good responses from our teachers for the programs we've initiated. I think teachers are interested in knowing something that's good, something that will help them improve the school. The results we see there [in learning about new programs] are mainly due to our curriculum people. When individual schools want to improve something, they often go to the curriculum folks for advice. If our teachers and principals see something going on somewhere else, they get a speaker to come talk to their whole faculty. [Where do they pick up new ideas?] At different conferences, mostly. Also, [the local university] has a number of small meetings organized for us. Everyone, including myself, is expected to attend.

In Sunnyview as in Richland, principals formally evaluate teachers annually. And as in Richland, the results of those evaluations form the basis of future goals for teacher improvement:

> [From the assistant superintendent:] We monitor the principals' evaluations closely. We want to know what principals are doing to help mediocre or poor teachers improve. Where is the help coming from? How closely is that teacher monitored in terms of change? We have a small, cohesive system here. If the teachers don't get adequate instructional leadership from someone in their own school, then the central office gives help. [How does the central office help?] We send people to observe the teacher, to talk with her about her goals and techniques, to make suggestions. We might also send her to see some especially excellent teacher somewhere else in the district. We draw up a plan for improvement with the principal and teacher involved. Then the teacher is re-evaluated periodically. We take care with teachers to help them improve—they want to improve—I think we have one of the best school systems in the state.

Implicit in both Richland and Sunnyview's policy are norms of continuous renewal and the expectation that ineffective teachers can improve once principals identify their needs—a sort of pedagogical triage—provide sufficient learning resources, and take their assessments anew. Further, as we saw in the inservice of principals, district-level policies appear to convey an explicit understanding of the symbiotic relationship between evaluation of teachers, goals for their improvement, and continuous monitoring of those goals. In moving districts, then, principals may be well advised to share their technical bounty with less fortunate teachers and wield the power of their expertise with humanity and discretion.

In reality, however, most districts provide only limited opportunity for teacher learning. For one thing, the average inservice teacher receives fewer than three days of staff development, and little of that training deals with instructional problem-solving (Joyce, Bush, & McKibbin 1981). For another, the most common types of inservice training consist of one-time "pullout" programs designed by district office administrators that have little if any immediate or sustained effect on teachers' instructional improvement (e.g., Little 1984; Walberg & Genova 1982).

Moving districts intentionally decentralize learning opportunities; teachers diagnose their own learning needs and design school inservice programs to directly address those needs. Teachers, then, receive personalized rather than standardized help. Assistance is therefore useful enough for teachers to avail themselves of relevant opportunities for professional growth and challenge. And because districts grant individual faculties the autonomy and discretion to shape their own learning, teachers more likely discuss new techniques, strategies, and ideas, and collaborate about their implementation. In this way they may enlarge their pedagogical repertoires and decrease the likelihood of routine classroom instruction. Furthermore, moving districts' progressive agenda to individualize teacher learning spoke implicitly to the nonroutine treatment of students.

Teacher Learning in Stuck Districts. In each stuck district, central office personnel rather than schools decide budgetary allocations, curriculum and textbook selection, and inservice content. None runs a fully operational resource center for teachers; nor do their curriculum or staff development specialists render on-site assistance to teachers and principals. The superintendents instead relegated their work to the central office.

Opportunities for learning in stuck districts put teachers up there with Oliver Twist, one of the great undernourished characters of English literature. Consisting entirely of the five state-mandated "pullout" days, inservices are delivered routinely. Teachers meet across schools by grade level to "discuss instruction." Sometimes exemplary teachers singled out by districts lead others at their grade level in discussion. Occasionally, districts hire one-shot outside speakers to address an assembly of the entire elementary school faculty. Jefferson's assistant superintendent comments first on some of these practices, followed next by Eastside's:

> Last year's inservice was a farce. We had an inservice planned for teachers and principals. There were no leaders [chosen from district schools] for some of the groups. [What happened?] They just didn't show up.

> We don't do much to keep teachers up-to-date. They mostly have to pick it up themselves. Of course, the better teachers are more in tune with the latest things than others. We sometimes ask those people to conduct inservices on special topics. [Do you think those inservices are successful?] I really don't know. We don't do any follow-up. [Do you monitor attendance?] No, not really.

The evaluation of teachers in all stuck districts is an act performed exclusively at the discretionary pleasure of the principal. This offers one account for stuck teachers' impertinence about their conclusions, recalling Chapter 4. From the assistant superintendent of Hillcrest, we have:

> We don't have good guidelines for principals to follow evaluating teachers. The form is only a page long. Principals are expected to evaluate untenured teachers every year, and tenured teachers are supposed to be evaluated every 4 years. But really, we know that doesn't happen in many schools. For example, the principal we have at Washington School has been there for 32 years. That's entirely too long. It's gotten to the point where the principal just does a factory job. He needs an assistant or something.

What is remarkable here, as elsewhere in this chapter, is that rather than setting clear performance expectations for principals and a basis for assessing them, rather than creating corresponding feedback mechanisms that apprised principals about their performance (and perceptions of their performance by others), rather than sponsoring remedial assistance where needed, stuck districts do little but transfer them to another school. Stuck superintendents even mentally shield themselves from demoting or retiring those principals who are clear impediments to their school's instructional and behavioral processes. This only exacerbates the problems and the paucity of solutions we have seen in stuck schools. Stuck principals in stuck districts are, it seems, patently cut adrift, entirely on their own.

Indeed, even in principals' meetings with district personnel, the agenda, according to all three assistant superintendents, seems of a mind-numbing caliber. No discussion of any clarifying rigor—be it technical or manage-rial—can take place in a context where fervent conviction (outside of the superintendent's) is frowned upon. The assistant superintendent's fre-quently voiced desire to follow through a sequence of ideas had to give way most of the time to the impressionistic, breezy flitting of the superintendent from announcement to announcement. Talk was not penetrating. Illumina-tion might only slow the routine flow. It is not surprising, then, that stuck districts provided no training of principals in evaluation techniques or strat-egies to help teachers learn.

Given all of this, Hillcrest's assistant superintendent assessed the conse-quences of too few district-sponsored learning opportunities for teachers:

> Some teachers experience a high degree of frustration. For example, a teacher recently called me up and asked me to come out and tell her what her principal's evaluation meant. She said the principal wouldn't do that [explain the mean-ing]. A lot of the teachers feel like there's no one to support them, to listen to them, or even to see them. So they feel like they have no control. It's sad. Some teachers want to be movers, shakers, or doers. But they lack the knowledge or the know-how to do it.

Here we can foresee the atrophy of new teachers, the dampening of the fire of commitment. So seemingly unprepared for what they saw politically, and so clearly lacking viable strategies for dealing with it, they tend to slide quickly and tragically into modes of reaction that are self-destructive and self-defeating—to say nothing of their loss of classroom effectiveness. And as their professional lives withered or ultimately ended, how is it possible to be fully aware of this and not lose respect for those responsible or com-plicitous? Lacking any framework into which they could place the punitive treatment they receive at the hands of districts and principals, they seem to embody in their own classrooms, ironically and yet unavoidably, precisely the same punitive values they initially abhor. As they discover the moral void at the heart of stuck schools they are shocked, astonished, trans-formed; but they tend to have nowhere to go with their vision of the void but straight into it, and in most of them go, losing themselves in what they initially feared and opposed.

The brisk pedagogical wind that tends to urge them upward at the be-ginning of their careers seems to have dropped, stilled by the implacable silence of their learning-impoverished districts, leaving them to drift each year into deeper, more stagnant waters.

To illustrate, when discussing his school visitations, Hillcrest's superin-tendent made perfectly clear that his interest lay neither in monitoring school progress nor in helping teachers solve technical problems:

> I'll be honest with y'all. I taught between 1964 and 1967. That's it. How am *I* going to tell a first grade teacher how to teach? I always tell teachers, "If you're employed, it will be for one thing and one thing only. That is to stay in the classroom and teach those children. If you have the ability to graduate from

college, you have the ability to teach. Now *that* depends on how hard you want to work.''

This superintendent's consciousness that teaching success depended primarily on teachers' own efforts again denies any district responsibility for their learning. When confronted with ineffective tenured teachers, therefore, the superintendent or district staff took no remedial action. To the contrary, those teachers, like the ineffective principal, were merely transferred to another school:

> There comes a time when you have to transfer a poor teacher and no principal wants the teacher. In those cases, I give the most undesirable teachers to the stronger principals. At that point, I just have to do it. That doesn't make me real popular. But I tell the principal, "If you do have a problem with this teacher, tell me and I'll have her moved after one year." It's gotten to the point on occasion where I have said, "I'm giving you this teacher, period. Now who do you want me to take out?"

In this policy it is plain to see how transfer teachers become social isolates in new schools, the objects of gossip but no help. Their past reputations may hound them, like a patient suffering recurrent bouts of a tropical disease. Strife-ridden probationary teachers likewise apparently receive no district-sponsored remedial help. Instead Hillcrest's superintendent gave them "the opportunity to save face" before firing them:

> I'll give her the opportunity to resign before I say that I won't reelect [rehire] her. I say, "Oh, it's really better for you. Think about it." I give them the opportunity because I would want them to give *me* the opportunity.

In a like manner, Eastside's superintendent revealed no consciousness of, or responsibility for, teacher learning:

> I don't really know. You know we're close to [a local college], and I think, most teachers stay pretty abreast of things. [What do you do when teachers don't seem to be doing a good job?] Teachers are evaluated by principals. And the [district] supervisor goes in three times every five years. Now we're getting into the State model. But to really use that plan, the teachers have to be completely evaluated every four years and *I don't think principals can stand that.* I'll probably have the principals talk with the teachers and if there's anything that needs correcting, they'll have until Christmas to get it straightened out and then if they don't and it's still a problem in March, they won't be rehired. [That's for probationary teachers, right? What about tenured teachers?] If it's a tenured teacher, then we're in trouble; there isn't much you can do about it.

That ineffective teachers cannot be helped to improve strikes a familiar reiterative cord and may account for the absence of meaningful principal and teacher inservice, the absence of district monitoring of school goals and teacher improvement, and, from Chapter 4, principal and teacher attitudes toward poorly performing colleagues.

We didn't ask Jefferson's superintendent about remedial practices for poorly performing teachers. There was no need to. Early in the interview he proudly announced that he had been the first superintendent ever in his district to issue formal reprimands to teachers. At this point he passed the interviewer a copy of a letter addressed to a tenured teacher, a fierce and unrelentingly hostile attack for her inadequate supervision of students, with the conclusion that this constituted grounds for dismissal.

Jefferson's superintendent was on the attack, like a field marshall probing for a weakness in the enemy lines, looking for a way in:

> I look for things, I hunt for things. When I see something bad, I do something. Transfers. Reprimands. It would have been so easy to get rid of incompetent teachers. Principals don't really have the guts to face the Board, NEA, to get rid of incompetent teachers. I don't think that they [the teachers] can be helped. Every time you reprimand one, you have NEA and the Tennessee School Board Association on your back. Reprimands are needed. If you grew up in X community and went to X school, and you come back and teach in X school, after 20 years you own X school. If a teacher owns her school, I see to it that she's transferred. For example, I was in one school, and the teacher told me she had raised some money to buy a new piano. And after that she told me what I should order. My face got red. I left, and she followed me, talking. I turned around and said to her, "What are you doing?" and she said, "Talking to you." And I said, "Go back to your classroom." I left. I felt angry. I returned to this school. She [the teacher] was out of the room. But she knew the big dog was there. She came in real quick and put on a record and began singing to the kids. Anyone could do it. I asked her for her lesson plan. She didn't have one. I reprimanded her right there to the point that if it ever happens again, she'll be before the board. I'll bet she's got lesson plans now.

As Jefferson's superintendent consumes himself with the dizzying swiftness of change—using a blunt hatchet rather than a delicate scalpel—teachers receive a painful impression of their present leader. There is a sense of the surface of things being stripped away, of the underside of their organizational lives lying exposed to view. Teachers themselves reflect the panic they feel in the face of their newly defined reality—their dramatic loss of psychic rewards:

> [From a stuck school:] The district has completely ruined teachers' morale in this county. It's definitely the politics of the county. School board people and the superintendent are elected who have no understanding of what it means to teach. Many of them have only a high school education themselves. Sometimes they come into the school to observe teachers and they don't have the vaguest idea about what they're seeing. They can't talk intelligently about what goes on in classrooms, and yet they make decisions all the time about what we should be doing. You get so depressed thinking about what they're *not* doing to help teachers that after a while it starts to affect your teaching. I've stopped reading the newspaper about the district and their decisions anymore because it is so *demoralizing* I just don't want to teach. You just have to close your eyes to that part, and hope that you can ignore the district and do in your classroom what you think is best.

[From a moving school:] Morale has really dropped around here. I can't say that there's been enough pressure put on my teaching to make me want to quit. This is probably because our principal really stands behind us. But this has been a trying time because of our new superintendent. We never know what's expected of us. He is very sarcastic and unpredictable. Expectations are never clear. You get the feeling that he's out to get you, but you never know when your time will be. The superintendent says he's "straightening out bad stuff" that's going on—tightening up the reins. [How has this affected your teaching?] Well, I like to do what I think is good for my students. Now it's a lot harder to do that here. [Could you give me an example?] Now we have to have field trips approved directly by the superintendent. You never know what will happen— it may or may not be approved. For example, I would like to take my students to the planetarium. Actually seeing the planets will give them a lot better idea of how the solar system works and will be a lot more meaningful for them. Similar trips have been rejected by the superintendent. I'm just afraid this one will be.

In opportunities for teacher learning, then, we confront another profound contrast between stuck and moving districts. In Sunnyview and Richland, superintendents' perceptions that teachers can improve if only provided with the proper resources to do so leads to actions that mobilize those critical district resources—to take courage out of adversity. In Hillcrest, Eastside, and Jefferson, superintendents' perceptions that improvement depends entirely on teachers' personal initiative leads them to abandon ship at the first bit of stormy weather. Again these varied task conceptions run parallel to principal behavior in stuck and moving schools and to analysis of variance results.

Dissemination of Our Findings to Districts and Principals

We received the most illuminating data contrasting stuck and moving districts through our own experiences in delivering principal inservices and in disseminating school-level findings to superintendents. The superintendent or assistant superintendent coordinated and both attended the principal inservice in each moving district. Sweet cinnamon rolls—the kind that stick to the tips of your fingers—were delivered piping hot from the high school cafeteria. Coffee was available. There was a feeling at once of ease and sociability between central office staff and principals. Each seemed to enjoy a trusting and close relationship with the other; there was much joking, laughing, and bantering before the inservice began. Once it started, however, all attended carefully to the information presented as evidenced by substantial note-taking and numerous requests from different participants for clarification or expansion. At the end of the presentation, at least one principal asked if there were a paper available to them that summarized the content. At this point, superintendents responded with such verve and directness that every word tended to remind us of the act of learning and the eagerness and pleasure of that act. Principals would receive individual school reports and conferences. The results might be useful in setting new goals for school improvement.

> [From Richland:] This information is not intended to evaluate you. I will not use it for that purpose. I want you instead to consider each measure of your school and think about its importance, in what ways these things can be improved. We have some things that everyone can improve upon. You might want to consider some of them when you set your school goals next year.

> [From Sunnyview:] This is very useful information. We're not going to use it in any sort of evaluation of you. We want *you* to use it, if you think it is accurate, and if you think it can help to improve your school. So look it over carefully, and if there are concerns you want some help with, we can work on those together.

Our inservice experiences in Eastside and Jefferson were at once depressing and remarkably similar. Neither superintendent attended, delivering a powerful symbolic message to principals about the value of their learning. Each assistant superintendent, also not in attendance, had nonetheless made all necessary arrangements. While principals were generally attentive at the onset, sitting in prearranged rows of chairs much like a routine high school classroom, their attention soon began to wander. A few remained fairly attentive, but the majority lolled wearily, unanimated. Eye contact with the presenter was fairly infrequent. In fact, one Eastside principal fell soundly asleep shortly after the presentation began, with his rather loud breathing occasionally interrupting the presenter's train of thought. Eventually, an adjacent colleague aroused him with an elbow in the ribs. In general, the group seemed unresponsive, tired, and preoccupied; anecdotes that had provoked considerable laughter in other districts produced nary a smile here. Only one principal in each district took notes, and none asked any questions.

At the nadir of irresponsibility was Hillcrest. Here the superintendent insisted that the *researchers* notify principals of the inservice to be held on a specific date and time that *he* had set. Accordingly, a month prior to the inservice, letters were sent to each elementary school principal, informing them of its time, location, and purpose. When we arrived, no principals were present (nor did any ultimately show up). The superintendent, in greeting us upon our arrival, showed no surprise—he clearly didn't expect any principals to attend:

> Now you understand that I left the arrangement of this meeting up to you. I've only gotten a call from one principal [today]. I don't know where the others are. I'm not sure how many you'll have.

He didn't comment on whether the principal who had called intended to come or not. When we asked where we could wait to see if any of the principals would arrive, he escorted us to a room where a large table and two chairs were situated at the back of the room. It seemed obvious, given the lack of chairs and general disorder of the room, that no principals were expected. When we asked, "Where are the principals?" the assistant superintendent replied, embarrassed and apologetically:

> Well, they're supposed to be in schools today. Many of them are just inundated with things. This meeting may well have gone over their heads. I know that several of them went to a state meeting today. This time might just not have been convenient for them. We can help share your information at the next principals' meeting.

At the conclusion of our interview with the assistant superintendent and the director of staff development, we explained the graphs of individual schools. We then were to interview Hillcrest's superintendent. When we asked if we should bring the graphs to show him, the director of staff development responded, "No, he probably won't have time for anything like that. He's very busy." Indeed, in concluding our interview, we noted that the superintendent never mentioned the principal inservice or the failure of any principals to attend. Nor did he ask a single question about the study or its findings.

SUMMARY AND CONCLUSIONS

This chapter explored district-level differences in teacher commitment and the practices that might explain them. Aggregating individual respondent survey data to the district level, we found significant differences between districts on each of the variables empirically related to teacher commitment, including commitment itself. To explore quantitative findings in greater detail, we conducted interviews with superintendents and their assistants to examine specific district-level practices that seemed relevant to findings in Chapter 6. Although highly exploratory in nature, data that contrasted districts with the most and least committed teachers and schools revealed that their policies of selecting principals and teachers, the extent of task autonomy, and learning opportunities superintendents appeared to delegate to schools and to principals and teachers within them articulated especially well with analysis of variance results.

However, at least three factors limit the extent to which these initial findings can be interpreted with complete confidence. First and foremost is the comparison of only eight districts, a sample size insufficient to command any assuredness and too small for multivariate analysis.

Second, per-pupil expenditure may have confounded some of the findings presented here. Unlike stuck county school systems that rely exclusively on the state for funding, moving city systems generate additional sources of revenue and thus hold substantially greater resources to devote to learning opportunities of teachers, to hire and encourage teachers to seek greater educational attainment, and so forth. Further, stuck more than moving teachers reported a stranglehold on such bedrock necessities as instructional supplies and materials with which to teach (workbooks, pencils, paper, etc.).

Nonetheless, there are still some lingering questions as to how fiscal resources are allocated in districts. Specifically, stuck districts disperse a greater proportion of their fiscal resources to noninstructional activities (maintenance of buildings and grounds, administrative costs, capital outlay) while moving districts allocate a higher proportion of their fiscal resources to instructionally related activities (contracted services for instruction, instructional supplies, instructional personnel at the district) (Tennessee Department of Education 1984). It would be foolhardy, then, to consider the question of fiscal resources without also taking into account what those resources purchase.

The third problem confounding our results is the fact that stuck districts have elected rather than appointed superintendents, while the opposite is true of moving districts. For one thing, appointed superintendents and their staffs spend more time dealing with instructional activities, while elected superintendents spend more time in managerial and political activities that are highly visible *symbols* of educational progress to the community. Similarly, appointed superintendents' operational goals relate primarily to curriculum and instruction, whereas elected superintendents tend to articulate managerial goals. Appointed superintendents all hold Ed.D. degrees and possess prior experience or training for their present office. Elected superintendents and their assistants hold only B.A. degrees and no prior experience for their present positions. In short, there is something decidedly bleak about the lack of preparation and expertise of elected superintendents. By contrast, moving superintendents command greater mastery of their role expectations vis-à-vis schools and more technical knowledge, not only because of their preservice and former inservice preparation but also because of their personal commitment to continuous technical growth.

These limitations notwithstanding, some general implications buttressed by other research on district effects are suggested here. At its very core is the nature of interorganizational control in an uncertain technical culture. In moving districts superintendents trust teachers with discretion to (1) help select key school personnel, (2) help principals set school goals, (3) allocate fiscal resources, (4) select appropriate teaching materials, and (5) determine their own inservice needs. If the technical culture available to implement organizational goals is uncertain, successful superintendents tend to delegate authority, precisely because schools confront such complex work. Rather than control being secured by minute descriptions of tasks and their procedures as in stuck districts, moving districts rely heavily on delegated authority. That is, the work of teachers takes place within a structure of guidelines that they helped shape, granting them considerable discretion over technical decision-making and at the same time holding them account-able for those decisions.

The larger points to recognize here are that strategies to improve schools should maximize teachers' control of the instruction, making them feel less uncertain and more worthwhile, while administrators at all levels find participatory ways to mobilize teachers in addressing critical school problems, and then supply the appropriate resources that respond directly to those problems. Administrators need to balance their roles, to season force with humanity, realism with high expectations. In constructing their shared reality of continuous school improvement and commitment, both moving superintendents prepared their agendas in a forum explicitly open to principals and teachers. Stuck superintendents talked more about super-ficial change, tending substantively toward the status quo with heavy-handed vigilance against empowering principals and teachers. They either did not care about their own and subordinates' professional growth and commitment or they mistakenly and naively assumed that their practices would produce better schools. If our data are any indication, coercive dis-trict control is the mark of an unsuccessful superintendent; a powerful school citizenry is the mark of a successful superintendent. The object of this point should be clear enough: to assure that schools will be healthy educative places, teachers must share responsibility for their professional destiny by engaging in the decisions through which that destiny is forged.

Those decisions begin with an understanding of the school as a work-place and of the source of its problems and possibilities. With those under-standings implicitly in hand, moving superintendents themselves tend to model the way principals should treat teachers, and teachers should treat students. Perhaps nowhere was this more apparent than in superintendents' consciousness about the need for continuous growth for themselves, their principals, and their teachers. There is little want of commitment in moving districts, because superintendents take responsibility and proactive mea-sures to improve the performance (and ostensibly the psychic rewards) of teachers and principals alike. Where the problem of teacher commitment looms largest, stuck superintendents simply transfer problematic staff to different schools to suffer even more egregious professional embarrassment and failure. Stuck superintendents seem to move in the wrong direction—faulting principals and teachers for the primacy of their workplace commit-ment over the shallow frivolities of district compliance. And as these super-intendents punitively grasp for routine solutions from logjam to logjam, they appear to have forgotten, overlooked, or sorely underestimated the fact that a professional culture does not tend toward bureaucratic compli-ance; that task decisions are not routine in nature; that the information required for effective decision-making cannot be standardized; that teach-ers, especially those in successful schools, feel a strong need for task auton-omy; that they are confident of their ability to work without the need for tightly controlled supervision; and that they regard their participation in decision-making as legitimate and see themselves as able to contribute (Hall 1977).

All of this suggests that superintendent certainty about a technical culture may determine the extent of interorganizational coupling. Successful superintendents seek out and satisfy teachers' professional needs while stuck superintendents conspicuously ignore them. Thus, under conditions of higher uncertainty, managerial and technical activities at the district level are only marginally if at all linked to schools' technical activities. Under conditions of lower uncertainty, there is tighter congruence between the behaviors of superintendents, principals, and teachers; activities that occur at the district level align more closely with, and facilitated, activities that occur at the school level. That is, where there seem greater certainty and fewer threats to their self-esteem, superintendents mobilize district resources in pursuit of interorganizational goals. How much misery might teachers have been spared—what myths, what tyranny, what armed and defensive teachers and principals might have vanished from the school landscape, had stuck superintendents understood schools in their vast complexity?

8

School Reform

The central lesson to be drawn from this research is that the social organization of schools renders meaning to the nature of teaching. Whatever impact education policy has on school success compared to other factors (e.g., SES, heredity) it is significantly affected by the quality of the linkages between policy and the intended beneficiaries of that policy, namely, teachers and students. As we have stressed throughout, the question of what teaching is, how it is performed, and how it is changed cannot be divorced from the social organization in which it occurs.

Only recently has research been perceived by investigators, and perhaps more importantly by policymakers, as being significant enough and relevant enough to substantially influence practice. As advocacy about a technical culture for education grows, so too have the number of researchers who raise serious questions about the scientific merit, validity, and consistency of those findings. That is, how much credibility should we place in available research to develop policy and to suggest changes in educational practice? With this question at the forefront, the concluding chapter reviews major findings of our study. The second section discusses the study's primary limitations. We then address problems and prospects of enhancing school quality that have gained considerable currency nationwide, including how to set priorities and direction for contemporary education reform.

This study, however, will not end in a tour de force of minute policy implications. In light of the way policymakers' recent enthusiasm for the "effective schools" and the "effective teaching" research has resulted in legislated practice, some of which seems blatantly inimical to school improvement (Rosenholtz 1987; Shannon 1986), there is more than ample reason for caution. We are just beginning to understand how schools' social organization can be altered in ways to make teaching a more professional activity. The descriptive work does give us some targets, some rich possibilities from which to formulate hypotheses and develop testable propositions, but given the vast complexities and differences between and within schools, it does not yield clear policy prescriptions. Thus we accept the challenge of advocacy along with the responsibility of reporting only to the extent that our findings will enable practitioners to draw their own enlightened implications. In this spirit, we agree whole-heartedly with Fenstermacher's (1983) response to the question of how research findings should be brought to bear on practice:

> The answer argued for here is to convey the knowledge and understanding generated by this research to those who may use it to improve what they do; it is not to elaborate this knowledge structurally and organizationally. Instead of asking how the implications shall be used, we might ask who is to decide what the implications of research for practice are. . . . The most pertinent question is, Will teachers and school administrators be helped to discover what research reveals, or will they merely be recipients of someone else's judgment of what the answers are? (Fenstermacher 1983: 498–499)

Owing that practitioners are the ultimate arbitrators of education policy, we turn next to the study's central findings.

TEACHERS' WORKPLACE: A SUMMARY

Shared Goals

We began with the multitude of ways teachers think about teaching: relating a story, enacting a resolution, concocting an excuse, or dreaming a dream. Through their workaday lives teachers tended to learn habits of understanding, methods of reasoning, ranges of feeling, and chains of explanations.

In high consensus schools, principals and teachers appeared to agree on the definition of teaching and their instructional goals occupied a place of high significance. These schools revealed a style, an attitude, a single-minded characterization. In their out-of-classroom work they culled and socialized the brightest or best educated novices with all the wholeness and harmony of group solidarity. They seemed attentive to instructional goals, to evaluative criteria that gauged their success, and to standards for student conduct that enabled teachers to teach and students to learn. Teachers appeared to partake in shared school goals because their thoughts were not merely their own, but inspired by a multitude of supportive collegial voices.

Their sense of community and their own identity led most of them to persist unassailably in their goals of student learning. Teachers spoke boldly, nobly, building big hurrahs of ideas for classroom instruction, tending to create for their students and themselves beginnings instead of endings. Student mastery of basic skills appeared the common factor that united them, the force that welded all the separate autonomous teachers into one common voice.

By contrast, in low consensus schools, few teachers seemed attached to anything or anybody, and seemed more concerned with their own identity than a sense of shared community. Teachers learned about the nature of their work randomly, not deliberately, tending only to follow their individual instincts. For want of common purpose there was little substantive dialogue. Without shared governance, particularly in managing student conduct, the absolute number of students who claimed teachers' attention seemed greater, and their experiences left bitter traces and tarnished hopes as their time and energy to teach vaporized into thin air. Colleagues talked of frustration, failure, tedium, though not in their own person: they managed to transfer those attributes to the students about whom they complained, themselves remaining complacent and aloof. In swapping disconsolate stories, teachers appeared to buy in easily to a painful sense of futility without feeling remorse over the high-quality work they once had earnestly wanted to render. With ambitions lost, teachers tended to go underground, staying topside only long enough to do little more than required.

Teacher Collaboration

Dreams of possibility were not likely the domain of isolated workplaces. Inertia seemed to overcome teachers' adventurous impulses, and listlessness devoted itself to well-trodden paths. In their ordered routines, teachers' self-reliance appeared not to be a civic sin, an act of selfishness against the community; it seemed rather a moral imperative. And because no one wished to challenge school norms of self-reliance, in times of classroom crisis most teachers skirted the edges of catastrophe alone and somehow managed to lead themselves to a safe haven. Teacher leaders were those who remained politically unassuaged, active in their union, or those who could empathize with colleagues' myriad problems.

Principals of isolated schools, seemingly unsure of their technical knowledge and concerned with their own self-esteem, did teachers and students an enormous disservice. In protecting their turf, even the smallest attempts by teachers to solve school or classroom problems were met by distance, intimidation, or defeat. Most often it was here teachers learned the unassailable lesson that they must shoulder classroom burdens by themselves. Indeed, their scattered classroom motifs suggested where the boundaries of self-reliance were drawn: no teacher could impose upon another.

Norms of self-reliance seemed as implacable as a hurricane, shattering novices' humanitarian intent. Initially they tried to identify and encourage in themselves those noble beliefs that gave evidence of their idealistic eminence. But soon most discovered in the course of communication that they had also acquired the instinctive cringe against asking for advice and assistance. This would be the first indication that they had not passed unmarked through their early socialization.

Diametrically, in the choreography of collaborative schools, norms of self-reliance appeared to be selfish infractions against the school community. With teaching defined as inherently difficult, many minds tended to work better together than the few. Here requests for and offers of advice and assistance seemed like moral imperatives, and colleagues seldom acted without foresight and deliberate calculation. Teacher leaders were identified as those who reached out to others with encouragement, technical knowledge to solve classroom problems, and enthusiasm for learning new things.

We also encountered collaborative principals who uniquely rewove schools that had come altogether unraveled. They shook loose new elements of collegial interdependence, seeming to vastly expand teachers' sense of possibility and their instincts for improvisation. Old rigidities all but collapsed, and old leadership and the past lost its legitimacy, jarring teachers from complacency, although not always without a struggle and a redefinition of roles.

Teacher Learning

The implications of goal consensus, principal evaluation, and teacher collaboration led us next to explore teachers' learning opportunities. In learning-impoverished schools, there appeared a numbing sameness, a routine lurking in teachers' work: the same questions, the same answers, no shared or common purpose, and little helpful leadership by principals, who instead mostly assumed the posture of a burrowing animal. Norms of self-reliance encouraged the view that learning to teach was as easy and quick to master as some sort of user-friendly software for computers. One either grasped it or not. No one, not even principals, tended to lay claim for the responsibility of helping struggling teachers improve.

In learning-enriched settings, an abundant spirit of continuous improvement seemed to hover schoolwide, because no one ever stopped learning to teach. Indeed, clumped together in a critical mass, like uranium fuel rods in a reactor, teachers generated new technical knowledge, the ensuing chain reaction of which led to greater student mastery of basic skills. Principals' frequent and useful evaluations seemed also a powerful mechanism for delivery on the promise of school improvement as they also served as guides for future work. Principals often orchestrated collaborative relations between more and less successful teachers, explicitly acknowledging that improvement was possible, necessary, and expected. Teachers saw that working with others seemed to reduce their endemic uncertainty and increase their classroom success. Such was the power of teacher learning that, like good, it became its own propagator.

Teacher Certainty

In exploring the uncertainty of teaching, we found both routine and non-routine technical cultures. In routine technical cultures, teachers mostly had only their own observations, their personal habits of narration, that seemed to yoke one's misery to another's in Aesopian sadness. With lax deportment and effort in their classrooms viewed as the fruit of parental depravity, and with gossip by teachers about parents and children running rampant, suspicion often gave way to punitive and routine procedures. Teachers' code of honor tended toward privacy, based on something other than instruction. They seemed to console themselves with the thought that somehow, at some level, someone else shouldered blame for each and every classroom failure. Teachers seemed ready to topple—teetering over an abyss. Yet each punitive and routine step was a measure of the school's failure to protect, to nourish its teachers psychically and with a body of technical knowledge, to actively engage its parent citizenry, to set standards for orderly student conduct, in short, to make teachers feel more certain and committed to student learning and their own professional growth.

The opposite seemed true in nonroutine technical cultures. With greater certainty about instructional practice and technical knowledge, teachers tended to search for reasons and ways to help, not for excuses for their failures. They often found what they were looking for in the sage counsel of principals and colleagues, and in the cooperation, trust, and support of parents. With more nonroutine and humanistic treatment came personal promises fulfilled: the sweet promise of helping children learn, the glittering promise of societal contribution, the warm promise of freedom from failure, from lack of faith in themselves and their technical culture.

Teacher Commitment

Next we observed that without learning opportunities, task autonomy, and psychic rewards, teachers' sense of commitment seemed choked by a string of broken promises. Most lost faith in their talents and values; they no longer cared enough to devote their energies to doing good works; they became so despairing that they couldn't recognize the consequences of abandoning their students. It was an appealing idea to them under the circumstances to simply let go, though it seemed a heavy burden to carry this weight of destructive skepticism.

Even in an era of political tribulation, moving schools were uplifted like iron fragments to a giant magnet. Here teachers frequently experienced the edifying sensation of hopes fulfilled as they invented new school futures. They were like Geiger counters calibrated to precious values, their commitment beating stronger and faster in the rich, rarified atmosphere of their workplace. It was one of the charms of moving teachers that, unlike the stuck, they were not fatalistic people. Most teachers from moving schools held an ideology that seemed the reverse of fatalism: everything was possible. The demands of their work brought forth virtues of ingenuity, loyalty, community, and mutual support and concern that seemed in increasingly short supply within stuck schools.

In the main, teachers from stuck schools looked through the wrong end of the telescope. They seemed interested in freedom *from;* they thought little of freedom *to.* The range of teacher unfreedoms was wide, subtle, and often alarming. Boredom, punitiveness, and self-defensiveness were unfreedoms. Feeling helpless and unable to cope was a state of unfreedom. Yet even those teachers who wished to be out of their present circumstances were cagey survivors. When stuck in a state of unfreedom, they frequently contrived their own covert liberty, created their own inner freedom and respite. As a form of freedom from distressing work, teachers often absented themselves in one-day breaks, much to the detriment of their schools and students.

District-Level Differences

Finally, we took a more expansive view of teacher commitment by looking into district-level practices. Superintendents ranged from makers of professionalism who worked frontiers, found new channels, and invented new lives, to those who thought they should regulate every aspect of teachers' daily lives. Moving superintendents appeared to tear down barriers to professionalism, while stuck superintendents only seemed to build them higher.

As elected officials, stuck superintendents ran their school systems with an ever-genial façade of masquerade, but frequently threatened the freedom and commitment of teachers and principals with transfer (as if that was no more significant than shuffling a deck of cards). Theirs seemed an uncertain subculture, and thus they stood ready at the drop of a hat to split a hair, squash an opinion, or contest an idea. Stuck superintendents appeared implicitly to deny the existence of a technical culture of any worth through their miasma of authoritarianism, and uniquely threatened moving schools' self-evident professionalism by appealing to coercive political power whenever their adamant convictions were in any way challenged. In stuck schools, superintendents helped make teachers into Robinson Crusoes surrounded by a sea of potentially helpful colleagues. Teachers felt alienated from a political system in which they had no voice and sometimes threatened by elaborate surveillance.

Strict regimentation and harsh coercive measures were not the bailiwick of moving superintendents. Rather their agenda for schools and teachers within them aimed toward innovation and growth. Coaxing improvement from principals and teachers seemed achieved through superintendents' technical knowledge, encouragement, and presence. Appropriate affect and leadership tended to mute the tension schools experienced in dealing with less able teachers or principals; there was, in fact, some indication that being treated professionally turned more than a few of them around. As advocates of professionalism and all that it entailed, superintendents tended to nurture those freedoms without paying the price of systemwide anarchy. Instead, they held schools accountable for the commitments they had made, and having promised, schools had moral reason to keep them.

Stuck superintendents revealed little understanding of schools and teachers, and their movement as elected rather than appointed officials appeared to involve much out-of-school political pandering. The division between stuck and moving superintendents went far beyond ideologies. Where moving districts pulled one way, giving teachers more autonomy to learn and improve their work, stuck districts pulled doggedly in the other. A decorous process of teacher and principal selection and socialization characterized moving districts, a sociopolitical agenda operated in stuck districts. Moving superintendents seemed continually to reach for victory and unity and organization, whereas stuck superintendents, anticipating nothing better than poor performance (from teachers, principals, and/or school boards), seemed to sink deeper into the labyrinth of their own political chicanery. Thus, in this study, both stuck and moving superintendents were near-perfect mirrors for how principals treated teachers, and teachers treated students.

Overall these findings identify broad conditions under which teachers engage in either professional or production-line work. But like any other study they, too, must be tempered with caution. The following discussion reviews major limitations of the study that must be considered before any implications for practice can be drawn.

LIMITATIONS OF THE STUDY

Most cautions about research are related to such concerns as the size and nature of the sample, its generalizability, methods of analysis, levels of analysis, problems of operationalization, uncontrolled variance, and the amount of inference researchers draw from their data. Our study is certainly no stranger to these issues. Apart from the problem of causal inference discussed in Chapter 1, the study's small elementary school sample and its predominantly low SES and rural character may limit the generalizability of its findings.

The level of analysis introduced two other methodological weaknesses. One is the small sample size that limited the number of variables considered in the quantitative analyses. The second is that in emphasizing the school, we sometimes overlooked its individual activities. For example, in less accomplished schools we did find small collaborative cadres, goal-setting by teachers at particular grade levels, and successful classroom management. Not all teachers in learning-impoverished schools, to be sure, allowed themselves to wither professionally. In a like manner, not all principals of successful schools beckoned for greater teacher involvement, raising their level of commitment. In short, school-level analysis misses many of the nuances of individual schools and teachers' attitudes and behaviors within them.

And then, of course, there is the confounding variable of elected versus appointed superintendents and the strength of their effects on individual schools. Is the elected superintendency the appropriate province for the marketplace of educational ideas, or is it a disastrous mistake? In the appointed superintendency, ideas that are fraudulent can be corrected by the educative maneuvers of those who succeed them, with the board of education clearly at the helm. But in the world of political advocacy, of elected superintendents, there seems no such thing as a fraudulent idea: there may be useless proposals, totally unworkable schemes, as well as very sound proposals that may receive imprimatur through districts' majoritarian system of election. Our data are not unequivocal on this issue (i.e., there was not a perfectly linear relationship between appointed superintendents and the policies of moving districts, or between elected superintendents and the policies of stuck districts) and the issue of whether the elected superintendency is a risky wild card in a serious game of chance is a question for further study.

Perhaps the most serious methodological challenge to our quantitative findings is the problem of multicollinearity; that is, when two of the independent variables are related to each other, the first variable entered into the equation is likely to emerge as the most significant predictor. The problem is particularly acute not only because of some close linkages in questionnaire items used to measure independent and dependent variables, but also because when data are aggregated, random error tends to decrease. Although these problems are somewhat tempered by the relatively high variance of each scale and the general fit of quantitative to qualitative data, the tentative nature of these findings and the need for replication studies to validate the relationships found cannot be overemphasized.

Another limitation of the study is substantive, arising from the national scramble to find ways to enhance the capability of schools to foster higher academic achievement. It is that test scores and school grades are weak indicators of the ability of schools to enhance either students' ultimate capacity to be successful and self-assured or the nation's store of productive human capital. Most parents and policymakers, we suspect, will find it hard to accept the findings of a recent synthesis of 35 studies examining the relationship between academic performance and post-school achievement and circumstances. In this study, Samson, Grave, Weinstein, and Walberg (1984) concluded that measures of students' academic achievement such as grade point average and scores on conventional standardized tests accounted, overall, for *less than 3 percent* of the difference found in occupational performance measures such as income, job satisfaction, and work effectiveness. Moreover was the fact—not one to be ignored—that academic achievement and occupational status were most positively related in some areas conventionally thought to require strong interpersonal skills and sensitivities (such as business and nursing) and weak or nonexistent in areas thought to be strongly related to traditional measures of academic performance (such as engineering, teaching, medicine, and work requiring a Ph.D.).

One should not, of course, overreact to these findings. Many factors beyond the scope of schools determine occupational success and one's sense of personal well-being deriving from it. And there are limits to the studies analyzed. The simple point is that conventional measures of academic achievement may be weak and inadequate indicators of the quality of our schools. It seems essential to keep in perspective claims that we will know we are meeting the needs of the nation's children—and the nation—when we attain substantial increases in achievement test scores for most of the country's students. It is interesting to mention in this regard that, in a recent national survey, 4000 American personnel directors from the private sector ranked nonacademic traits and skills substantially higher than academic performance as factors important to workplace success (Crain 1984; see also Bills 1988).

All of this is not to raise questions about the importance of basic skills mastery or to suggest that the same school conditions described herein would not also be successful in fostering other types of learning.

There is no question that the focus on basic skills mastery, especially in the context of serious doubts about the nation's teachers to provide quality education, has led to a preoccupation with standardized test scores and routine academic work. Policymakers have launched a major mission to rescue the public schools from their perilous slide. Lest schools educate away other capabilities, it seems important that policymakers find ways to emphasize and include students' interpersonal skills, reflection, analysis, judgment, and inventiveness. By ignoring capabilities such as these, we submit, policymakers put a dangerously low evaluation on more essential forms of human fulfillment, forms that will likely determine how much of life's joys and benefits people experience.

At the onset we noted that the most important lesson drawn from our research is that the success of elementary schools is in no small way determined by its social organization. The policy options that seem most promising and the obstacles that seem most pressing now follow from this conclusion.

PROBLEMS FOR EDUCATION REFORM

A recurring theme of current school reform is the call for the enhancement of teaching as a profession; for serious reflection and critical analysis by teachers about the meaning and scope of their work. While this call comes primarily from professional educators, the possibility is being entertained, albeit grudgingly in many quarters, by policymakers themselves. Yet when we examine the specific reform agendas that have gained considerable currency nationwide, none directly addresses this lofty ambition, yet most share one pervasive characteristic: they bring under one master, typically the State Education Agency (SEA), vastly different student needs, as teachers unwillingly subordinate themselves to hierarchical control (Darling-Hammond & Wise 1985; Rosenholtz 1987; Shannon 1986).

Teachers have become the touchstone for every imaginable contemporary debate on education, particularly as a totem for political assault. Policymakers think that teachers have too much freedom: all engine, no brakes, the great vehicle careering all over the road, the lowest common denominator at the wheel. With the current onslaught of commission reports, a number of prominent Americans believe that public education is not merely doomed but undeserving of survival (e.g., *A Nation at Risk*). Much negative publicity has resulted, and the public climate of opinion has become increasingly hostile; there has been an abrupt and utter evaporation of confidence in the nation's teachers, and consequently, of their own confidence in themselves.

This harsh and subversive judgment of the teaching profession as a whole has resulted in even greater demands for accountability, and, by virtue of the way reforms have been implemented, has debited the present (and perhaps future) attractiveness of teaching for academically talented teachers, who, we have seen, show the greatest promise for helping students learn. Many of the recently passed reforms try to regulate both the content and process of education in the hopes that teacherproof instruction will increase the quality of schooling. Legislators and administrators seek to enforce hierarchical control over teachers through such routine devices as management-by-objectives, standardized curriculum packages, and minimum competency testing. These reforms live now in enormous indebtedness that is inescapably to be paid, not in money, but in wasted human potential, school mediocrity, and lost teacher commitment. As in war, where territory can be won only at everybody's cost, the winners of education reform are also likely to become the losers.

That schools may now more exclusively be given over to production-line work implies that teachers are nothing more than semiskilled workers, and education itself nothing more than specific parts waiting for assembly. But studies conducted over the last twenty years show that students vary in how they learn and how fast they learn; they learn differently at different stages of development, and in different subject areas (for a review, see Good & Brophy 1987). This body of findings and our own research strongly suggests that the successful school is a nonroutine technical culture where teaching professionals are asked to make reflection and its requisites the master of action and its requisites.

Indeed, insofar as teachers exchange information and experiences with each other, insofar as they owe allegiance to their peers and the profession, and insofar as they seek control of their work in light of their own shared standards and common identity, they can claim extensive technical knowledge and task autonomy that rivals any other profession. In this spirit, teachers empowered by technical knowledge presently resist the necessity of taking orders from bureaucratic superiors and are not reluctant to test the limits of their professional jurisdiction—to continue to exercise judgment and discretion on a daily basis in the course of performing their work. They discover loopholes, technicalities, and elegant circumventions to approach their work with purposive disregard for reforms that do not advance their educative intention (see Rosenholtz 1987). But how long this may continue is now an uneasy question.

We suspect not too long. A twenty-year decline in teachers' job commitment has exponentially paralleled increasing bureaucratic rather than professional control in schools. Data on attitudes toward teaching show that the proportion of teachers who probably or certainly would not choose teaching if they could choose again increased from 11% in 1961 to 36% in 1981. Plans to remain in teaching also changed. Those saying that they planned to remain only until something better came along increased from 10% in 1976 to 19% in 1981 (National Education Association 1983). With the simple-mindedness of bureaucratic control, the task autonomy under which the brightest and best teachers once entered the workplace has steadily eroded during the same time that America's school-age population has grown. The prospects of hiring and retaining the best and the brightest given stronger bureaucratic control seem gloomy at best (e.g., Chapman 1983). With recent reform, then, efficacious teachers are not likely to long tolerate the paternalistic will of a distant bureaucracy that treats them as an ignorant group. In brief, hierarchical control and professionalism, like sibling rivals, do not get along well with each other.

It seems reasonable to assume that the dramatic plunge in workplace commitment of the best teachers would shock policymakers into realizing that it cannot mandate prescriptions without major territorial concessions. But as long as public support for the nation's schools wanes, policymakers will not be easily persuaded to loosen their grip on the nation's teachers. Events of the past few years make it equally apparent that if policymakers are to maintain their hegemony, it will have to be through coercive control and perhaps at the cost of the nation's best schools (Darling-Hammond & Wise 1985; Rosenholtz 1987; Shannon 1986).

As we have implicitly framed it, the choice is between a professional, egalitarian culture whose visible hands nourish highly qualified teachers with technical growth, with optimism about change, with spirited inventiveness, and with growing liberty from classroom failure, versus an unyielding bureaucracy who sees in the empowerment of teachers only the threat of lost control; in their participatory decision-making the victory of mediocrity; in their professionalization the specter for even greater educative disorder.

Perhaps we seriously oversimplify the choice between bureaucracy and professionalization, between coercive control and egalitarianism, capturing neither the regularities of most schools nor the variations and possibilities of school governance. To feel compelled to choose between bureaucracy and professionalism is to forget that not all bureaucracy is necessarily bad and that not all aspects of professionalism are necessarily good. Nor should we gainsay all education reformers. They are not automatically ignorant. In the educational marketplace, there are, as always, good ideas and bad ideas.

In reality, however, not enough comprehensive and useful information about teachers and schools is known to provide a steadfast base from which policy changes can be confidently launched. In the wake of increasing activity on the part of states and localities, the paucity of information about the features of schooling that policymakers are now seeking to change is felt more acutely than ever before. Where purposive efforts to improve school quality are mounted, they may hit with highly uneven impact if their effects are not properly anticipated. In addition, without a satisfactory "feedback" mechanism to policymakers, there is no avenue to supply insight, constructive criticism, and dispassionate scrutiny to assist them in knowing whether their efforts are well designed interventions that solve actual school problems or merely cosmetic changes that never penetrate beneath the surface.

While research on successful school practice offers substantial evidence that schools do make a difference, this research also suggests, consistent with our emphasis on seeing the school as a social organization, that the success of any given strategy depends in large part on its context. There is no easy formula, and there are no guarantees. But there are clues and guidelines, and the key to unlocking sustained improvement is for educators to develop their own adaptations of the general strategies often found to be successful (Berman & McLaughlin 1977; Huberman & Miles 1984).

In our view, then, the first problem for policymakers is not how to regulate schools but how to deregulate them so that they are still responsive to community needs; not how to put more power into bureaucratic hands but how to get more power into the hands of local teachers and principals. Schools can (and should) stand for public accountability and the common good without making a centralized bureaucracy its only instrument.

To accomplish this, however, policymakers will have to learn to trust teachers, something too few politicians and bureaucrats seem capable of doing. And to trust them when they err as well as when they act wisely. For without mistakes, there is no learning; without learning there are fewer psychic rewards; with fewer psychic rewards there is lower commitment; and with lowered commitment there is far less student growth.

Yet trust of teachers, at least in the present climate of reform, seems an unlikely prospect at best. With negative sentiment about teacher quality still running high, especially as manifest by the public's unwillingness to appropriate greater funding for education, schools are caught in something of a self-fulfilling prophecy: To prop up populist support, hierarchical chains of command have increasingly tightened to keep schools accountable and thereby to offset fiscal losses due to declining federal funding and increased dependence on states and localities. At the same time, teachers disenfranchised by greater bureaucratic control tend to quell student learning, making school accountability far less likely. And the more public support drops, the greater local and state policy maneuvering, a more tangled web for the next encounter. The result may be a profusion of rules and regulatory detail that confounds teachers' best interests and commitment, and the academic needs of students. The second problem confronting policymakers, then, is one of reconciling schools' indispensable autonomy with the accountability necessary for local or state support.

This brings up a third difficulty faced by policymakers. With increased fiscal constraints and greater hierarchical control comes the inability to recruit and retain more academically capable teachers. For one thing, pecuniary rewards are a decisive factor in people's initial occupational choice, persuading those who once chose teaching to now seek more prosperous and professionally fulfilling careers. At the same time, the problem of low workplace commitment and early defection from teaching that the loss of professional autonomy and discretion engenders applies especially to academically talented teachers. In short, there is a real danger that increased political brokering and policy maneuvering—at a time when the teacher workforce is already numerically and academically weak—may force the nation into an even greater educational recession.

Another major issue policymakers confront is also related to fiscal constraints—the ability of states and localities to provide appropriate and meaningful learning opportunities for all education practitioners, from superintendents to teachers, and those in between. Common sense suggests that people engaged in the process of educating others should also be allowed their own learning, critical inquiry, and debate. Those with limited opportunity for professional growth are not only ill-equipped for an inherently changing environment, but they unwittingly become programmed for sameness and routine, exacting costs of incalculable proportion. If the spate of state interventions does little to boost student learning outcomes, it is probably because teachers and principals have been disenfranchised from any reflective activities of their work, and that their learning needs have not been adequately met, leading to a sharp decrease in their psychic rewards and a substantial decline in their workplace commitment.

PROSPECTS FOR EDUCATION REFORM

Against these problems, rhetoric aside, can we ever bring any kind of real professionalism to the field of teaching? If policymakers finally say no to bureaucratic control, can we offer them something to say yes to? The point of this analysis is not that all news is bad; there are promises of change and hopes for a reprieve.

Helping policymakers understand the workplace conditions that enhance teachers' learning opportunities, their psychic rewards, their freedom from uncertainty, and their commitment to the profession is paramount in creating a compelling rationale for well-conceived changes. In this light, our data on schools' social organization are propitiously aimed at providing a basic description of the teaching environment. But their usefulness extends far beyond description. They offer the basis for an expanded understanding of teacher quality and school success, one that considers several education outcomes together with data about what teachers actually think and do in the course of their work. Moreover, these data shed light on critical issues such as teacher commitment and student learning that can be linked to the workplace conditions in which teachers find themselves. In addition to providing detailed explanations of why commitment decisions are made, for instance, these data suggest the specific features of schools that may be altered in ways to enhance those decisions.

For their part, there are many important tasks SEAs or local districts can assume as they delegate authority for school improvement (Turnbull 1985). First, they can specify broad parameters with which to develop programmatic goals and permissive variations for local adaptation. Second, they can monitor local implementation and provide helpful feedback directed at the improvement. Third, they can allocate sufficient resources—both fiscal support and appropriate technical assistance—organized around programmatic goals. Resources not only include teaching materials but also information on model programs for dissemination, replication, or adaptation; release time for local staff to observe exemplary practices; personnel who steer teachers and principals toward useful resources; specialists who furnish helpful information and long-term, on-site assistance.

These are some of the services that can be rightfully accomplished by states or districts. But those technical tasks and decisions for which they are unfit are more likely to be accomplished by local schools with an engaged citizenry who consensually devise self-regulation through ongoing negotiation, than by a distant bureaucracy where virtue often gives way to utility, reason to conformity, and teacher welfare to self-interest.

A different and much more exalted conception of teaching, a conception in which hope replaces despair, might begin with the core idea that professionalism is the product, not the enemy, of schools as institutions. However, before educators' legitimacy as professionals can be claimed, there is need for major and fundamental redefinitions of their roles both in and out of classrooms and schools. Teachers, principals, and superintendents as professional educators need to accept a broader definition of their responsibilities, a definition under which they would not simply yield to minimum state requirements but rather actively endorse and enlarge their spirit, or else *openly* challenge their underlying principles. For this to occur, educators need (a) to understand what constitutes a healthy school environment, (b) to seek the skills or personnel necessary to create one, and (c) to be open and receptive to change as their technical culture grows.

The issue of the school principal as instructional leader also requires serious attention. The now automatic belief in the "great person" theory of leadership as the sole requirement to building a professional culture invites rethinking. Great principals do not pluck their acumen and resourcefulness straight out of the air. In our data, successful schools weren't led by philosopher kings with supreme character and unerring method, but by the steady accumulation of common wisdom and hope distilled from vibrant, shared experience both with teacher leaders in schools and colleagues districtwide. This is not to say that teachers fulfilled their individual capabilities without the generous contributions of principals. But of all their activity, perhaps most enriching and sustaining for schools, like backstage rigging for a theatrical performance, was principals' capacity to facilitate and empower teachers with a network of technical knowledge that connected them one to the other in pursuit of a common ideal.

Related to this, the issue of the most propitious level for change is also of concern, given recent understandings about district policies and the way those policies come to affect the performance of principals and teachers. It is difficult if not impossible to create a professional culture in districts that offer curriculum, fixed strategies, or specific teaching behaviors as the whole answer, rather than as alternative ingredients to the diversified classroom or school. Indeed, successful schools in stuck districts marked the victory of reflection over dogma, of variation over routinization, of empowerment over censorship.

Finally, to offer a more vital model of the school as a workplace, one that would encourage and even demand teacher participation, states and localities might begin by insisting that classroom teaching is in many ways only one significant act of the professional. New expectations for professional responsibility involve analytic reflection on their practices among colleagues and, as an outgrowth, continuous classroom experimentation (e.g., Good and Brophy 1987).

Altering teachers' perceptions of their work is no easy task, and, as numerous scholars have argued, their capacity to resist change is enormous (e.g., Goodlad 1983). In light of strong norms of self-reliance, there is also reason to doubt whether teachers are either willing or prepared to surrender their classroom isolation for collaborative relations. In studies by Ashton and Webb (1986) and Kasten (1984), isolated teachers emphatically denied that they suffered professionally from their solitary confinement. In the normative reality they shared, it could hardly be otherwise. They saw isolation as a given; an immutable part of their workaday lives. Teachers' attitudes and behaviors are susceptible to change only if, as a result, they perceive themselves as more certain of and successful in their practice. If collaboration is to become one of the standard accoutrements of schools, it needs facilitative hands reaching out to help—hands from districts, school principals, and teacher leaders. The appeal of unthreatening sharing with colleagues, as we saw in Chapters 3 and 5, may gradually spread from a small hybrid group to a wider audience, diminishing teachers' uncertainty, augmenting their psychic rewards, increasing student learning, and finally inducing teachers to end their long silence.

In this regard, new evidence documenting the role of practitioners as researchers in their own settings is another viable strategy (Lieberman & Rosenholtz 1987). Teachers work in teams with researchers, enlarging their own capacity to identify problems and collect and interpret data. In some models, the process or the product of the research becomes professional development for an expanded group of teachers. This means that teachers not only inquire into their own practices, but also assume responsibility for the learning of their colleagues. This organic model puts teacher leaders in positions of authority to develop learning opportunities for both experienced and new teachers, working one-on-one and in groups. New roles such as these then begin to set new definitions, new realities of what it means to be a teacher: not only to teach in one's classroom, but to learn to enhance one's craft on a continuous basis, to inquire into problems of pedagogy, and to organize for and facilitate the professional development of one's peers.

Participation of this sort requires the strengthening not of the vertical ties between teachers, principals, and superintendents, but of the neglected lateral ties between them. Instead of directly controlling activities, principals and superintendents need to learn how to set general directions, and to structure environments that enable teachers to work together to discover and receive acknowledgment for their own skills and talents. We call, in other words, for a vigorous participatory politic in which teachers, principals, and superintendents collaborate in making self-regulation a genuinely shared responsibility. By rejecting the idea that task autonomy and school quality are necessarily opposed to each other, professional educators would make it much more difficult for policymakers to dismiss their moral authority in the name of devotion to excellence.

One final issue begs clarification. In successful schools, it might be argued, the problem of professional autonomy may arise at that intersection where competing individual freedoms and communal needs collide. The question is: Do healthy schools experience the perennial American conflict between individual autonomy and community responsibility, between personal aspirations and communal goals? We think not. Our own research suggests that though the premium on individual effort is never lost, a communal choreography of the school eventually takes over. Every assigned role on the roster potentially can and often does change with each child, or with each technique, or with each teacher's considered talent. The subsequent interactions among all faculty expand in incalculable ways. When in the thrall of these communal aspects—problem-solving or sharing new technical knowledge—individual initiative often gives way to collective strategizing, and willing acts of sacrifice for cooperation. Whether on administrative or educative matters, virtuoso soloists arrange themselves into an ensemble. The idiosyncratic ways of the lone performer appear to be subdued by a free institution. Finally, in successful schools, regardless of all past history, shared principles govern. We find most often in successful schools a capacity to cherish individuality and inspire communality that is the hallmark of our loftiest institutions.

References

Aderman, D. & Berkowitz, L. (1985). Observational set, empathy, and helping. *Journal of Personality and Social Psychology. 14*, 141–148.

Amato, P.R. & Saunders, J. (1985). The perceived dimensions of help-seeking episodes. *Social Psychology Quarterly. 48*, 130–137.

Ashton, P.T., Crocker, L. & Olejnik, S. (1987). *Does teacher education make a difference? A literature review and planning study.* Prepared for the Florida State Department of Education. Gainesville, FL: University of Florida.

Ashton, P.T., Webb, R. B. & Doda C. (1983). *Teachers' sense of efficacy and student achievement.* Final report to the National Institute of Education. Gainesville, FL: University of Florida.

Ashton, P. T. & Webb, R. B. (1986). *Making a difference: Teachers' sense of efficacy and student achievement.* New York: Longman.

Azumi, J.E. & Madhere, S. (1983). *Professionalism, power and performance: The relationships between administrative control, teacher conformity, and student achievement.* Paper presented at the Annual Meeting of the American Educational Research Association, Montreal.

Becker, H.S. (1953). Becoming a marihuana user. *American Journal of Sociology, 59*, 235–242.

Becker, H. J. & Epstein, J. L. (1982). Teachers' reported practices of parent involvement: Problems and possibilities. *Elementary School Journal, 83*, 103–113.

Beckerman, T.M. & Good, T.L. (1979). The classroom ratio of high- and low-aptitude students and its effect on achievement. *American Journal of Education, 18*, 317–327.

Berger, P. L. & Luckmann, T. (1966). *The social construction of reality.* Garden City, NY: Doubleday.

Berkowitz, L. (1970). The self, selfishness, and altruism. In J. Macaulay and L. Berkowitz (eds.), *Altruism and helping*. New York: Academic Press.

Berman, P. & McLaughlin, M.W. (1977). *Federal programs supporting educational change: Factors affecting implementation and continuation*. Santa Monica, CA: Rand Corporation.

Bidwell, C.E. & Kasarda, J.D. (1980). Conceptualizing and measuring the effects of schools and schooling. *American Journal of Education, 88*, 401–430.

Bills, D.B. (1988). Educational credentials and promotions: Does schooling do more than get you in the door? *Sociology of Education, 61*, 52–60.

Bishop, J.M. (1977). Organizational influences on the work orientations of elementary teachers. *Sociology of Work and Occupations, 4*, 171–208.

Blankenship, R. L. (1973). Organizational careers: An interactionist perspective. *The Sociological Quarterly, 14*, 88–98.

Blase, J.L. (1986). A qualitative analysis of teacher stress: Consequences for performance. *American Educational Research Journal, 23*, 13–40.

Brophy, J. (1985). Teacher-student interactions. In J. Bruner (ed.), *Teacher expectancies*. Hillsdale, NJ: Erlbaum.

Chapman, D. W. (1983). A model of the influences on teacher retention. *Journal of Teacher Education, 34*, 43–49.

Cohen, E. G. (1981). Sociology looks at team teaching. *Research in Sociology of Education and Socialization, 2*, 163–193.

College Blue Book. (1985). 20th Edition. New York: Macmillan.

Crain, R.L. (1984). *The quality of American high school graduates: What personnel officers say and do about it*. Center for the Social Organization of Schools, Report 354. Baltimore: Johns Hopkins University.

Crittenden, K.S. & Wiley, M.G. (1985). When egotism is normative: Self-presentational norms guiding attributions. *Social Psychology Quarterly, 48*, 360–365.

Darling-Hammond, L. (1984). *Beyond the commission reports: The coming crisis in teaching*. Santa Monica, CA: Rand Corporation.

Darling-Hammond, L. & Wise, A. (1985). Beyond standardization: State standards and school improvement. *Elementary School Journal, 85*, 315–335.

Denscombe, M. (1985). *Classroom control: A sociological perspective*. London: Allen & Unwin.

DeYoung, A.J. (1987). The status of American rural education: An integrated review and commentary. *Review of Educational Research, 57*, 123–148.

Dornbusch, S. & Scott, W.R. (1975). *Evaluation and the exercise of authority*. San Francisco: Jossey-Bass.

Eberts, R.W., Kehoe, E. & Stone, J.A. (1984). *The effect of school size on student outcomes*. Eugene, OR: Center for Educational Policy and Management, University of Oregon.

Educational Research Service. (1985). *Educator opinion poll*. Arlington, VA.

Ekstrom, R. (1975). *The relationship of teacher aptitudes to teacher behavior. Beginning teacher evaluation study: Phase 2*. Final report, Vol. 6. San Francisco: Far West Laboratory for Educational Research and Development.

Epstein, J. L. (1986). Parents' reactions to teacher practices of parent involvement. *Elementary School Journal, 86*, 277–293.

Epstein, J. L. (1987). Parent involvement: What research says to administrators. *Education and Urban Society, 19*, 119–136.

Farber, B. (1984). Stress and burnout in suburban teachers. *Journal of Educational Research, 77*, 325–331.

Fenstermacher, G.D. (1983). How should implications of research on teaching be used? *Elementary School Journal, 83*, 496–499.

Fisher, J.D., De Paulo, B.M. & Nadler, A. (1981). Extending altruism beyond the altruistic act: The mixed effects of aid on the help recipient. In J. P. Rushton & R. Sorrentino (eds.). *Altruism and helping behavior.* Hillsdale, NJ: Erlbaum.

Gecas, V. & Schwalbe, M.L. (1983). Beyond the looking-glass self: Social structure and efficacy-based self-esteem. *Social Psychology Quarterly, 46*, 77–88.

Gersten, R., Cavnine, D., Zoref, L., & Cronin, D. (1986). A multifaceted study of change in seven inner-city schools. *Elementary School Journal, 86*, 257–276.

Gibson, S. & Dembo, M.H. (1984). Teacher efficacy: A construct validation. *Journal of Educational Psychology, 76*, 569–582.

Glidewell, J.C., Tucker, S., Todt, M. & Cox, S. (1983). Professional support systems: The teaching profession. In A. Madler, J. D. Fisher, & B. M. DePaulo (eds.), *Applied research in help-seeking and reactions to aid.* New York: Academic Press.

Good, T. L. & Brophy, J. E. (1987). *Looking in classrooms.* New York: Harper & Row.

Goodlad, J. I. (1983). *A place called school.* New York: McGraw-Hill.

Griffin, G.A., Barnes, S., Hughes, R., O'Neil, S., Defino, M.E. & Hukill, A. (1983). *Clinical preservice teacher education: Final report of a descriptive study to the National Institute of Education.* Austin: University of Texas.

Gross, A.E., Fisher, J.D., Nadler, A., Stiglitz, E. & Craig, C. (1979). Initiating contact with a women's counseling service: Some correlates of help-utilization. *Journal of Community Psychology, 7*, 42–49.

Hackman, R.J. & Cammann, C. (1977). What makes a group work successfully? In Hackman, J. R., Lawler, E. E. & Porter, L. W. (eds.) *Perspectives on organizational behavior.* New York: McGraw-Hill.

Hackman, R.J. & Oldham, G.R. (1980). *Work redesign.* Reading, Mass: Addison-Wesley.

Hall, R. H. (1977). *Organization: Structure and process.* Englewood Cliffs, NJ: Prentice-Hall.

Huberman, A.M. & Miles, M.B. (1984). Rethinking the quest for school improvement: Some findings from the DESSI study. *Teachers College Record, 86*, 34–54.

Johns, G. & Nicholson, N. (1982). The meaning of absence: New research strategies for theory and research. In *Research in organizational behavior, Vol. 4.* New York: JAI, 127–172.

Johnson, D.W. & Johnson, R.T. (1975). *Learning together and alone: cooperation, competition and individualization.* Englewood Cliffs, NJ: Prentice-Hall.

Joreskog, K. G. & Sorbom, D. (1978). *LISREL IV users guide.* Chicago: National Educational Resources.

Joyce, B., Bush, R. & McGibbin, M. (1981). *Information and opinion from the California staff development study: The compact report.* Sacramento: California State Department of Education.

Kanter, R.M. (1968). Commitment and social organization: A study of commitment mechanisms in utopian communities. *American Sociological Review, 33*, 499–517.

Kanter, R.M. (1975). *Men and women of the corporation*. New York: Basic Books.

Kanter, R.M. & Brinkerhoff, D. (1981). Organizational performance: Recent developments in measurement. *Annual Review of Sociology, 7*, 321–349.

Kasten, K.L. (1984). The efficacy of institutionally dispensed rewards in elementary school teaching. *Journal of Research and Development in Education, 17*, 1–13.

Katzman, M.T. (1971). *The political economy of urban schools*. Cambridge, MA: Harvard University Press.

Kerr, D.H. (1983). Teaching competence and teacher education in the United States. In L.S. Shulman & G. Sykes (eds.), *Handbook of teaching and policy*. New York: Longman.

Koehler, V. (1985). Research on preservice teacher education. *Journal of Teacher Education, 36*, 23–30.

LaRocque, L. & Coleman, P. (1987). *School district effectiveness and district ethos: Monitoring progress as an administrative practice*. Vancouver, BC: Simon Fraser University.

Lieberman, A. & Rosenholtz, S. (1987). The road to school improvement: Barriers and bridges. In J.I. Goodlad (ed.), *The ecology of school renewal*. Eighty-sixth Yearbook of the National Society for the Study of Education. Chicago: University of Chicago Press.

Litt, M.D. & Turk, D.C. (1985). Sources of stress and dissatisfaction in experienced high school teachers. *Journal of Educational Research, 78*, 178–185.

Little, J. W. (1982). Norms of collegiality and experimentation: Workplace conditions of school success. *American Educational Research Journal, 19*, 325–40.

Little, J.W. (1984). Seductive images and organizational realities in professional development. *Teachers College Record, 86*, 84–102.

Lortie, D. (1975). *Schoolteacher: A sociological analysis*. Chicago: University of Chicago Press.

March, J.G. & Simon, H.A. (1958). *Organizations*. New York: Wiley.

Marcus, P.M. & Smith, C. B. (1985). Absenteeism in an organizational context. *Work and Occupations, 12*, 251–268.

Maslach, C. (1982). *Burnout: The cost of caring*. Englewood Cliffs, NJ: Prentice-Hall.

McLaughlin, M.W. & Pfeifer, R.S. (1988). *Teacher evaluation: Improvement, accountability, and effective learning*. New York: Teachers College Press.

Metz, M. H. (1978). *Classrooms and corridors: The crisis of authority in secondary schools*. Berkeley: University of California Press.

Murnane, R.J. (1975). *The impact of school resources on the learning of inner city children*. Cambridge, MA: Ballinger.

Murnane, R.J. (1981). Interpreting the evidence on school effectiveness. *Teachers College Press, 83*, 19–35.

Murphy, J. & Hallinger, P. (1987). Characteristics of instructionally effective school districts. *Administrator's Notebook*.

National Education Association. (1983). *Status of the American public school teacher*.

Natriello, G. (1983). *Evaluation frequency, teacher influence, and the internalization of evaluation processes: A review of six studies using the Theory of Evaluation and Authority*. Eugene, OR: Center for Educational Policy and Management.

Natriello. G. (1984). Teachers' perceptions of the frequency of evaluation and assessments of their effort and effectiveness. *American Educational Research Journal, 21,* 579–595.

Pallis, A.M., Entwisle, D.R., Alexander, K.L. & Cadigan, D. (1987). Children who do exceptionally well in first grade. *Sociology of Education, 60,* 257–271.

Perrow, C. (1970). *Complex organizations: A sociological review.* Belmont, CA: Wadsworth.

Perrow, C. (1979). *Complex organizations: A critical essay,* 2nd ed. Glenview, IL: Scott, Foresman.

Peters, T.J. & Waterman, R.H. Jr. (1982). *In search of excellence: Lessons from America's best-run companies.* New York: Harper & Row.

Peterson, P.L. & Barger, S.A. (1985). Attribution theory and teacher expectancy. In J. Bruner (ed.), *Teacher expectancies.* Hillsdale, NJ: Erlbaum.

Peterson, P.L., Janicki, T.C. & Swing, S.R. (1981). Ability treatment interaction effects on children's learning in large-group and small-group approaches. *American Educational Research Journal, 18,* 453–473.

Rosenholtz, S.J. (1985). Effective Schools: Interpreting the evidence. *American Journal of Education, 93,* 352–388.

Rosenholtz, S.J. (1987). Education reform strategies: Will they increase teacher commitment? *American Journal of Education, 95,* 534–562.

Rosenholtz, S.J. & Simpson, C. (in press). School organization and the rise and fall of teacher commitment. *Sociology of Education.*

Rosenholtz, S.J. & Simpson, C. (1984). The formation of ability conceptions: Developmental trend or social construction? *Review of Educational Research, 54,* 31–63.

Samson, G.E., Grave, M.E., Weinstein, H.J. & Walberg, H.J. (1984). Academic and occupational performance: A quantitative synthesis. *American Educational Research Journal, 21,* 311–322.

Schneider, B.L. (1985). Further evidence of school effects. *Journal of Educational Research, 32,* 30–43.

Scott, W.R. (1981). *Organizations: Rational, Natural, and Open Systems.* Englewood Cliffs, NJ: Prentice-Hall.

Seligman, M.E.P. (1975). *Helplessness: On depression, development, and death.* San Francisco: Freeman Press.

Shannon, P. (1986). Merit pay and minimum competency testing. *Reading Research Quarterly, 21,* 20–35.

Sizemore, B., Brossard, C.A., Harrigan, B. (1986). *An abashing anomaly: The high achieving predominantly black elementary school.* Washington, DC: Mason University Press.

Snyder, M.L. & Wickland, R. A. (1981). Attributional ambiguity. In J.P. Rushton & R. Sorrentino (eds.) *Altruism and helping behavior.* Hillsdale, NJ: Erlbaum.

Spunk, D.W. (1974). Reward structures in the public high school. *Educational Administration Quarterly, 10,* 18–34.

Staub, E. (1981). Promoting positive behavior in schools, in other educational settings, and in the home. In J. Harvey, W. Tackes & R. Kidd (eds.) *New directions in attribution research, Vol. 3.* Hillsdale, NJ: Erlbaum, 247–276.

Tennessee Department of Education (1984). *Statistical Report for the Scholastic Year Ending June 30, 1984.*

Tetlock, P.E. (1981). The influence of self-presentational goals on attributional reports. *Social Psychology Quarterly, 44*, 300–311.

Thompson, J.D. (1967). *Organizations in action*. New York: McGraw-Hill.

Thompson, J.D. & McEwen, W. J. (1958). Organizational goals as an interaction process. *American Sociological Review, 23*, 23–31.

Turnbull, B.J. (1985). Using governance and support systems to advance school improvement. *Elementary School Journal, 85*, 337–352.

U.S. Department of Education, Office of Planning, Budget and Evaluation. (1985). *State education statistics*. Washington, DC.

Walberg, H.J. & Fowler, W.J. (1987). Expenditure and size efficiencies of public school districts. *Educational Researcher, 16*, 5–13.

Walberg, H.J. & Genova, W.J. (1982). Staff, school and workshop influences on knowledge use in educational improvement efforts. *Journal of Educational Research, 76*, 69–80.

Wise, A.E., Darling-Hammond, L., McLaughlin, M.W. & Bernstein, H.T. (1985). Teacher evaluation: A study of effective practices. *Elementary School Journal, 86*, 61–121.

Wise, A.E., Darling-Hammond, L. & Berry, B. (1987). *Effective teacher selection: From recruitment to retention*. Santa Monica, CA: Rand Corporation.

Index